STEPS IN ENGLISH

BOOK TWO

BY

A. C. McLEAN, A.M.
FORMERLY PRINCIPAL OF LUCKEY SCHOOLS, PITTSBURG, PA.

THOS. C. BLAISDELL, Ph.D.
PROFESSOR OF ENGLISH IN MICHIGAN STATE AGRICULTURAL COLLEGE

AND

JOHN MORROW, M.S.
SUPERINTENDENT OF SCHOOLS, ALLEGHENY, PA.

NEW YORK ∴ CINCINNATI ∴ CHICAGO
AMERICAN BOOK COMPANY

Copyright, 1903, 1911, by
AMERICAN BOOK COMPANY.

Entered at Stationers' Hall, London.

STEPS IN ENGLISH, TWO.

Plim. 43

Alvina
Heldt

Arnold Heldt
Ogden
Iowa

Arnold Weldt
Ogden
Iowa
7th Grade

PLAN AND PURPOSE.

THIS book is intended to provide a practical teaching manual of English for the three years preceding the high school.

It consists of two parts, a Grammar and a Composition, which should be studied together. While each part is complete in itself, constant inter-reference welds the two into a unit. In many instances the same subjects are treated in both parts, in the one rather from the side of theory, in the other more directly from the side of practice. It is believed that this dual arrangement makes each part more logical, more practical, and more pedagogical.

The lessons both in the Grammar and in the Composition are largely inductive. From usage as seen in sentences and in selections the pupil is led to develop the principles of correct speaking and effective writing. Rules and definitions are made clear before they are stated.

As valuable knowledge comes only from doing, many examples and illustrative exercises are provided. Where practicable these examples are given in contrast, that the pupil by comparison may discover principles and make distinctions which, otherwise presented, might not be clear.

As adequate expression in language can be acquired only by talking and writing, under proper guidance, about that which is familiar, all composition work is based on the child's experiences,—on the things he himself has done or has seen done. In dwelling on these experiences the fact also has been emphasized that real appreciation of literature depends largely upon a vivid remembrance of details and of acts seen and performed; without such remembrance the suggestions in literature can not be understood.

The practical value of grammar is emphasized in the Composition. Its use and importance are constantly kept before the pupil by the application of its principles in oral and written work. In other words, the fact that a book on English must help to make fluent, correct, and effective speakers and writers has been the guiding principle in the preparation of this work.

The Grammar is divided into three parts, and the same is true of the Composition. The time given to the book in each week should be divided about equally between grammar and composition. The importance of the subjects seems to call for at least a daily lesson in each, — an ideal that some schools may be unable to attain.

For the courtesy of permitting the use of copyrighted selections the authors wish to express their appreciation to Charles Scribner's Sons for selections from F. Hopkinson Smith, Paul du Chaillu, and Robert Louis Stevenson; to the Century Company for selections from Jacob A. Riis and General Grant; to Houghton, Mifflin and Company for the selections and passages from Thomas Bailey Aldrich, Charles Dudley Warner, Lucy Larcom, Emerson, Longfellow, Whittier, Holmes, Hawthorne, and Bronson Alcott, which are used by permission of and by special arrangement with this firm, the authorized publishers of the writings of these authors; to Harper and Brothers for the poem by Kate Putnam Osgood and the letters by Macaulay and Lowell; and to the other publishers and authors who are mentioned in connection with the selections.

CONTENTS.

I. GRAMMAR.

PART I. THE SENTENCE AND ITS ELEMENTS. WORDS AND THEIR USES IN THE SENTENCE.

PAGES

The Sentence (Classified by Use) 7–10
Subject and Predicate 10–24, 31
Independent Elements 15, 19
Words in Apposition 20
The Parts of Speech 25–48
Modifiers 33
Phrase Modifiers 37

PART II. THE SENTENCE AND ITS ELEMENTS (Continued). COMPLEMENTS, PHRASES, AND CLAUSES.

Complements 49–58
The Indirect Object 56
Infinitives and Participles 58–67
Phrases and Clauses 68–79
The Simple Sentence 80
The Complex Sentence 82
The Compound Sentence 84–88
Summary of the Sentence 88–93

PART III. THE PARTS OF SPEECH. THEIR CLASSIFICATION, INFLECTIONS, AND RELATIONS.

The Noun 94–126
The Pronoun 126–144
The Verb 144–192
The Adjective 193–205, 209
The Adverb 205–210
The Preposition 211–214
The Conjunction 214–217
Words Variously Used 217–221

II. COMPOSITION.

PART I. NARRATIVES AND LETTERS. ACTS THAT SHOW CHARACTER. PUNCTUATION.

"How to Write" 223
Letters 227, 232, 234, 244, 250, 252
Words to Watch 230, 239, 247, 253, 262

CONTENTS

PAGES

Punctuation 233, 235, 243, 245, 251, 256
Suggestion in Literature 240
Telegrams 256

PART II. ACTS THAT SHOW FEELING. PUNCTUATION.

Suggestion of Feelings 265–268, 292
Postal Cards 272, 278
Words to Watch 272, 281, 297, 302, 303
Punctuation 275–277, 284–288, 290–292, 295, 302, 305
Description 299
The Note of Invitation 304

PART III. DETAILS THAT PICTURE. MISCELLANY.

Practical Descriptions 308
Bills and Receipts 312
Words to Watch 314, 325
The Pronoun: Some Dangers 316
The Letter of Introduction 319
Advertisements 324, 340
Suggestive Words 326–332
Persuasive Writing 332
Organization and Conduct of a Society or Meeting 337
Principles of Composition 343

SELECTIONS FROM LITERATURE.

A Kind Act (School Work) . . 226	A Lady's Mistake (Warner) . . 293
The Whistle (Franklin) . . . 226	The Mountain and the Squirrel (Emerson) 297
Letter (Lowell) 228	A Pleasant Room (Alcott) . 298, 299
A Sudden Shower (Riley) . . . 230	Grant's Bargain (U. S. Grant) . 304
Letter (Macaulay) 232	The Other Fellow (William Hawley Smith) 306
Letter (Stevenson) 234	
Three Boys and a Dog (School Work) 238	The Eel Trap 308
Oliver Horn (F. Hopkinson Smith) 241	Leaving the Old Home (Lucy Larcom) 309
A Gentleman (Lucy Larcom) . 250	Joyous Days 314
The Foreign Gentleman (Alcott) 255	The Den (Alcott) 317
A Boy's Song (James Hogg) . . 258	Snaring Fish (Warner) . . . 318
Christmas Morning (Alcott) . . 263	A Night Afield (Hamlin Garland) 321
Heavy Hearts (Alcott) 265	Winter (Shakespeare) 325
Merton's Promise 266	A New England Scene (F. Hopkinson Smith) 326
The Rescue 269	
The Heroism of John Binns (Riis) 273	Seadrift (Aldrich) 330
How I Made an Anchor . . . 278	The Poet's Song (Tennyson) . . 332
Driving Home the Cows (Kate Putnam Osgood) 282	What the Long Night Said (du Chaillu) 336
Elegy Written in a Country Churchyard (Gray) 292	The Boy to the Schoolmaster (Edward J. Wheeler) . . . 341

PICTURES 237, 249, 260, 271, 289, 301, 311, 323, 335
ADDITIONAL EXERCISES 346

I. GRAMMAR.

PART I.

THE SENTENCE AND ITS ELEMENTS.
WORDS AND THEIR USES IN THE SENTENCE.

(*To be studied in connection with Part I of the Composition on pages 223–264.*)

1. THE SENTENCE.

When we wish to express a thought clearly, we must arrange our words so that taken together they form what is called a sentence. If we arrange words without relation to one another, we express only disconnected ideas; as,

Beautiful the on hillside trees.

These words may be made to convey a meaning by changing their order and thus relating them; as,

Beautiful trees on the hillside.

As they are now arranged, these words are related and have some meaning; but they do not completely express a thought, and can not properly be called a sentence. The question arises, "What about the beautiful trees on the hillside?" To answer this question we must supply a predicating word or expression:

Beautiful trees **grow** *on the hillside;* or,
Beautiful trees on the hillside **were blown down.**

The word *grow* and the words *were blown down* predicate, or tell, something about the trees, and thus complete the expression of a thought.

DEFINITION. A *Sentence* is the complete expression of a thought in words.

Exercise.

Study the following expressions, and distinguish the five that are sentences. Change those that are parts of sentences into sentences by supplying appropriate words:

1. Birds in the tree.
2. Trees growing on the hillside.
3. Youth is the springtime of life.
4. On the 22d of February.
5. Trying to cross the river.
6. Merit wins the soul.
7. But the sweet face of Lucy Gray.
8. Electricity in the air.
9. A penny for your thoughts.
10. Knowledge is power.
11. The boys study their lessons.
12. The boys, studying their lessons.
13. If you want learning you must work.
14. Better late than never.

(*For additional exercises see p. 346.*)

2. KINDS OF SENTENCES.

Sentences are used to express three different kinds of thoughts. Observe the following sentences and select:

1. Those that are used **to tell** something.
2. Those used **to command or request** something.
3. Those used **to ask** a question.

1. We have only twenty-six letters in our alphabet.
2. The Japanese have forty-seven letters.
3. Do they write as we do?
4. Come, let us visit a Japanese school.
5. Notice how they write.
6. Do they write with pens or pencils?
7. No, they have brushes much like those we use for water colors.
8. All men are equal; there is naught in birth;
   'Tis Virtue only makes the difference.

THE SENTENCE

DEFINITIONS. A sentence that tells, or declares, something is a *Declarative Sentence*.

A sentence that commands or requests is an *Imperative Sentence*.

A sentence that asks a question is an *Interrogative Sentence*.

When a declarative, an imperative, or an interrogative sentence is used to express emotion, such as sorrow, surprise, or impatience, it is called an *Exclamatory Sentence;* as,

1. *Few, few shall part where many meet!*
2. *Woodman, spare that tree!*
3. *Where, oh, where was Roderick then!*

Which of these sentences tells something? Which commands? Which asks a question? Why are they followed by exclamation points?

RULES OF CAPITALIZATION AND PUNCTUATION. In writing, the first word of every sentence should begin with a capital letter. (Comp. 17,[1] p. 243.)

The close of a declarative or an imperative sentence is usually marked by a period (.). (Comp. 17.)

The close of an interrogative sentence is usually marked by an interrogation point (?). (Comp. 17.)

When a sentence is exclamatory it is followed by an exclamation point (!). (Comp. 70, pp. 305, 306.)

Exercises.

Ex. I. *Tell whether each of the following sentences is declarative, interrogative, or imperative, and give reasons. Mention those that are also exclamatory:*

1. There is nothing so imperishable as a book.
2. Wear the old coat and buy the new book. — *Phelps.*
3. Truth needs not the foil of rhetoric. — *Middleton.*
4. Who ever knew truth put to the worse in a free and open encounter? — *Milton.*
5. Vain pomp and glory of the world, I hate thee! — *Shakespeare.*

---

[1] References to the Composition, which occupies the latter part of this book, are indicated in this manner.

6. The world globes itself in a drop of dew. — *Emerson.*
7. Who can direct when all pretend to know? — *Coleridge.*
8. How soon a smile of God can change the world![1] — *Browning.*
9. He who quells an angry thought is greater than a king.
10. What mighty contests rise from trivial things![1] — *Pope.*
11. Do noble things, not dream them, all day long. — *Kingsley.*

12.   Where'er the wide old kitchen hearth
    Sends up its smoky curls,
    Who will not thank the kindly earth,
    And bless our farmer girls! — *Whittier.*

Ex. II. *Select from another book five declarative, five interrogative, five imperative, and five exclamatory sentences. Tell whether each of the exclamatory sentences is declarative, imperative, or interrogative in meaning.*

3. SUBJECT AND PREDICATE.

Two words, at least, are needed in the English language to express a thought completely, — one to name something, and one to say, or state, something about what is named.

When we say "Trees grow," we use the word *Trees* to name something, and the word *grow* to state, or assert, something about what is named. If we say "Beautiful trees grow on the hillside," we use *Beautiful trees* to name something, and *grow on the hillside* to assert something about what is named.

DEFINITION. In a sentence the word or group of words naming that about which something is asserted, is called the *Subject;* and the word or group of words that asserts (predicates) something of the subject, is called the *Predicate.*

[1] Exclamatory sentences that begin with *how* or *what*, and are not interrogative in meaning, are sometimes called *purely exclamatory* and classified as such, instead of being called exclamatory declarative.

SUBJECT AND PREDICATE

NOTE. Strictly speaking, in an interrogative sentence the subject names that about which something is *asked* (not *stated*), and the predicate *asks* something about that which is named by the subject. So in an imperative sentence the predicate *commands* or *requests*, instead of stating, telling, asserting, or the like. For convenience, however, the word *assert* may be applied to all three kinds of sentences.

The subject and predicate are the two essential, or necessary, parts of every sentence.

Note how these parts are illustrated in the following sentences:

1. *Plants\breathe.*
2. *Sponges\are animals.*
3. *Penn \ founded Pennsylvania.*
4. *The busy \ have no time for tears.*
5. *Push and pluck \ will work wonders.*
6. *To do right \ is our duty.*

The separation of a sentence into its parts, or elements, according to their use is called **Analysis**.

Illustrating the analysis of a sentence by means of some plan, or drawing, is called **Diagramming**.

ORAL ANALYSIS. — Sentence. Why? Kind of sentence. Why? Subject. Why? Predicate. Why?

MODEL. — *A blade of grass \ is a mystery.* This is a *sentence*, because it is the complete expression of a thought. It is a *declarative sentence* because it declares, or tells, something. *A blade of grass* is the subject, because it names that about which something is asserted; *is a mystery* is the predicate, because it tells what is asserted of the subject.

TO THE TEACHER. When the pupil has learned to recognize the sentence, and is able to distinguish readily its parts, a formal analysis in which every child follows the same order, should not be insisted on. Such work is apt to become mechanical. Be satisfied at all times if a pupil shows that he understands clearly, and expresses his understanding intelligently.

Exercise.

Analyze the following declarative sentences, and then diagram each according to the illustrations given:

1. Oranges grow.
2. Oranges are sweet.
3. Sweet oranges are most expensive.
4. Oranges that are sweet grow in Florida.
5. Growing oranges is very profitable.
6. Shallow waters make most noise.
7. Mountain sheep go in flocks.
8. A good book is the best teacher.
9. To choose time is to save time.
10. The truest self-respect is not to think of self.
11. Our good deeds live after us.
12. The path of industry is the path to success.
13. Seconds are the gold dust of time.
14. The first step towards greatness is honesty.
15. The evil that men do lives after them.
16. Every difficulty yields to the enterprising.
17. The mold of a man's fortune is in his own hands.

4. SUBJECT AND PREDICATE OF INTERROGATIVE SENTENCES.

An interrogative sentence usually has a form different from that of the declarative sentence, and, to determine its subject and predicate, it is usually necessary to change the form to that of the declarative; as,

Has every pupil a book?
every pupil ╲ *Has a book*

Did Longfellow write "Excelsior"?
Longfellow ╲ *Did write Excelsior*

SUBJECT AND PREDICATE

Exercise.

Change the following interrogative sentences, as nearly as possible, to the declarative form; tell the subject and the predicate of each; and place each in a diagram as in the preceding exercise:

1. Do sponges grow?
2. Did Columbus discover America?
3. When did Columbus discover America?
4. Are not the autumn leaves beautiful?
5. How deep is the river?
6. Did you study your lesson?
7. Have you read "Lives of the Hunted"?
8. Why does a leaf fall face downward?
9.[1] Who can paint like nature?
10. How many were present?
11. Which of the two rivers is the longer?

5. SUBJECT AND PREDICATE OF IMPERATIVE AND EXCLAMATORY SENTENCES.

Every sentence has a subject and a predicate; but in an imperative sentence the subject is usually omitted, because it represents the person or persons spoken to, and it is unnecessary to name a subject of this kind; as,

1. (*You*) *Behold.*   2. *Don't* (*you*) *do that.*

Exercise.

In the following numbered sentences supply the subjects that are omitted, and then diagram to show the subject and the predicate, as in the preceding lessons.

---

[1] Some interrogative sentences have the arrangement of declarative sentences. This is true when an interrogative word (*who, which, how,* etc.) is used as the subject or as a modifier of the subject.

NOTE. That any part of a sentence has been supplied may be indicated in the diagram by inclosing in parentheses ( ) the word or words supplied; as,

$$(you) \wedge \underline{Don't\ do\ that}$$

1. Hear me for my cause.
2. Do not weary of well doing.
3. Give us this day our daily bread.
4. Look before you leap.
5. Please excuse me.
6. You study your lesson.
7. Don't you accept it.
8. Ask questions in order to learn.
9. Do the duty that lies nearest thee.

The directions for determining the subject and predicate of declarative, interrogative, and imperative sentences apply to the exclamatory sentence according to the form in which the exclamation is expressed.

DECLARATIVE FORM:
Here we are at last!
we $\wedge$ *are Here at last*

INTERROGATIVE FORM:
Was ever poet so trusted before!
poet $\wedge$ *Was ever so trusted before*

IMPERATIVE FORM:
Don't you touch that wire!
you $\wedge$ *Don't touch that wire*

6. INCOMPLETE EXPRESSIONS OF THOUGHT.

A single word that is neither the subject nor the predicate word, may convey a thought without giving it complete expression. In answer to the question "Are you happy?" the single word *Yes* conveys the same thought that is expressed by the sentence "I am happy." Given as a com-

SUBJECT AND PREDICATE

1. In the declarative sentence the subject usually precedes the predicate. This is called the **Natural Order**.

SUBJECT.   PREDICATE.
Every pupil | *has read "Hiawatha."*

2. In the interrogative sentence the subject usually follows either the predicate or some part of it:

PART OF PREDICATE.   SUBJECT.   REST OF PREDICATE.
Has   *every pupil*   *read "Hiawatha"?*

3. In the imperative sentence the subject is generally omitted. When expressed, in literature, it often follows part of the predicate:

PART OF PREDICATE.   SUBJECT.   REST OF PREDICATE.
Praise   *ye*   *the Lord.*

Exercise.

Select from your reader two sentences to illustrate the position of the subject and of the predicate in each of the different kinds of sentences.

TO THE TEACHER. — Pupils who have not studied Book One of this series may need additional practice in the analysis of sentences in their natural order before taking up the next lesson. Each teacher knows the needs of her class, and should give additional drill when necessary.

8. SUBJECT AND PREDICATE OUT OF NATURAL ORDER.

In some declarative sentences the predicate, or some part of it, precedes the subject. This occurs when we wish to emphasize a certain part of the sentence.

Observe the arrangement of the subject and predicate in the following declarative sentences:

PREDICATE.   SUBJECT.
1. *There stands*   *the man.*

Part of Pred.	Subj.	Rest of Pred.
2. *Brightly glow*	*the stars*	*at night.*

Change the arrangement of these sentences to their natural order and note the different effect:

1. *The man stands there.*
2. *The stars glow brightly at night.*

In such sentences we may determine the subject by putting **who** or **what** before the predicate to form a question; as in the first sentence above, "**Who** stands there?" The answer to the question thus formed is the subject.

Exercise.

Determine the subject and the predicate of the following sentences, arrange them in their natural order, and diagram:

1. Down the chimney Santa Claus came.
2. Slowly and sadly we laid him down.
3. Far above the old Potomac stands a mansion.
4. Halfway up the stairs it stands.
5. Into the valley of death rode the six hundred.
6. On a tree near by sat a robin.
7. Up spake our own little Mabel.
8. No more was seen the fairy isle.
9. Little by little all tasks are done.
10. In the cottage yonder I was born.
11. By the wayside, on a mossy stone, sat a hoary pilgrim.
12. Far away to the northwest shines the blue Mediterranean.
13. Around my ivied porch shall spring each fragrant flower that drinks the dew.
14. Somewhat back from the village street stands the old-fashioned country-seat.
15.
    By the shores of Gitche Gumee,
    By the shining Big-Sea-Water,
    Stood the wigwam of Nokomis.

9. INTRODUCTORY WORDS.

When the predicate in a declarative sentence is placed before the subject for the purpose of emphasis, it is often preceded by the word **there** as an introductory word; as,

There is a time for all things.

The word *there* is often thus used to introduce a sentence. Omit it and notice how incomplete the sentence sounds.

When used in this manner *there* is commonly called an **Expletive** — a term that means *to fill out*. In diagramming it should be set apart from the rest of the sentence; as,

$$\underline{There}$$
$$\underline{a\ time\ for\ all\ things \wedge is}$$

CAUTION. The word *there* is not always an expletive when it introduces a sentence. Note its use in each of the following sentences:

1. **There** (expletive) *is no royal road.*

$$\underline{There}$$
$$\underline{no\ royal\ road \wedge is}$$

2. **There** (part of predicate) *he saw a narrow road.*

$$\underline{he \wedge saw\ a\ narrow\ road\ There}$$

Exercise.

Analyze the following sentences to determine the subject and the predicate, and then diagram them:

1. There is nobility in truth.
2. There is no sorrow there.
3. There are two fives in ten.
4. There we discovered the way.
5. There he saw a stranger standing.

6. There's no slipping up hill. — *Eliot.*
7. There is a pleasure in the pathless woods.—*Byron.*
8. There was a manhood in his look. — *J. Taylor.*
9. There never was a good war. — *Franklin.*
10. There's no wound deeper than a pen can give. — *J. Taylor.*
11. There is no new thing under the sun. — *Bible.*

10. WORDS IN APPOSITION.

When the word **it** is used as the subject of a sentence, a group of words often follows the predicate to explain what is meant by the subject. These words are not a part of the predicate; they belong to the subject. As,

1. It *is noble to seek the truth.*

   $It = to\ seek\ the\ truth \wedge is\ noble$

2. It *is true that plants breathe.*

   $It = that\ plants\ breathe \wedge is\ true$

In the first of these sentences, the words *to seek the truth* explain or make known the idea for which the word *it* stands. *It* merely introduces the sentence and fills the office of subject without telling what the subject means. Words used to explain some other word are said to be in **Apposition**. Apposition means *placed by the side of.*

In the diagram, words that are *in apposition* should be placed by the side of the words they explain, and connected with them by an equality sign.

RULE OF PUNCTUATION. **When an appositive expression follows the word it explains, it is generally set off by commas;** as, *Grammar, or the science of language, treats of the laws of speech. Daniel Boone, the pioneer, was one of the founders of Kentucky.* (Comp. 53, pp. 284–286.)

Exercise.

Diagram the following sentences, and observe how they are punctuated:

1. It is wrong to tell a lie.
2. It is true that lost time is never found again.
3. It is not good to wake a sleeping hound. — *Chaucer.*
4. It is a well known fact that sponges are animals.
5. It's good to be merry and wise.
6. It's good to be honest and true.
7. It was my privilege to be present.
8. It is traitorous to desert one's flag.
9. It was his desire to act the part of a gentleman.
10. It has been finely said that lost time is never found again.
11. Golden beams, the little children of the sun, came to brighten the earth.
12. Elmwood, the home of Lowell, is in Cambridge.
13. Mabel, his little daughter, came quietly into the room.
14. Lucy Larcom, the author of many charming stories for children, lived in Beverly.
15. She was a personal friend of Whittier, the Quaker poet of Amesbury.
16. By Whittier the statement was made that simple duty hath no place for fear.

11. SUBJECT AND PREDICATE — COMPOUND.

Two or more subjects are often connected and used with one and the same predicate; as,

1. { *Rice grows in a warm climate.*
    Cotton grows in a warm climate.

    SUBJECTS CONNECTED.

2. *Rice and cotton ∧ grow in a warm climate.*

DEFINITION. **Two or more connected subjects having the same predicate form a** *Compound Subject*.

Two or more predicates are often connected and used with the same subject ; as,

SUBJECT.   CONNECTED PREDICATES.
Hope \\ *ebbs and flows.*

DEFINITION. **Two or more connected predicates having the same subject form a** *Compound Predicate.*

Sometimes a sentence has both a compound subject and a compound predicate; as,

COMPOUND SUBJECT.   COMPOUND PREDICATE.
Hill and dale \\ *blossom and sparkle.*

Exercises.

Ex. I. *Construct or select from your reader five sentences with compound subjects, three with compound predicates, and two in which both subject and predicate are compound.*

Ex. II. *Diagram each sentence to show the subject and the predicate.*

12. REVIEW.

TO THE TEACHER. The pupil should now be able to recognize the sentence, and to distinguish its logical elements of subject and predicate without much difficulty. This power rather than the mastery of definitions should be the test of the pupil's fitness to proceed further. The following sentences have been arranged to give additional practice.

EXERCISE. *Select the subject and the predicate of each of the following sentences:*

1. Knavery and flattery are blood relations. — *Lincoln.*
2. Joy comes and goes. — *Arnold.*
3. The air, the earth, the water, teem with delightful existence. — *Wm. Paley.*

SUBJECT AND PREDICATE

4. True wisdom is the price of happiness. — *Young.*
5. He watched, and wept, and prayed for all. — *Goldsmith.*
6. Flow gently, sweet Afton. — *Burns.*
7. With the talents of an angel a man may be a fool. — *Young.*
8. Lucky is he who has been educated to bear his fate.
— *Thackeray.*
9. Four gray walls and four gray towers overlook a space of flowers. — *Tennyson.*
10. It is not all of life to live.
11. It was impossible to retreat.
12. A thing of beauty is a joy forever.
13. It requires perseverance to succeed.
14. What is your name, my brave little man?
15. There is a large elm between the house and the river.
16. Great heaps of yellow apples lay under the trees.
17. The fleecy clouds rest on the mountain side.
18. To bear is to conquer our fate.
19. Fragrant blossoms fringe the apple boughs.
20. Somewhere the birds are singing evermore. — *Longfellow.*
21. That we are never too old to learn is a true saying.
22. Full often wished he that the wind might rage. — *Wordsworth.*
23. In the core of one pearl are all the shade and shine of the sea.
24. The flowers of sweetest smell are shy and lowly.
— *Wordsworth.*
25. A soft answer turneth away wrath.
26. The leaders of industry are virtually the captains of the world. — *Thomas Carlyle.*
27. The navigation of the Mississippi we must have. — *Jefferson.*
28. There is no defense against reproach except obscurity.
— *Addison.*
29. The lover of books is the richest and happiest of the children of men. — *John Alfred Langford.*
30. Flag of my country! In thy folds are wrapped the treasures of the heart.
31. Let us glory in the title of American citizens. — *John Conway.*
32. For my voice, I have lost it with hollowing and singing of anthems. — *Shakespeare.*
33. Lincoln stands forth on the page of history, unique in his character and majestic in his individuality. Like Milton's angel, he was an original conception. He was raised up for his times. He was a leader of leaders. By instinct the common heart trusted him.

He was of the people and for the people. He had been poor and laborious. Greatness did not change the tone of his spirit. It did not lessen the sympathies of his nature. His character was strangely symmetrical. He was temperate without austerity. His love of justice was only equaled by his delight in compassion. His regard for personal honor was only excelled by love of country. His self-abnegation found its highest expression in the public good. His integrity was never questioned. His honesty was above suspicion. He was more solid than brilliant. His judgment dominated his imagination. His ambition was subject to his modesty. His love of justice held the mastery over all personal consideration. Not excepting Washington, Lincoln is the fullest representative American in our national annals. He had touched every round in the human ladder. He illustrated the possibilities of our citizenship. We are not ashamed of his humble origin. We are proud of his greatness.

—*From an Address by Bishop Newman.*

TEST QUESTIONS. 1. In expressing our thoughts, does it make any difference in what order we speak or write our words? 2. Does a group of words, if properly arranged, always make a sentence? 3. How can you determine whether or not a group of words is a sentence? 4. What do we call sentences that make statements? 5. Those that give commands? 6. Those that ask questions? 7. Give an example of each kind. 8. When is a sentence exclamatory? 9. How do the tones in which people speak help you to understand them? 10. In writing, what helps us to understand sentences? 11. Give orally a sentence in the form of a question that would need an exclamation point after it. 12. Give four rules for beginning and closing sentences in writing. 13. What are the two essential parts of every sentence? 14. In what kind of sentence is one of these parts frequently omitted? 15. Why? 16. Which part of a sentence is called the subject? 17. Why is the other part called the predicate? 18. What is meant by an incomplete expression of thought? 19. How do we punctuate a word used in a sentence as a term of address? 20. What is the usual order of the subject and the predicate in the different kinds of sentences? 21. What is a word called when used merely to fill out the sentence? 22. When used in exclamation? 23. What does the word *apposition* mean? 24. When is a word in apposition with another? 25. Give the rule for punctuating appositives.

13. THE PARTS OF SPEECH.

We have learned that a sentence is the complete expression of a thought in words, and that it consists of two parts, the subject and the predicate. We now come to consider the words used in forming the subject and the predicate, and in so doing we take up the study of grammar proper.

Grammar shows how words are put together in sentences, how they change their forms, and why certain forms and not others are correct.

In studying words and their different forms we first divide them into classes, or families, according to their various uses in the sentence.

DEFINITION. The classes into which words are divided according to their uses in the sentence are called *Parts of Speech*.

14. THE NOUN.

One of the largest and most important classes of words is made up of names. It would be impossible to express our thoughts unless we had names for the things about which we wish to speak or to write.

Select in the following sentences the words that are used as names:

1. Flowers bloom.
2. Beauty charms.
3. Health has gone.
4. Exercise invigorates.
5. George Washington was honored.
6. Mount Vernon attracts thousands.

Notice that these names represent:

1. Things that occupy space, as a person, a place, or a thing; as, *George Washington* (person); *Mount Vernon* (place); *flowers* (thing).

2. Things that do not occupy space, as a quality, a condition, or an action; as, *beauty* (a quality); *health* (a condition); *exercise* (an action).

These names are called **Nouns**.

DEFINITION. A *Noun* is the part of speech used as the name of something.

REMARK. It is the name, and not the thing itself, that is a noun. A boy is not a noun, but the word *boy* is.

15. KINDS OF NOUNS.

Write the following nouns in two columns; the first column to contain all those naming things that occupy space; the second column, all those naming things that do not occupy space:

House, hope, book, truth, health, kindness, king, carpenter, New York, cruelty, Longfellow, city, poverty, child, childhood, man, manhood, sun, brightness, Charter Oak, smoke, sky, virtue, sickness, color, fashion, Schenley Park, perseverance, industry, laughter, Henry, Monday,[1] October, 1492.

These columns represent two different kinds of nouns: The nouns in the first column name things that exist in space, and are called **Concrete Nouns**; those in the second column name things that do not occupy space, and are called **Abstract Nouns**.

[1] Occupies space of time.

DEFINITIONS. A *Concrete Noun* is the name of a person, place, or thing that exists in space.

An *Abstract Noun* is the name of a quality, condition, or action — something that does not occupy space.

TO THE TEACHER. This distinction of nouns as concrete and abstract is important not so much on account of its grammatical significance as for the help it gives the pupil to recognize the noun, — not only as the name of a person, place, or thing, but as the name of everything that has existence or being, whether that being is recognized through the senses or by mental abstraction.

If pupils can comprehend it, an abstract noun may be defined as the name of a quality, condition, or action withdrawn or abstracted in thought from the object to which it belongs.

Exercise.

Make a list of the nouns in the following sentences, and tell whether they are concrete or abstract:

1. The oriole uses wool, hair, and flax for her nest, and shapes it like a purse.

2. There is a mountain in Arcadia where the four winds prepare to take breath for their courses on the earth, whence force shall resound on force, and softness be answered by softness. — *Greek Oracle.*

3. All mischief comes from idleness: — hence gambling, luxury, dissipation, ignorance, calumny, envy, and forgetfulness of God.

— *Pascal.*

4. Until the appearance of the steamboat in 1812, the merchants of Pittsburg, Cincinnati, Louisville, and a host of other towns in the interior bought the produce of the Western settlers, and floating it down the Ohio and the Mississippi sold it at New Orleans for cash, went round to the east coast by sea, and with the money purchased goods at Baltimore, Philadelphia, and New York, and carried them over the mountains to the West. — *John Bach McMaster.*

16. THE PRONOUN.

It often becomes necessary to refer to the same person or thing more than once in a sentence ; as,

1. *Alexander the Great wept because Alexander the Great could find no more worlds to conquer.*
2. *Flowers bloom, and shed flowers' fragrance on the air.*

This repetition of names makes the sentence cumbersome and inelegant. It may be avoided by writing the sentences as follows:

1. *Alexander the Great wept because* **he** *could find no more worlds to conquer.*
2. *Flowers bloom, and shed* **their** *fragrance on the air.*

What nouns have been left out of these sentences? What words are used instead of them? Such words are called **Pronouns** (for or instead of nouns).

DEFINITION. A *Pronoun* is a word used instead of a noun.

The principal pronouns are: **I, my, mine, me, he, his, him, she, her, hers, it, its, you, your, yours, we, our, ours, us, they, their, theirs, them, who, whose, whom, which, that, what.**

These little words are used very frequently, and they are often used incorrectly. You will learn their correct uses in subsequent lessons.

Exercise.

Note the indicated pronouns, and tell for what noun each is used:

1. Animals are such agreeable friends — **they** ask no questions, **they** pass no criticisms. — *George Eliot.*
2. A man may well bring a horse to the water,
   But **he** can not make **him** drink without **he** will.
   — *John Heywood.*
3. The tree is known by **its** fruit. — *St. Luke.*

4. What is wealth to the man **who** can't use **it** to better **himself** and **his** fellow man?

5. Come to **me**,[1] O ye children,
For **I** hear **you** at **your** play. — *Longfellow.*

6. Be England what **she** will,
With all **her** faults **she** is **my** country still. — *Churchill.*

7. Be wiser than other people if **you** can; but do not tell **them** so. — *Lord Chesterfield.*

8. A sensitive plant in a garden grew,
And the young winds fed **it** with silvery dew,
And **it** opened **its** fanlike leaves to the light,
And closed **them** beneath the kisses of night. — *Shelley.*

9. I doubt if **he**[2] **who** lolls **his** head
Where idleness and plenty meet,
Enjoys **his** pillow or **his** bread
As those[3] **who** earn the meals **they** eat.

DEFINITION. The word, or group of words, for which a pronoun stands is called its *Antecedent*.

Exercise.

Turn to page 265, select all the pronouns in the selection "Heavy Hearts," and tell the antecedent of each.

17. SUBSTANTIVES.

In addition to pronouns, other words, and frequently groups of words, perform the office of nouns. It is therefore convenient to use a term that can be applied to every expression used as a noun. The term **Substantive** is properly applied to such expressions.

DEFINITION. A *Substantive* is a noun, or any word or group of words used as a noun.

[1] Refers to the speaker.   [2] A person.   [3] Persons.

Exercise.

The substantives are indicated in the following sentences. Tell of each whether it is a noun, a pronoun, or a group of words used as a noun:

1. **God** has lent **us** the **earth** for our **life**. — *Ruskin.*
2. **To be prepared for war** is **one** of the most effectual **means** of preserving **peace**. — *Washington.*
3. **I** am an **expansionist**. **I** am glad **we** have acquired the **islands we have acquired**. **I** am not afraid of the **responsibilities** which **we** have acquired; but neither am **I** blind to **how heavy those responsibilities are**. — *Roosevelt.*

18. THE VERB.

When we say, "Flowers bloom," we use the noun *flowers* as a name, and the word *bloom* to tell, or to make an assertion, about the things named.

Flowers **bloom.** *Beauty* **charms** *the eye.* *Health* **has gone.** *George Washington* **was honored** *by all.*

The words *bloom*, *charms*, *has gone*, and *was honored* are used to tell, or assert, and are called **Verbs.**

DEFINITION. A *Verb* is the part of speech used to make an assertion.

Most verbs assert action; as, Horses *trot*, *eat*, *jump*, *run*. A few verbs do not assert action; as, They *rest;* God *exists;* John *has* a vase; It *contains* flowers; They *own* a farm.

The noun, the pronoun, and the verb, being used as the chief words in forming the subject and predicate, are the principal parts of speech in the sentence. No sentence can be formed without a verb.

Exercise.

Point out the verbs:

1. Silence gives consent. — *Goldsmith.*
2. Slow and steady wins the race. — *Lloyd.*
3. Small pitchers have wide ears. — *Heywood.*
4. The path of duty leads to happiness. — *Southey.*
5. The world exists for the education of each man. — *Emerson.*
6. The wicked flee when no man pursueth. — *Bible.*
7. England, with all thy faults, I love thee still. — *Cowper.*

8. God bless the noble workingmen,
    Who rear the cities of the plain;
    Who dig the mines, who build the ships;
    And drive the commerce of the main!

9. The weakest kind of fruit
    Drops earliest to the ground. — *Shakespeare.*

10. The bloom of a rose passes quickly away,
    And the pride of a butterfly dies in a day.

19. SIMPLE SUBJECT AND PREDICATE.

Let us examine once more the following sentence:

Beautiful trees grow on the hillside.

The complete [1] subject of this sentence is *Beautiful trees*, and the complete [1] predicate is *grow on the hillside*. If we omit the word *trees* from the subject and the word *grow* from the predicate, do the remaining words, *Beautiful on the hillside*, express a thought or make a sentence? If we omit all but the words *trees grow*, is a thought expressed? The word *trees* and the word *grow* are the two parts of speech in this sentence which, taken together, make a statement, and are called the simple [2] subject and predicate; as,

---

[1] Or "modified." [2] Or "grammatical."

COMPLETE SUBJECT.   COMPLETE PREDICATE.
Beautiful trees ⋀ *grow on the hillside.*

SIMPLE SUBJECT.   SIMPLE PREDICATE.
trees   ⋀   *grow.*

REMARK. Hereafter, when we wish to speak of the simple subject and simple predicate, we shall speak of them as *subject* and *predicate;* and when we wish to speak of them and their modifiers, the terms *complete subject* and *complete predicate* will be used.

TO THE TEACHER. It should be made clear to pupils that the terms *subject* and *predicate* are applied to the words themselves, and not to what is represented by the words. In the sentence *Boys play*, the subject of the sentence is the word *Boys*, and the predicate is the word *play*. The subject of thought, however, is the boys themselves, and the thought predicate is the action expressed by the word *play*.

Exercise.

Select the subject and the predicate in each of the following numbered sentences, and then diagram each sentence according to the example given below.

Observe in the diagram that a single part of speech fills the place of the subject, and that a single part of speech occupies the place of the predicate. The remaining parts of the complete subject, you will notice, are arranged on a vertical line placed under the subject-line and joined to it. The same is true of the remaining parts of the complete predicate:

A beautiful tree ⋀ *stands there.*

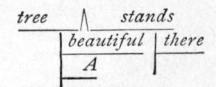

1. The cold wind blows violently.
2. The beautiful snow falls fast.
3. The snow-drifts grow rapidly.
4. Now comes the sport.
5. The flag waves triumphantly.
6. They strolled along carelessly.
7. The frightened hare ran away.
8. Softly the evening came.
9. The children played happily.
10. The robin sang cheerfully.

Two or more words taken together may form a verb; as,

The wind **does blow.**
The wind **will blow.**
The wind **is blowing.**
The wind **has been blowing.**
The wind **may have been blowing.**

The words that form a verb are **often** separated in the sentence by other words; as,

The wind **did** *not* **blow.**
The wind **will** *not always* **blow.**

Exercise.

Select the verbs in the following sentences, and determine those that are made up of two or more words:

1. She must weep, or she will die. — *Tennyson.*
2. The birds are singing in the leafy galleries.
3. Who can paint like nature?
4. Hope may vanish, but can not die.
5. The day is done, and the darkness falls from the wings of night.
6. The sun has drunk the dew that lay upon the morning grass.
7. What can not be cured must be endured.
8. Nature had nursed me in her lap, and I had grown a dark and eerie child.
9. The rain comes when the wind calls.
10. The fox barks not when he would steal the lamb.

20. MODIFIERS.

In diagramming sentences (Gr. **19**) you learned that certain words are joined to the subject, and others, to the predicate. These words are used to modify, or change, the meaning or application of the words to which they are joined.

In the following sentence substitute *small* for *beautiful*, and *in the orchard* for *there*, and note the change in meaning:

A beautiful *tree stands* there.

DEFINITION. A *Modifier* is a word, or a group of words, added to another to change the meaning.

A modifier changes the meaning by limiting (usually narrowing) the application of a word. The word *trees* applies to trees in general and means all trees. If we add the modifier *beautiful*, the modified word means only such trees as are beautiful.

21. ADJECTIVES.

Refer to the sentences you diagrammed on page 32, and select the words that are used to modify the meaning of nouns.

These words are called **Adjectives**.

DEFINITION. An *Adjective* is the part of speech used to modify the meaning of a noun or pronoun.

Consult a dictionary for the derivation and meaning of the word *adjective*.

Exercise.

Fill the blanks with appropriate adjectives, and tell what each modifies:

1. _____ clouds gathered.
2. A _____ heart's worth gold.
3. A _____ laugh is sunshine in a house.
4. A _____ son maketh a _____ father.
5. There is _____ _____ word as fail.
6. A _____ stone gathers _____ moss.

7. Washington, _____ _____ President of _____ United States, was born on _____ _____ day of February.
8. Patience is the _____ remedy for _____ trouble.
9. How doth _____ _____ _____ bee
   Improve _____ _____ hour,
   And gather honey all _____ day
   From _____ _____ flower.

22. ADVERBS.

The class of words joined to the predicate in the sentences you have diagrammed (Gr. 19) are called **Adverbs,** because they are generally used with verbs to modify their meaning.

They are not always used, however, to modify the meaning of verbs. Sometimes an adverb modifies the meaning of another modifier; as,

A **very** *beautiful* tree **stands** *quite* **near**.

```
tree         stands
|beautiful   |near
 |very        |quite
 |A
```

In this sentence the adverb *very* modifies the adjective *beautiful,* and the adverb *quite* modifies the adverb *near*.

DEFINITION. **An *Adverb* is the part of speech used to modify the meaning of a verb, an adjective, or an adverb.**

Exercise.

Fill blanks with appropriate adverbs, and tell what each modifies:

1. Write _____.
2. Don't read _____ _____.

3. Speak _____ to the erring.
4. The earth revolves _____ _____.
5. What is worth doing at all is worth doing _____.
6. Build thee _____ stately mansions, O my soul!
7. Though the mills of God grind _____, yet they grind exceeding small.
8. The world will _____ note, nor _____ remember, what we say here; but it can _____ forget what they did here.

23. TO RECOGNIZE ADJECTIVES AND ADVERBS.

An adjective usually modifies by showing **what kind, which one,** or **how many**; as,

What kind *of tree?*	Beautiful *tree.*
Which one *of the trees?*	The first *tree.*
How many *trees?*	Several *trees.*

The words *beautiful, the, first,* and *several* are adjectives, and show what kind, which one, and how many.

An adverb usually modifies by showing **how, when,** or **where**; as,

The snow falls **how?**	*The snow falls* softly.
The snow falls **when?**	*The snow falls* now.
The snow falls **where?**	*The snow falls* here.

The words *softly, now,* and *here* are adverbs, and show how, when, and where the snow falls.

Exercise.

In the following tell which of the indicated words are adjectives and which are adverbs.

Point out the part of speech that each modifies, and tell what it shows; thus,

Beautiful *snowflakes fall* **softly.**

Beautiful is an adjective used to modify the meaning of the noun *snowflakes* by showing what kind of snowflakes.

Softly is an adverb used to modify the meaning of the verb *falls* by showing how the snow falls.

1. We **often** praise the evening clouds,
   And tints **so gay** and **bold**,
   But **seldom** think upon our God,
   Who tinged these clouds with gold.— *Sir Walter Scott.*

2. **Here delicate** snow-stars out of the cloud
   Come floating downward in **airy** play,
   Like spangles dropped from the **glistening** crowd
   That whiten by night the milky way;
   There broader and **burlier** masses fall;
   The **sullen** water buries them all —
      Flake after flake —
   All drowned in the **dark** and **silent** lake.

   And some, as on tender wings they glide
   From their **chilly** birth-cloud, **dim** and **gray**,
   Are joined in their fall, and, **side by side**,[1]
   Come clinging along their **unsteady** way;
   As friend with friend, or husband with wife,
   Makes **hand in hand**[1] the passage of life;
      Each mated flake
   Soon sinks in the **dark** and **silent** lake.
   — *William Cullen Bryant.*

24. PHRASE MODIFIERS.

Note the indicated groups of words used as modifiers in the numbered sentences, and tell what they modify; thus,

The flakes **of snow** *sink* **in the lake.**

Of snow is used as an adjective to modify the meaning of the noun *flakes*, by telling what kind.

[1] *Side by side* and *hand in hand* are used as single adverbs.

In the lake is used as an adverb to modify the meaning of the verb *sink*, by showing where.

1. The clouds hang **over the lake.**
2. **Out of the clouds** come flakes of snow.
3. They come **in airy play.**
4. **On tender wings** they glide.
5. Some hover awhile **in the air.**
6. They sink **in the depths of the lake.**
7. We live **in deeds,** not years,
   In thoughts, not breaths ;
   In feelings, not **in figures on a dial.**

DEFINITION. **A group of words not containing a predicate verb and used as a single part of speech is called a** *Phrase.*

Exercise.

Analyze and diagram the following numbered sentences according to models here given:

Very soon the deep crimson blush of morning appeared.

ORAL ANALYSIS. First give kind of sentence and point out subject and predicate; then give the modifiers of the subject and predicate. Thus:

This is a declarative sentence ; *blush* is the subject, and *appeared* is the predicate.

The subject *blush* is modified by the adjectives *the* and *crimson* and by the phrase *of morning;* and *crimson* itself is modified by the adverb *deep*. The predicate *appeared* is modified by the adverb *soon*, and *soon* is modified by the adverb *very*.

```
blush        \    appeared
 |crimson         |soon
   |deep            |Very
 |the
 |of| morning
```

1. Soon we came to the lake.
2. The silvery moon watched over them.
3. A ray of light shone through the window.
4. On the mountain-side a sunbeam falls.
5. Pretty blue violets bloom early in the spring.

6. Many beautiful lilies are found in Japan.
7. The birds are singing in the leafy galleries.
8. Around the garden beds hosts of devouring insects crawl.
9. Very tall trees grow from acorns.
10. Strike for the green graves of your sires!
11. The fountain of truth will never fail.
12. Words, without thoughts, never to Heaven go.
13. In winter the reindeer feeds upon moss.
14. Potatoes grow well in Peru.
15. White strawberries grow in Chile.
16. On the motionless branches of some trees, clusters of autumn berries hung.

25. PREPOSITIONS.

In diagramming the sentences in the last exercise we found that phrases were used as modifiers. Notice also the following sentences:

1. *We came* to the boat.
2. *The moon watched* over them.

Note that these modifying phrases are made up of a substantive — a noun or pronoun (*boat*, a noun; *them*, a pronoun) — and another word used to connect the substantive to some other word.

Omit the word *to* and note the loss or lack of connection: *We came boat.* *To* links or joins *boat* to *came*.

These connecting words also indicate, or show, a relation in sense between the parts of speech they connect.

Note the different relation of *boat* to *came* indicated by substituting *on* for *to*.

We came { to *the boat,*
{ on *the boat.*

To denotes the place to which we came.
On denotes the manner of our coming.

Most connective words that show relation are called **Prepositions.**

The word *preposition* is from a Latin word meaning *placed before*, and refers to the early use of such words before verbs as prefixes; as, *To* up*hold*, in*close*, over*look*, with*draw*, for*give*, under*stand*.

Their use as connectives requires them to be placed, for the most part, before the substantive with which they are used; as, *shafts* **of** *sunshine* **from** *the west*. They may, however, come after them; as,

Ten thousand men that fishes gnawed **upon.** *— Shakespeare.*

$$\frac{fishes \wedge gnawed}{\quad | upon\, |\, that}$$

The substantive that is used with a preposition is called its **Object.**

The pronoun *that* in the above sentence is the object of the preposition *upon*.

Everything came to her from on high.

$$\frac{Everything \wedge came}{\quad | to\, |\, her \atop | from\, |\, on\ high}$$

The pronoun *her* is the object of the preposition *to*, and the substantive phrase *on high* is the object of the preposition *from*.

REMARK. In this sentence we may supply the word *place* as an object of *from*, and consider *high* as the object of *on*.

$$\frac{Everything \wedge came}{\quad | from\, |\, (place) \atop (a) \atop on\, |\, high}$$

THE PARTS OF SPEECH

Every preposition must have an object. Omit the objects of the following prepositions, and note the loss or change of meaning:

1. We should count time by (heart-throbs).
2. He gave the book to (me).
3. I shot an arrow into (the air).
4. A man of (honor) speaks the truth.
5. The boy fell behind (the house).[1]
6. The child fell down (stairs).[1]

We may determine the object of a preposition by using *what* or *whom* after the preposition to form a question; as,

We should count time by what?   *By* heart-throbs.
He gave the books to whom?   *To* me.

DEFINITION. A *Preposition* is the part of speech used to connect a substantive with some other word, and to indicate a relation between them.

Exercises.

EX. I. *Note the prepositions in full-face type in the following sentences, determine the object of each, and point out the part of speech with which each object is connected:*

1. The wisdom **of** the wise and the experience **of** ages may be preserved **by** quotation. — *Disraeli.*
2. It is the people's government, made **for** the people, **by** the people, and answerable **to** the people. — *Webster.*
3. A freeman contending **for** liberty **on** his own ground is superior **to** any slavish mercenary **on** earth. — *Washington.*
4. Let reverence **of** the law be breathed **by** every mother **to** the lisping babe that prattles **on** her lap; let it be taught **in** schools, . . . preached **from** pulpits, proclaimed **in** legislative halls, and enforced **in** courts of justice. — *Lincoln.*

---

[1] Some words are used either as prepositions or as adverbs. *Behind* and *down* are words of this kind. When the object is omitted they become adverbs.

Ex. II. *Diagram the following sentences according to the example given:*

The early settlers of New York and Pennsylvania traveled on horseback and in wagon trains.

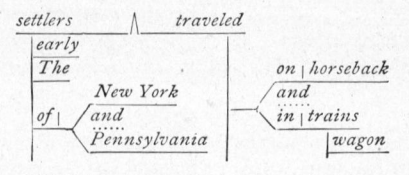

```
        settlers  \    traveled
        early
        The                    on | horseback
                New York       / and
        of |   / and           \ in | trains
               \ Pennsylvania        wagon
```

1. He pleaded for life and liberty.
2. Coffee grows in Mexico and Brazil.
3. People now travel by rail or in automobiles.
4. In summer and winter the reindeer feeds upon moss and lichens.
5. Three years she grew in sun and shower.   (During three years.)
6. With mirth and song the halls resound.

26. CONJUNCTIONS.

Note how the connective word *and* is used in the sentence diagrammed in the preceding lesson. Unlike the preposition it does not join two parts of speech so that one helps to modify the other. It merely indicates that two words, or groups of words, are to be taken together. A connective word of this kind is called a **Conjunction** — a word that means *joining together.*

When words or phrases are joined by conjunctions they are *in the same grammatical construction;* that is, they are used as like parts of speech in the sentence.

In the sentence diagrammed in the preceding lesson, *New York* and *Pennsylvania* are two nouns used alike as object of the preposition *of.* They are joined together by the conjunction *and. On horseback* and *in wagon trains* are two phrases used alike as adverbial modifiers and joined together by a conjunction.

THE PARTS OF SPEECH

A conjunction may join two separate sentences into one.

SEPARATE SENTENCES.	SENTENCES CONNECTED.
1. *Thou shalt build.* 2. *I will burn.*	1. 2. *Thou shalt build* **and** *I will burn.*
3. *We may give advice.* 4. *We can not give conduct.*	3. 4. *We may give advice,* **but** *we can not give conduct.* 3. 4. *We may give advice,* **if** *we can not give conduct.*

DEFINITION. A *Conjunction* is the part of speech that joins sentences, or connects words or phrases that are in the same grammatical construction.

Exercises.

EX. I. *In the following sentences the indicated words are conjunctions. Tell what each connects, and note that the words and phrases connected are used in the same construction:*

1. He quaffed off the wine, **and** he threw down the cup.
2. A beautiful **and** lovely child ran **and** played beside her.
3. Slowly **and** sadly we laid him down.
4. Give me liberty, **or** give me death!
5. They sailed around **and** around the island.
6. Virtue is an angel, **but** she is a blind one.
7. What is liberty without wisdom **and** without virtue?
8. Wild is thy lay, **and** loud.
9. The world will little note, **nor** long remember, what we say here, **but** it can never forget what they did here.
10. Laws are not masters, **but** (they are) servants, **and** we rule them **if** we obey them.

EX. II. *Tell which of the indicated words in the following sentences are prepositions, and why. Tell which are conjunctions, and why:*

1. Do not squander time; **for** that is the stuff life is made of.
2. Cleverness is serviceable **for** everything, sufficient **for** nothing.
3. Wings are for angels, **but** feet for men.
4. All **but** him had fled.
5. You have done better **since** the last examination.
6. **Since** you refuse to go, I must ask some one else.

27. INTERJECTIONS.

There is a small class of words expressive of feeling or emotion, which have no grammatical connection with any other part of the sentence in which they are used.

Examine the use of the indicated words, and note the kind of feeling expressed in each sentence:

1. **Lo!** *the birds have flown!* (Surprise.)
2. **Hurrah!** *the birds have flown!* (Joy.)
3. **Pshaw!** *the birds have flown.* (Disappointment.)
4. **Ho!** *the birds have flown.* (Desire to call attention.)
5. *The birds,* **alas!** *have flown.* (Sorrow.)

```
            alas
         birds ∧ have flown
        |The
```

The indicated words, you observe, are independent; that is, they have no grammatical connection with any other part of the sentence. They are added or thrown in, as it were, merely to indicate the kind of feeling that the sentences are intended to express. From their use, these words are called **Interjections** — a word that means *something thrown in among other things*.

DEFINITION. An *Interjection* is an exclamatory word or expression used independently to indicate feeling or emotion.

As explained in Grammar **6** (pp. 14, 15), when some other part of speech is used as an interjection it may be equivalent to a sentence ; as,

1. **Behold!** *the sun has risen.*
2. **Away!** *we must not linger.*
3. **Impossible!** *it can not be.*

Some authors would complete these expressions, and classify the interjections as a verb, an adverb, etc. ; as,

1. *You* **behold.** (Verb.)
2. *We must go* **away.** (Adverb.)
3. *It is* **impossible.** (Adjective.)

It is probably better, however, to consider them as interjections.

Exercise.

Select the interjections in the following sentences, mention those that are generally other parts of speech, and name the kind of feeling probably expressed in each sentence:

1. Hurrah! the battle's won.
2. He died, alas! before the morn.
3. Hist, Ringan! seest thou there!
4. And lo! the ranks divide.
5. Strange! I did not see you.
6. "Ugh! Bah!" cried the fairy godmother.
7. Oh! I'm the chief of Ulva's isle.
8. O master! what is this I see!
9. Ah! what a shadow is praise!
10. But hush! hark! a deep sound strikes like a rising knell.

Strictly speaking, the interjection is not a "part of speech," since it is not joined with the other words in a sentence, but merely *thrown in among them* without connection. For convenience, however, it is included among the parts of speech, as is also the expletive (Gr. **9,** p. 19).

28. SUMMARY OF THE PARTS OF SPEECH.

From the preceding lessons it appears that there are nine functions, or uses, of words in speech, or discourse, and that words are classified accordingly into nine different parts of speech, as follows :

PRINCIPAL PARTS OF SPEECH.
1. **Noun.** — The part of speech used as the name of something.
2. **Pronoun.** — The part of speech used instead of a noun.
3. **Verb.** — The part of speech used to make an assertion.

MODIFIERS.
4. **Adjective.** — The part of speech used to modify the meaning of a noun or pronoun.
5. **Adverb.** — The part of speech used to modify the meaning of a verb, an adjective, or an adverb.

CONNECTIVES.
6. **Preposition.** — The part of speech used to join a substantive to some other word, and to indicate a relation between them.
7. **Conjunction.** — The part of speech used to join two sentences into one, or to connect words or phrases that are in the same grammatical construction.

INDEPENDENT EXPRESSIONS.
8. **Interjection.** — The part of speech used independently to express feeling or emotion.
9. **Expletive.** — The part of speech used independently to give fullness or euphony to a sentence.

These nine parts of speech include all the words of our language ; but it does not follow that a word is always the same part of speech. The same word may have different uses in the sentence, and hence may become different parts of speech according to its use and meaning.

Notice the different parts of speech Shakespeare has made of the word *round :*

THE PARTS OF SPEECH

1. *He wears upon his brow the* **round** (noun) *of sovereignty.*
2. *I will a* **round** (adjective) *unvarnished tale deliver.*
3. *The golden metal must* **round** (verb) *my brow.*
4. *The gold must* **round** (adverb) *engirt these brows of mine.*
5. *The sun hath gone* **round** (preposition) *the orbed earth.*

Exercise.

Note the words in full-face type, tell the part of speech each is, and give a reason for your classification:

1. A rolling **stone** gathers no moss.
2. **Stone** walls do not a prison make.

3. Trout **stay** in cool waters.
4. **Stay** is a charming word in a friend's vocabulary.

5. It is an **ill** wind that blows no good.
6. **Ill** fares the land, to hastening **ills** a prey.

7. The aged couple were **talking** about the past.
8. **Talking** is the disease of **age**.
9. Some persons **age** very rapidly.

10. Let them **fear** bondage who are slaves to **fear**.

11. **Deeds** survive the doers.
12. He **deeds** the property to his son.

13. The birds **nest** in the trees.
14. The bird's **nest** in the tree contains three blue eggs.

15. Heaven still guards the **right**.
16. Be sure you are **right** and then go ahead.
17. He will **right** the wrongs of the innocent.
18. And that my soul knoweth **right** well.

19. He is an **American**, and glories in the right of an **American** citizen.

20. His years **but** young, **but** his experience old.

21. Quick! **man** the lifeboat.

22.   **Man** wants but **little** here below,
      Nor wants that **little** long.

23.   A **little** rule, a **little** sway,
      A sunbeam in a winter's day.

29. REVIEW.

Ex. I. *Use each of the following words, first as a verb, then as a noun:* run; fish; blow; bark; paint.

Ex. II. *Use each of the following words, first as a verb, then as an adjective:* clear; dull; lean; tame; smooth.

Ex. III. *Use each of the following words, first as a verb, then as a noun, then as an adjective:* black; dress; iron; last; spring.

Ex. IV. *Use each of the following words as two different parts of speech, and tell how you have used them:* behind; by; mine; still; only; there; for; rest; fast.

TEST QUESTIONS. 1. Into how many classes are all the words of our language grouped? 2. What general name is given to these classes? 3. How do we determine what part of speech a word is? 4. Which class of words do we use as names? 5. Which part of speech is used to make an assertion? 6. Does a part of speech always consist of a single word? 7. Which part of speech must every sentence contain? 8. Define the subject and the predicate of a sentence. 9. What is the modified subject? 10. What is the difference between the subject of a sentence and the subject of thought in a sentence? 11. Name five concrete nouns. 12. Name five abstract nouns. 13. How do concrete and abstract nouns differ? 14. Why are pronouns convenient? 15. What is the antecedent of a pronoun? 16. What is a modifier? 17. How does one word modify another? 18. What is the difference between an adjective and an adverb? 19. What does the word *preposition* mean? 20. What is the object of a preposition? 21. How may we determine the object of a preposition? 22. How do prepositions and conjunctions differ? 23. In what are they alike? 24. What must be true of words and of phrases that are joined by conjunctions? 25. Why are interjections and expletives, strictly speaking, not parts of speech? 26. Of what use is each in communicating thought?

PART II.

THE SENTENCE AND ITS ELEMENTS (CONTINUED). COMPLEMENTS, PHRASES, AND CLAUSES.

(To be studied in connection with Part II of the Composition on pages 265-307.)

30. COMPLEMENTS.

1. Verbs of Complete Predication. In the sentences that you have thus far been required to analyze or diagram, the predicate has consisted of a verb which by itself made a complete assertion or predication. Such verbs are called **Verbs of Complete Predication**;[1] as,

1. *The ship* sank.
2. *She* must weep.

The verb in each of these sentences makes a complete assertion. We may use additional words to make the assertion more definite; as,

The ship sank **quickly**; or *sank* **slowly**; or *sank* **in the harbor**;

yet the verb *sank* makes a complete assertion without these additional words, and is, therefore, a verb of complete predication.

2. Verbs of Incomplete Predication. Some verbs usually require an additional word, or words, to complete the assertion. Such words are called **Verbs of Incomplete Predication,** or, briefly, **Incomplete Verbs;** as,

---

[1] Complete verbs are sometimes called **Attributive Verbs,** because they express in themselves the attribute ascribed to the subject.

1. *Washington* was.
2. *Washington* crossed.
3. *The weather* is.
4. *The weather* became.
5. *General Grant* said.

Each of these expressions contains a subject joined with a verb, yet it is incomplete as making an assertion, and we must supply additional words to complete the meaning of the predicate; thus:

1. *Washington was* president.
2. *Washington crossed* the Delaware.
3. *The weather is* fine.
4. *The weather became* settled.
5. *General Grant said*, "Let us have peace."

DEFINITION. That which is joined to a verb to complete the predication is called a *Complement*.

Exercise.

In each of the following groups of words tell whether the verb makes complete predication, and if the predication is incomplete, supply suitable complements:

1. The first president was
2. The earth is
3. The earth revolves
4. Romulus founded
5. The Romans built
6. Oranges are
7. Oranges taste
8. Florida produces
9. Roses bloom
10. The rose smells
11. Bees make
12. The weather seems
13. The sun rose
14. The problem appears
15. Marble feels
16. The children rested
17. Longfellow was
18. Dewey captured
19. Franklin discovered
20. General Grant became
21. Morse invented
22. Lawrence said
23. The flag waves
24. The flag looks
25. We honor

(*For additional exercises see p. 352.*)

31. KINDS OF COMPLEMENTS.

If you observe closely you will notice that the complements you supplied in the last exercise are of two kinds:

1. Complements that name the subject, or describe it by denoting some quality, or attribute, of it; as, *The first president was* **Washington**. The complement *Washington* names the subject. *The earth is* **round**. *Round* denotes an attribute of the earth.

2. Complements that name the object which receives the act performed by the subject and expressed by the verb; as, *The Romans built* **ships**. *Ships* is the object that receives the action performed by the subject *Romans* and expressed by the verb *built*.

In the twenty-five sentences of the preceding exercise (Gr. 30) you were required to supply twenty complements. Write these complements in two columns, placing in the first all those that name or describe the subject; in the second, all those naming the object that receives the action expressed by the verb.

The complements in the first column are called **Attribute Complements,** or, more briefly, **Attributes.** Why?

Those in the second column are called **Object Complements,** or, more briefly, **Objects.** Why?

DEFINITIONS. An *Attribute Complement* completes the predicate by naming or describing the subject.

An *Object Complement* completes the predicate by naming that which receives the action expressed by the verb.

Exercises.

Ex. I. *In the following sentences the indicated words are complements. Tell of each whether it is an attribute or an object:*

1. We smell the **roses**.
2. The roses smell **sweet**.
3. He tasted an **apple**.
4. The apple tasted **sour**.
5. The corn grows **tall**.
6. The farmer grows **corn**.
7. The boy turned the **grindstone**.
8. The boy that fell turned **pale**.
9. The mid-day sun feels **warm**.
10. The traveler feels the **heat**.
11. The coat becomes **old**.
12. The coat becomes the **boy**.
13. The hat becomes the **man**.
14. The boy becomes the **man**.
15. The conqueror very often becomes a **tyrant**.

Ex. II. Point out the complements in the following numbered sentences and tell whether they are object or attribute complements, and why. Diagram each sentence according to the following examples:

```
  earth ∧ is \ round           President ∧ was \ Washington
 |The                           |first
                                |The
```

```
  Romans ∧ built | ships
 |The
```

Notice that the top of the line before an attribute complement points toward the subject, but the line before an object complement is vertical.

1. The children are happy.
2. The children's poet is Longfellow.
3. Longfellow loved little children.
4. He wrote poems for them.
5. Cæsar was a great general.
6. Thrice he refused the crown.
7. Dispatch is the soul of business.
8. A statesman may make mistakes.
9. Punctuality is the politeness of kings.

32. COPULATIVE VERBS.

Incomplete verbs that require an attribute complement are called **Copulative Verbs**, or **Copulas**. They are so

COMPLEMENTS

called because they are used as joining words, or couplers, to join the subject to that which is asserted of it. Thus:

> *The dog* **seems** *cross.*
> *The dog* **is** *cross.*

DEFINITION. **A** *Copulative Verb,* **or** *Copula,* **is a verb that makes a predication by joining the subject to that which is asserted of it.**

Of the small number of verbs used as copulas, the verb **be** (**am, is, was, were, has been,** etc.) is the most common. Others are: **become, smell, sound, look,** etc.

These verbs are not always used as copulas. Even the word **be,** which is almost purely copulative, is sometimes used as a complete verb meaning *to exist;* as,

> God **is** *and ever shall* **be.**
> *Time* **was** *when no man lived here.*
> **To be,** *or not* **to be,** — *that is the question.*

A copula takes an attribute complement. It never has an object complement.

Exercise.

Turn to Grammar **31** *and make a list of all the verbs used as copulas in Exercises I. and II.*

CAUTION. Do not mistake words that are added as *modifiers* of the predicate for words that are added as *complements*. In the sentence "The girl writes well," the word *well* is used to modify the meaning of the verb and to tell *how* the girl writes. In the sentence "The girl writes a letter," the word *letter* is added to the verb to tell *what* the girl writes. A complement of a verb usually answers the question formed by placing **what? who?** or **whom?** after the verb. The girl writes **what?** *A letter.* A modifier of a verb usually answers the question formed by placing **how? when?** or **where?** after the verb. The letter was written **how?** *Well.*

Exercise.

In the following sentences the indicated words are either complements or modifiers. Point out the complements and tell whether they are attribute or object complements:

1. The child speaks the **truth**.
2. The child speaks **distinctly**.
3. The boy obeyed **promptly**.
4. The boy obeyed his **teacher**.
5. The pupils paint **well**.
6. The pupils paint **landscapes**.
7. The girl turned **quickly**.
8. The girl turned her **back**.
9. Arnold turned **traitor**.
10. He remained **there** for the rest of his life.
11. He remained **secretary** for the rest of his life.
12. He who loves **praise**, loves **temptation**.
13. He who loves **truly**, loves **always**.
14. The lady looked **pleasantly** at the child.
15. The red apple looked **good** to the boy.

33. OBJECTIVE COMPLEMENTS.

You have learned that verbs of incomplete predication require either an attribute or an object complement to complete their meaning. Some verbs require something in addition to an object complement to complete their meaning; as,

They made the boy _____.
This made him _____.

In these two groups of words we have subject, verb, and complement; yet they are not complete sentences. Additional words are required to complete the predicate:

They made the boy **captive**.
This made him **unhappy**.

The use of these complementary words *captive* and *unhappy* may be seen by comparing sentences of similar meaning:

They **made** *the boy* **captive** = *They* **captured** *the boy*.
This **made** *him* **unhappy** = *This* **disheartened** *him*.

COMPLEMENTS

Captive and *unhappy* each completes the predicate and at the same time describes the object.

DEFINITION. **A word or group of words used to complete the predicate and to describe the object is called an** *Objective Complement.*

The objective complement is sometimes called the **Factitive Complement,** because it is used only with *make* and verbs of similar meaning; the word *factitive* comes from a Latin word meaning *make*.

TO THE TEACHER. Special care is necessary to prevent confusing the objective complement with the object complement, because of the small difference in the names.

Exercise.

Point out the objective complements (or factitive complements) in the following numbered sentences, show that they belong to both the verb and the object, see whether the verb **make** *can be substituted, and diagram according to this model:*

$$They \;\backslash\; made/captive \;|\; boy$$
$$\qquad\qquad |the$$

In the diagram notice that the line before the object complement is vertical, as usual, and the line between the verb and the objective complement points toward the object, as the objective complement always describes the object.

1. They proclaimed Alphonso king.
2. They considered him great.
3. They named the city Rome.
4. Sympathy makes a person kind.
5. We pumped the well dry.
6. The carpenter planed the board smooth.
7. He sawed the board square.
8. He painted the board red.
9. He kept the board painted.
10. He made the board useful.
11. Haste can make you slipshod.
12. It can never make you graceful.
13. We can make our lives sublime.

[1] Pages 55–66 have been made somewhat simpler in this 37th printing than in the older printings of the book. Teachers using old and new books in the same class can obtain from the publishers copies of these simplified pages if desired.

34. THE INDIRECT OBJECT.

They made the boy a coat.

This sentence means: "They made a coat **for** the boy." *Coat* is the object complement, and *boy*, telling for whom the coat is intended, is called the **Indirect Object**.

```
They  \  made | coat
          |(for) | boy | a
                | the
```

The janitor gave the blackboard a coat of paint.

This sentence means: "The janitor gave **to** the blackboard a coat of paint." Here *coat* is the object complement, and *blackboard* is the indirect object.

DEFINITION. A noun or pronoun that tells for whom or what the object complement is intended, is called an *Indirect Object*.[1]

By a slight change in the order of the words, *to* or *for* may be placed before an indirect object; as,

1. *Owen wrote his mother a letter.*	1. *Owen wrote a letter to his mother.*
2. *She bought him a present.*	2. *She bought a present for him.*
3. *She gave him a book.*	3. *She gave a book to him.*

```
She  \  gave | book
         |(to) | him | a
```

These sentences show that the indirect object is a phrase modifier of the predicate, having the preposition *to* or *for* omitted. In analyzing, call the indirect object a modifier of the predicate, and place it as such in the diagram.

---

[1] When a verb takes an indirect object, the *object complement* may be called the *direct object* to distinguish it from the *indirect*.

INDIRECT OBJECT

Exercise.

Diagram the following sentences, mention the object of each, and tell for whom or what the object is intended:

1. Edith made her doll a dress.
2. Will you do me a favor?
3. The child told him the truth.
4. Forgive us our debts.
5. Sidney gave the dying soldier a drink.
6. I sent Dr. Noss an invitation.
7. Mr. Hart teaches us music.
8. You can't teach an old dog new tricks.
9. David sold the deacon a horse.
10. I wish you good luck.

35. REVIEW.

EXERCISE. *Select the complements in the following and tell the kind of each; also point out the indirect objects:*

1. The camel is a native of Arabia.
2. Camels are patient animals and carry heavy burdens.
3. The merchant gave the boy a chance.
4. He made the boy his secretary.
5. By industry he became a prosperous man.
6. Idleness is the mother of all the vices.
7. Poverty wants few things, avarice wants everything.
8. Nothing that is dishonest is profitable.
9. Faithfulness to duty brought him his reward.
10. Enthusiasm makes men happy.
11. Living is not breathing; it is acting.
12. Hunger makes coarse meats delicate.
13. A good cause makes a stout heart and a strong arm.

TEST QUESTIONS. 1. What is meant by a verb of complete predication? 2. What is a copulative verb? 3. Does a copulative verb ever have an object? 4. Why are some complements called attributes? 5. How many kinds of complements are there? 6. What parts of speech may be used as complements? 7. What is an indirect object? 8. How does an objective complement differ from an attribute complement? 9. From an object complement? 10. Write, or select from your reader, five sentences to show the use of the object; five to show the use of the attribute; two to show the use of the objective complement; two to show the use of the indirect object.

36. INFINITIVES AND PARTICIPLES.

From the foregoing lessons you have become familiar with the nine different parts of speech, and have learned their uses as the simple elements, or parts, of the sentence; namely, Subject, Predicate, Complement, Modifier, and Connective.

Besides these nine parts of speech there are two other classes of words which, although *not separate parts of speech*, have been given individual names — the **Infinitive** and the **Participle.** They are forms of the verb: they may always be modified by adverbs, and may have complements. They cannot, however, be used as predicates; but they are used as subjects, complements, and modifiers (like nouns, adjectives, and adverbs).

For example, *to read* and *to go* are infinitives; *reading* and *going* are participles. The infinitive and participle are called the *infinite* forms of a verb. All forms used as predicates are called *finite*.

37. THE INFINITIVE.

The common form of the infinitive is a verb with *to* before it, *to* having become merely the **Sign of the Infinitive,** and not a preposition; as, *to love, to walk, to strike, to eat.*

There are other forms of the infinitive also (Gr. 105, 111), but they are easily recognized by the word *to* preceding them. For example, all the infinitives of the verb *love* (an incomplete verb) and of *walk* (a complete verb) are:

To love. (To be loving.)	To walk. (To be walking.)
To have loved. (To have been loving.)	To have walked. (To have been walking.)
To be loved.	
To have been loved.	

THE INFINITIVE

The infinitive cannot be used as the predicate of a sentence. It can be modified by an adverb, and if incomplete it has a complement.

Uses of the Infinitive.

1. The infinitive is used most often as a *Noun:*

To study is to improve.

To study is the subject, and *to improve* is the attribute complement.

He likes to study English.

In this sentence the infinitive *to study* is the object complement of *likes.*

It is wise to study hard.
Here *to study* is an appositive.

Nothing remains except to study.
To study is object of the preposition *except.*

Which one of the infinitives above is modified by an adverb? Which one has an object complement?

Ex. I. *Tell the use of each infinitive in the following, and diagram:*

1. To visit my friends pleases me. 2. I hope to go with my father. 3. I began to know the valley well. 4. It is a pleasure to visit my friends. 5. No way was left but to walk. 6. To walk was to miss the train.

2. The infinitive is sometimes used as an *Adjective:*

Subjects to study are many.

To study modifies the noun *subjects.* It means the same as the phrase *for study,* used as an adjective.

We have lessons to be studied.

The infinitive *to be studied* is used as an adjective to modify *lessons.*

I am to study till noon.

To study is an attribute complement. The phrase *till noon,* telling when, is a phrase used as an adverb.

Ex. II. *Tell the use of each infinitive in the following, and diagram:*

1. He is a man to be watched. 2. The chicken to be killed could not be caught. 3. There are prizes to win. 4. He is to go to the city soon. 5. He has work to do on Monday.

3. The infinitive is sometimes used as an *Adverb:*

He visited Washington to study the city.

$$\underline{He \setminus visited \mid Washington}$$
$$\mid to\ study \mid city$$
$$\mid the$$

To study modifies the verb *visited*. How is *city* used? Note that *to* in this sentence equals *in order to*. This is often true in the adverbial infinitive.

Grammar is hard to study.

$$\underline{Grammar \setminus is \setminus hard}$$
$$\mid to\ study$$

To study modifies the adjective *hard*.

Ex. III. *Tell the use of each infinitive in the following, and diagram:*

1. He was anxious to prevent a riot. 2. He crossed the street to speak to the leader. 3. He had come to listen. 4. I am happy to find you.

4. The infinitive has one use in which it has a subject. It is *not* a predicate, however, as it does not assert action. It names an action and *assumes* that it will be performed by the subject. The infinitive, then, is used as an *assumed predicate*.[1]

I expect you to study.

$$\underline{I \setminus expect \mid you \mid \setminus to\ study}$$

You is not the object of *expect*, as I am not saying that I expect you. *To study* is not the object of *expect*, as I am not saying that I expect to study. *You to study* is the object: I expect what? *you to study*. Here the act of study is named and I *assume* that you will perform the act. But *to study* does not assert action. The predicate line is left open at the top ($\mid \_ \setminus \_$) to show that the action is assumed, not asserted.

[1] For the assumed predicate use of the infinitive in the subject, see page 360.

THE INFINITIVE

Ex. IV. *Tell the use of each infinitive in the following, and diagram:*

1. He asked us to spend a day with him. 2. He invited his cousin to come. 3. I expected Mattie to accept the invitation. 4. He finally persuaded her to go. 5. She asked me to enter the store. 6. The general expected him to carry the message. 7. I ask you to allow me to examine everything. 8. Will you allow me to give you a little advice? 9. I ask you to mistrust that man. 10. I have ordered three men to search the river.

To, the sign of the infinitive, is usually omitted after the verbs *bid, dare, feel, hear, help, let, make, see*. After most of these verbs the infinitive is used as an assumed predicate.

He bade me go. $He \wedge bade \mid me \mid \setminus go$

Go is an infinitive.   The sentence means, *He ordered me to go.*

Ex. V. *Point out the infinitives, and diagram each sentence:*

1. I felt the rope shake in my hand. 2. Help me lift this box. 3. I heard three boys ask him to go. 4. This makes me suspect the man. 5. He did not dare approach the house. 6. Let us go to the woods. 7. I saw him enter the room. 8. Let me see the book. 9. He made a desert blossom.

DEFINITION. An *Infinitive* is a verb form usually preceded by *to* and used as a noun, an adjective, an adverb, or an assumed predicate.

Exercise.

Analyze or diagram, and tell how each infinitive is used:

1. The teacher wanted the boy to go to school.
2. To study is to improve.
3. The dog loves to follow his master.
4. Every attempt to capture the wolf failed.
5. Lucy went to visit her cousin.
6. They expect Tom to win the prize.

7. Tom expects to win the prize.
8. Tom is anxious to win the prize.
9. To win the prize is an honor.
10. The captain ordered the troops to advance.
11. Lucy was anxious to see her cousin.
12. Henry went to see the fire.
13. The farmer has apples to sell.
14. To shoot at crows is to waste powder.
15. To converse with historians is to keep good company.
16. To throw perfume on the violet is wasteful excess.
17. Music hath charms to soothe the savage breast.
18. It was his duty to obey promptly.
19. It is not all of life to live.
20. It was his aim to settle the strike.
21. Perseverance will help to conquer our difficulties.

THE PARTICIPLE.

The most common form of the participle is a verb with the added syllable *ing*, as *loving, walking, striking, eating.*

There are also other forms of the participle, which will be studied in later lessons (Gr. **39, 106**); for example, all the participles of the verb *love* (an incomplete verb) and of *walk* (a complete verb) are:

loving	being loved	walking
loved	having been loved	walked
having loved		having walked

The word **Participle** means *sharing* or *partaking*. This form of the verb is so called because, in its most common use, it partakes of the nature of both verb and adjective; for example, study this sentence:

The boy studying his lesson will improve.

```
boy  \ will improve
 |The
 |studying | lesson
           |his
```

In this sentence the participle *studying* expresses action, like other verbs; it does not, however, assert action of a subject. As an incomplete verb, *studying* takes an object complement; and like an adjective it is used to modify the meaning of a noun. Of what noun does it modify the meaning? Point out its object complement.

THE PARTICIPLE

The participle cannot be used by itself as the predicate of a sentence. It can be modified by an adverb, and if incomplete it has a complement.

USES OF THE PARTICIPLE.

1. Any participle may be used as an *Adjective:*

The boy studying his grammar is my brother.

Studying modifies the noun *boy*.

Having studied his grammar, the boy went to school.

Having studied modifies the noun *boy*.

One gets little benefit from lessons studied hastily.

Studied modifies the noun *lessons*.

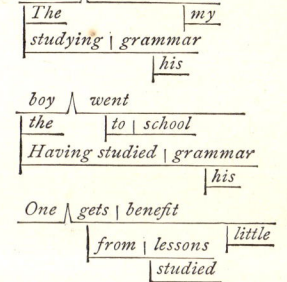

Ex. I. *Tell the use of each participle in the following sentences, and then diagram:*

1. One coming from Paris is surprised at the Spaniards. 2. They care nothing for pleasures procured by labor. 3. Favored by a beautiful sky, they have reduced life to its simplest form. 4. My uncle has a house situated in a yard sloping to the Hudson. 5. There is a courtyard covered with a vaulted roof pierced by small holes.

2. A participle which contains the ending *ing* may be used as a *Noun:*[1]

Studying is profitable.

Studying names an action but does not assert the action. It is the subject of *is*.

---

[1] Participles used as nouns are similar in construction to infinitives used as nouns. Thus, *Studying is profitable* means the same as *To study is profitable*.

The infinitive and participle used in this construction are sometimes classed as **Verbal Nouns**. When thus classified, the term **Gerund** is used by some grammarians to designate the *ing* form of the verbal. Others prefer to consider both *to study* and *studying* infinitives, and designate the latter as the **Infinitive in *ing***. The classification in this book is more easily understood by the pupil.

Studying grammar is profitable. $\underline{Studying \mid grammar} \wedge is \setminus profitable$

Here the participle *studying* takes an object complement. It is the subject of *is*.

Doing right is obeying God's law.

Here each participle has an object complement; one participle is used as a subject and the other as an attribute complement.

He was praised for studying grammar at home.

Here the participle is the object of the preposition *for*. It has both an object complement and an adverbial modifier.

Ex. II. *Tell the use of each participle in the following, and then diagram:*

1. She began preparing the meal. 2. Then they read the papers, besides singing ballads and playing the guitar. 3. They employ much time in doing nothing. 4. They prefer hunting rabbits, and by so doing they show their sense. 5. His lodgings cost him the trouble of spreading his cloak on the ground. 6. There a young man has no chance of making a success of life. 7. We are far from having attained their social equality.

3. The participle, like the infinitive, has a use in which it has a subject and assumes but does not assert action: the *assumed predicate* use.

I saw him studying. $I \wedge saw \mid him \mid \setminus studying$

Him studying is the object complement of *saw*. *Him* is an assumed subject, and *studying* is an assumed predicate. Notice that the predicate line is open at the top.

Ex. III. *Tell the use of each participle in the following, and diagram:*

1. He left the candle burning. 2. I saw a dozen men searching the woods. 3. I saw her eyes dancing. 4. I heard his father praising his work. 5. I saw the boys skating and heard their shouts ringing in the cold air. 6. I felt his pulse quickening.

4. For other uses of the participle, see pages 77, 361.

THE PARTICIPLE

DEFINITION. A *Participle* is a form of the verb (not preceded by *to*) used commonly as an adjective.

The participle containing the ending *ing*, as we have seen, may also be used as a noun, or as an assumed predicate.

A participle, remember, may be modified by an adverb, and may have a complement, but it cannot be modified by an adjective. If such a word is modified by an adjective it has lost its verb nature entirely and has become a pure noun; as, *The studying of grammar is profitable; He has a reputation for honest dealing.* Here *the* makes *studying* a pure noun, and *honest* makes *dealing* a pure noun.

Likewise, participles used immediately before nouns whose meaning they modify become pure adjectives; thus,

A **roaring** *sound was heard.*
Whispering *tongues can poison truth.*
We saw him in one of the **reserved** *seats.*

Exercises.

Ex. I. *In the following sentences classify the indicated words and tell how each is used in the sentence:*

1. **Rowing** a boat is healthful exercise.
2. The **rowing** of a boat is healthful exercise.
3. Constant **smoking** is injurious.
4. He was pleased at **winning** a prize.
5. **Reading** steadily affects the eyes.
6. Keep your **working** power at its maximum.
7. See! there is Jackson, **standing** like a stone wall.
8. The soldier was promoted for **doing** his duty.

Ex. II. *Analyze or diagram the following sentences and explain the use of each participle:*

1. A stream, winding through the meadow, flows into a sparkling lake.
2. Doing right is obeying God's law.
3. By doing nothing we learn to do ill.

4. Praising all is praising none.
5. Seeing the multitudes, he went up into a mountain.
6. By praising a man we sometimes injure him.
7. Mounting his horse, the general rode away.
8. The boy was punished for running away.
9. The squirrels playing about the Capitol are tame.
10. He heard his daughter's voice singing in the village choir.
11. Good reading aloud is an accomplishment.[1]
12. Your writing the letter so neatly secured you the position.[2]
13. Much depends on your going.
14. They were sure of winning a prize.
15. Tom's running away displeased his parents.

39. FORMS OF THE PARTICIPLE.

The Present Participle. A participle ending in *ing* is called the **Present Participle,** because it denotes action or being as still in progress; as, *playing, riding, being played.*

The present participle is used both as an *adjective* and as a *noun.*

The Past Participle. When a participle denotes action or being as finished, it is called a **Past Participle;** as, *played, ridden.*

The past participle generally ends in *d, ed, t, n,* or *en.* Its chief use is in forming the passive voice and the secondary tenses of the verb (Gr. 96, 110, pp. 156, 181). It is sometimes used as an *adjective,* but never as a noun.

The Perfect Participle. When a participle denotes action or being as completed just before the time represented by the predicate of the sentence, it is called a **Perfect Participle;** as, *having played, having been playing, having been played.*

The perfect participle may be used either as an *adjective* or as a *noun.*

---

[1] *Good* modifies *reading aloud.*
[2] *Your* modifies the phrase *writing the letter so neatly.* *You* is indirect object.

THE PARTICIPLE

Present Participle.	Past Participle.	Perfect Participle.
Playing Being played	Played	Having played Having been playing Having been played
Riding Being ridden	Ridden	Having ridden Having been riding Having been ridden

Exercise.

Tell the different kinds of participles in the following sentences; then analyze or diagram the sentences to show the use of each participle:

1. John, driving through the park, met his uncle.
2. John, driven through the park, met his uncle.
3. John, having driven through the park, met his uncle.
4. There came a thoughtful man,
    Searching nature's secrets, far and wide.
5. The ground-pine curled its pretty wreath,
    Running over the club-moss burrs. — *Emerson.*
6. Plunged in the battery smoke
    Right through the lines they broke. — *Tennyson.*
7. Genius is an immense capacity for taking trouble. — *Carlyle.*
8. But winter lingering chills the days of May.
9. Winds whispering from the west will bring them rain.
10. I shall cheerfully bear the reproach of having descended below the dignity of history. — *Macaulay.*

40. REVIEW.

TEST QUESTIONS.   1. What two forms of the verb have individual names?   2. Why are predicate verbs known as finite verbs?   3. What forms of the verb are not finite?   4. In the sentence "They ordered him to go," why is *to go* not a real predicate?   5. How many uses may the infinitive have in a sentence?   6. Write or select sentences to illustrate each of the different uses of the infinitive. 7. Define a participle. 8. In what respect do participles differ from infinitives? 9. In what respect are participles like verbs? 10. What uses may participles have in the sentence? 11. Select sentences from your reader to show the different uses of the participle. 12. How many forms has the participle? 13. Name and describe each. 14. Compose or select ten sentences, five containing present participles and five containing past participles, and tell how each is used. 15. Select or compose five sentences containing perfect participles.

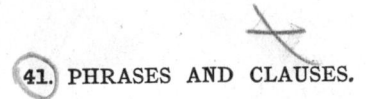

41. PHRASES AND CLAUSES.

Expanded Parts of Speech. The elements of a sentence (page 58) consist of the parts of speech of which the sentence is composed. Two or more different parts of speech, however, may be taken together as a single element and used to do the work of one part of speech.

Observe the following sentences and note that the single adjective *honest* is expanded into groups of two or more parts of speech which, taken together, do the work of the single adjective:

1. *An* **honest** *man speaks the truth.*
2. *A man* **of honesty** *speaks the truth.*
3. *A man* **that is honest** *speaks the truth.*

Observe also that the group of words in the second sentence, *of honesty*, does not contain a finite verb, or predicate, and that the group of words in the third sentence, *that is honest*, does contain a predicate.

The group of words in the second sentence is called a **Phrase.** The group in the third sentence is called a **Clause.**

In what respect are they alike? How do they differ?

PHRASES AND CLAUSES

DEFINITIONS. A *Phrase* is a group of words that does not contain a predicate and that is used to do the work of a single part of speech.[1]

A *Clause* is a group of words that contains a predicate and that is used to do the work of a single part of speech.

Exercise.

Tell which of the following groups of words are phrases and which are clauses:

1. In the White House.
2. Where the President lives.
3. Standing in the doorway.
4. Busied with public affairs.
5. Before leaving the city.
6. Before he left the city.
7. To enjoy his vacation.
8. At the seashore.
9. Among the Thousand Islands.
10. Of the St. Lawrence.
11. Where the gray birches wave.
12. In front of the train.
13. Before the train started.
14. When the train started.
15. As soon as the train started.
16. To ring the bell.
17. Ringing the bell.
18. If the bell rings.
19. Because the bell rings.
20. Did the bell ring?

42. KINDS OF PHRASES AND CLAUSES.

Note the indicated phrases and clauses in the sentences at the top of the next page, and tell for what part of speech each does the work:

---

[1] A distinction should be made between a **literary phrase** and a **grammatical phrase**.

A **grammatical phrase** is made up of two or more different parts of speech, exclusive of the finite verb, that can be parsed separately, and that taken together do the work of a noun, an adjective, or an adverb.

A **literary phrase** is any group of related words that convey an idea without making a predication; as, *Narrow walls of rock*, *From bowlder to bowlder*. (Comp. 88, p. 328.)

1. *An* earnest *man finds a way.*
2. *A man* in earnest *finds a way.*
3. *A man* that is in earnest *finds a way.*
4. *A tree grows* there.
5. *A tree grows* in that place.
6. *A tree grows* where it is planted.
7. **Labor** *brings reward.*
8. **To labor** *brings reward.*
9. **Whoever labors** *deserves reward.*

A phrase or a clause takes its particular name from the part of speech whose work it performs.

In earnest is called an **Adjective Phrase** because it is used as an adjective to modify, or make more definite, the meaning of the noun *man* in the second sentence.

DEFINITION. An *Adjective Phrase* is one that does the work of an adjective.

In that place is an **Adverbial Phrase,** used to modify the meaning of the verb *grows* in the fifth sentence.

DEFINITION. An *Adverbial Phrase* is one that does the work of an adverb.

To labor is a **Noun Phrase,** used as the subject of the eighth sentence.

DEFINITION. A *Noun Phrase* is one that does the work of a noun.

Point out the **Adjective Clause** in the above sentences. What is an adjective clause? (Make your own definition.)

Point out the **Adverbial Clause** in the above sentences. Define an adverbial clause.

Point out the **Noun Clause** in the above sentences. What is a noun clause?

REMARK. Phrases are sometimes named from the part of speech that introduces them; thus, *in earnest* may be called a **Prepositional Phrase,** it being introduced by the preposition *in*. This, however, gives undue prominence to the structure of the phrase, rather than to its use, and gives prepositional phrases, owing to their frequent occurrence, special prominence over others.

It is the use, or office, of a part of speech that determines its importance in the sentence, and since a phrase is used to do the work of a part of speech, it is better that it take its name from the part of speech whose work it performs. This is true also of clauses.

Exercise.

Turn to p. 308 and select from the description of " The Eel Trap" five adjective phrases and ten adverbial phrases, and tell what part of speech each modifies.

43. NOUN PHRASES.

Note how the phrases are diagrammed in the following, tell how each is used in the sentence, and for what part of speech it stands:

1. *To ask him a question was to wind up a spring in his memory.*

2. *The child wanted to ask him a question.*

3. *The child had no idea of asking him a question.*

4. *It is hard to ask him a question.*

The subject of the first sentence is the phrase *to ask him a question*, and the attribute complement is the phrase *to wind up a spring in his memory*.

In the second sentence the phrase *to ask him a question* is used as the object complement; and in the third sentence the phrase *asking him a question* is used as the object of the preposition *of*.

Thus it is clear that a **noun phrase** may be used as **subject,** as **object complement,** as **attribute complement,** as **object of a preposition,** and **in apposition.**

Exercise.

Diagram the following sentences according to examples given above:

1. To work industriously is to gain promotion.
2. The child hopes to win the prize.
3. The child is capable of winning the prize.
4. His winning the prize depends on his effort.
5. Over the fence is out.
6. All shouted, "Over the fence!"
7. In the field is over the fence.
8. Politeness is to do and say the kindest things in the kindest way.
9. To improve the golden moment of opportunity is the great art of life.
10. To labor rightly and earnestly is to walk in the golden path of contentment.

44. ADJECTIVE CLAUSES.

Analyze each of the following sentences; note how the clauses are connected, and how the connecting words are indicated in the diagram:

PHRASES AND CLAUSES

1. *He who ordained the Sabbath loves the poor.*

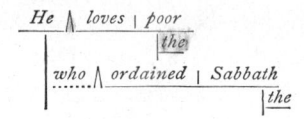

```
        He \ loves | poor
                   |the|
        who \ ordained | Sabbath
                       |the
```

ORAL ANALYSIS. The main part of the sentence as already given (page 38). *Who ordained the Sabbath* is an adjective clause used to modify the pronoun *he*. The connective is *who*.

2. *This is the artist whose work you admired.*

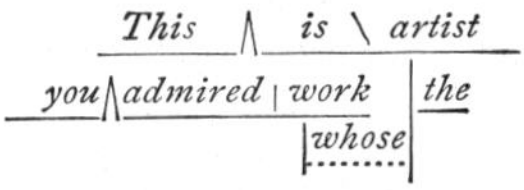

```
        This \ is \ artist
        you \ admired | work | the
                      |whose|
```

3. *The freeman is he whom the truth makes free.*

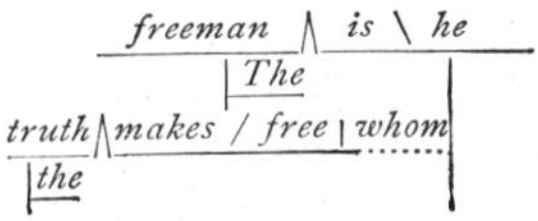

```
        freeman \ is \ he
                |The
        truth \ makes / free | whom
        |the
```

4. *Our to-days and yesterdays are the blocks with which we build.*

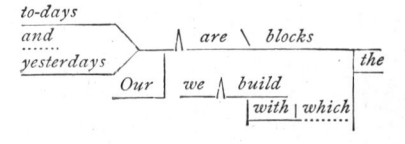

```
        to-days
        and
        yesterdays      \ are \ blocks
                                      |the
                   Our | we \ build
                              |with | which
```

5. *Happy is the man that findeth wisdom.*

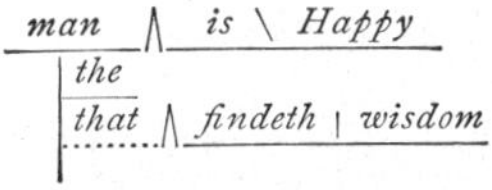

```
        man \ is \ Happy
        |the
        |that \ findeth | wisdom
```

Observe that the words used to connect the adjective clauses in the preceding exercise are pronouns: *who, whose, whom, which,* and *that*.

What pronoun is used as a connective in the first sentence? To what word in the main part of the sentence does it directly relate as its antecedent? What pronoun is the connective in each of the other four sentences, and to what antecedent does each relate? Why are these pronouns placed on a dotted line (..........) in the diagram? Since they fill the office of both a conjunction and a pronoun, they may be properly called *Conjunctive Pronouns*, but

They are commonly called **Relative Pronouns**.

Tell why they are so called.

Exercise.

Expand the adjectives in the following sentences to adjective clauses:

1. Health and plenty cheer the industrious man.
2. Regular exercise is the secret of health.
3. A wounded soldier lay on the field of battle.
4. A wise son maketh a glad father.
5. A narrow mind begets obstinacy.

45. THE CONJUNCTIVE ADVERB.

Notice in the following that the connective *when* is equivalent to the adjective phrase *on which:*

I remember the day when (on which) they sailed.

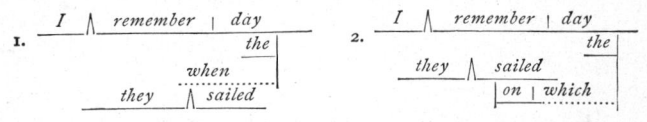

```
        I | remember | day                    I | remember | day
1.                     the         2.                       the
             when                        they \ sailed
      they \ sailed                           | on | which |
```

The use of *when* in this sentence is the same as that of the phrase *on which;* that is, it connects the clause and as an adverb it modifies the verb *sailed.* (In each sentence the clause modifies *day*.) A connective that does the work of both a conjunction and an adverb is called a **Conjunctive Adverb**, and if desired its use both as a connective and as a modifier may be shown (see diagram 2, page 76).

Exercise.

Analyze or diagram the following sentences and tell the kind of connective used in each:

1. This is the house that Jack built.
2. They have rights who dare (to) maintain them.
3. We visited Titusville, where the first oil well was sunk.

PHRASES AND CLAUSES

4. No one is useless in this world who lightens the burden of it for another.

5. There are parts of California where roses are always in bloom.

6. Smiles, which are the soul's sunshine, cost little or nothing.

7. Longfellow, who wrote beautiful poems, lived in Cambridge.

8. Many of the poems that he wrote were written for children.

9. Children celebrate the day when he was born.

10. He lived in a house where Washington had lived.

11. He lives happily who lives for others.

12. Those who bring sunshine to the lives of others can not keep it from themselves.

13. He that would thrive must rise at five.

14. He whose house is made of glass must not throw stones at another.

15. He only is exempt from failure who makes no effort.

16. Know ye the land where the cypress and myrtle are emblems of deeds that are done in their clime?

PUNCTUATION. Give a reason for the use of the commas in sentences 3, 6, 7. Why are the clauses in the other sentences not set off by commas? (See Comp. **53**, pp. 284–286, for punctuation.)

46. ADVERBIAL CLAUSES.

1. Since an adverbial clause does the work of an adverb, it may be used to modify the meaning of a verb, an adjective, or an adverb.

Note the adverbial clauses in the following sentences, determine what part of speech each modifies, and point out the words used as connectives:

1. *No one despises him because he is poor.*

2. *What is worse than dishonesty?*

3. *He is so dishonest that no one trusts him.*

```
He | is \ dishonest
      | so
      | that
      one \ trusts | him
           | no
```

In these sentences the connectives **because, than,** and **that** are neither pronouns nor adverbs. They are used merely to introduce clauses and to connect them with the elements they modify. Connectives of this kind are called **Subordinate Conjunctions.**

Can you tell why they are so called?

2. When a subordinate conjunction denotes **time, place, manner,** or **degree,** it is usually classified as a **Conjunctive Adverb.** If desired, its use both as a conjunction and as an adverb may be shown in the diagram by placing it on a dotted line as in diagram 2 below. Sometimes it is desirable to show this double use.

Go where duty calls thee.

```
1. (You) | Go              2.   (You) | Go
         | where                duty | calls | thee
         duty | calls | thee         | where
```

To the Teacher. The classification of the conjunctive adverb is of slight grammatical importance, and its distinction in the diagram may be omitted if desired.

Care should be taken that such distinctions do not take rank over more important ideas, and thus destroy the simplicity and value of the subject.

The diagram has no equal as a device for saving time in the recitation and for prompting pupils to make a careful study of the use and meaning of each element in the sentence, but it should never lead to distinctions that bear no importance to the interpretation of thought or to its correct expression.

Exercise.

Determine the adverbial clauses in the following sentences, tell what part of speech each modifies, point out the connectives, and diagram the sentences:

1. He succeeds because he is industrious.
2. What is better than success (is)?
3. He is so industrious that he succeeds.
4. The rain is falling where they lie.
5.[1] Tobacco is an American plant, as Raleigh found it here.
6. Heaven's blue is larger than its clouds (are).
7. Childhood shows the man as morning shows the day.
8. If you fear difficulties you will fail.
9. When school commenced, Henry was in his seat.
10. He remained in his seat, though he was quite ill.
11. Where the heart is well guarded, temptation can not enter.
12. Before men made us citizens,[2] great Nature made us men.[2]
13. No nation can be destroyed while it possesses a good home life.
14. Man can be great when great occasions call.
15. Laziness travels so slowly that poverty soon overtakes him.
16. Wagner, when he composed "Siegfried," arrayed himself in mediæval garb.

47. THE ABSOLUTE PHRASE.

An **Absolute Phrase** has for its principal word a noun or a pronoun that is the *subject only of a participle*. An absolute phrase is an abridged clause, and is usually adverbial in office. Thus,

Because our time was occupied (adverbial clause), *we could not attend.*

Our time being occupied (absolute phrase), *we could not attend.*

---

[1] In sentence 5 and some others the clauses may be said to modify the principal member as a whole. In diagramming such sentences the clause is treated as if it modified the verb. [2] Gr. 33, pages 54-55.

The use of the *absolute phrase* should not be confused with the use of *a participial phrase as the subject* of a sentence. An absolute phrase is always set off by a comma. A participial phrase used as a subject is never set off by a comma (Comp. 53, pp. 284–286). Thus:

ABSOLUTE PHRASE.

(*Set off by comma.*)

1. *He* (not *His*) *having arrived, the meeting was disorganized.*

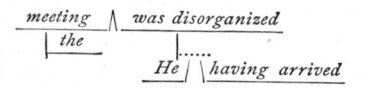

PARTICIPIAL PHRASE AS SUBJECT.

(*Not set off by comma.*)

1. *His* (not *He*) *having arrived disorganized the meeting.*

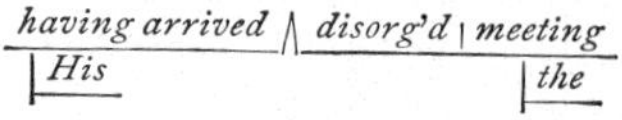

2. *They having returned, all rejoiced.*

3. *I refusing to comply, they withdrew.*

2. *Their having returned caused all to rejoice.*

3. *My refusing to comply made them withdraw.*

48. NOUN CLAUSES.

Examine the following sentences and note how the clauses are used:

1. *Where the violets bloom is a secret.*

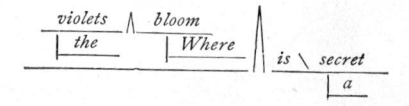

2. *This is where the violets bloom.*

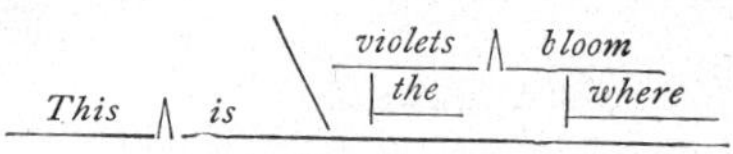

3. *I know where the violets bloom.*

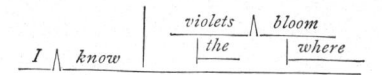

4. *I have no knowledge of where the violets bloom.*

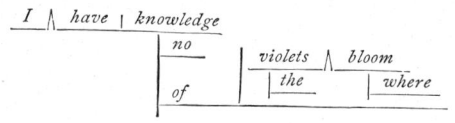

5. *The secret, where the violets bloom, was discovered by Helen.*

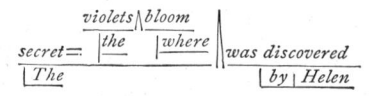

These sentences show the use of a **noun clause**, (1) as **subject**; (2) as **attribute complement**; (3) as **object complement**; (4) as **object of a preposition**; (5) as **an appositive**.

Note in the fifth sentence that the clause denotes the same thing as does the noun *secret*, which it explains.

A clause placed after a noun or pronoun to denote the same person or thing, and to explain or show more clearly what is meant by the noun or pronoun, is called an **Appositive Noun Clause**. (See page 20 for meaning of *apposition*.)

Exercise.

In the following sentences tell how the noun clauses are used. Diagram each sentence, observing the examples given above:

1. How he escaped is still a mystery.
2. Reputation is what[1] we seem.

[1] *What* is an attribute complement of *seem*.

3. Trouble teaches how much there[1] is in manhood.
4. The good is always the road to what is true.
5. The fact that lightning is electricity was discovered by Franklin.
6. Whatever makes men good Christians,[2] makes them good citizens.[2] — *Webster*.
7. Poor Richard's saying, "Lost time is never found again," should be remembered by all.
8. Who never tries will never win.
9. What is done wisely is done well.
10. Who keeps one end in view makes all things serve.

49. THE STRUCTURE OF THE SENTENCE.

We have learned in Part I. that sentences are classified *according to their use* into **declarative, interrogative, imperative,** and **exclamatory**. We are now prepared to study the sentence *according to its structure, or build*.

50. THE SIMPLE SENTENCE.

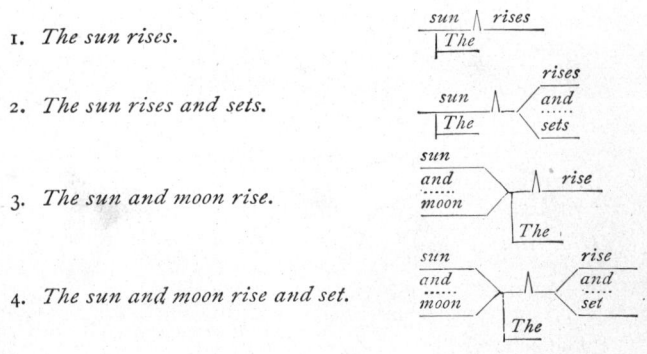

1. *The sun rises.*

2. *The sun rises and sets.*

3. *The sun and moon rise.*

4. *The sun and moon rise and set.*

---

[1] *There* is an expletive (page 19).
[2] Gr. 33, pages 54-55.

THE SIMPLE SENTENCE

Each of these sentences is made up of but one subject and one predicate.

In the second sentence the predicate is compound. What is a compound predicate? Which sentence contains a compound subject? Which contains both a compound subject and a compound predicate?

These sentences are called **Simple Sentences.**

DEFINITION. A *Simple Sentence* is one that contains but one subject and one predicate. Either or both of these may be compound.

It should be remembered that this classification depends wholly upon the structure of the sentence, and not upon the simplicity or complexity of thought. A sentence may be long and involved, having both the subject and the predicate modified by words and phrases; yet it is simple as long as it contains but one subject and one predicate.

Exercise.

The following are simple sentences; analyze or diagram each:

1. *The sun and moon rise in the east and set in the west.*

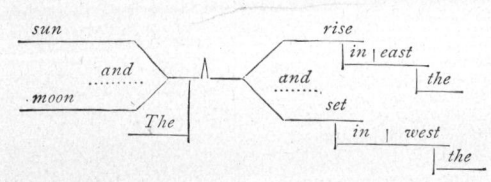

[diagram]

2. The Dutch mansion was usually built of brick.
3. Its gable-end, receding in regular steps from the base of the roof to the summit, faced the street.
4. The front door was decorated with a huge brass knocker, burnished daily.
5. The Connecticut mistress spun, wove, and stored her household linens in crowded chests.
6. The Dutch matron scrubbed and scoured her polished floor and woodwork.

7. The happy burghers breakfasted at dawn, dined at eleven, and retired at sunset.

8. The great patroons living along the Hudson, supported by their immense estates and crowds of tenants, kept up the customs of the best European society of the day.

51. THE COMPLEX SENTENCE.

1. *When the day ends, night begins.*

```
  night ∧ begins
         | When
           day ∧ ends
           | the
```

2. *Whoever digs a pit shall fall into it.*

```
  Whoever ∧ digs | pit ‖
                 | a     shall fall
                           | into | it
```

Each of these sentences contains two subjects and two predicates.

What are the subjects and predicates in the first sentence? In the second sentence?

In the first sentence the part *night begins* contains the principal subject and predicate of the sentence and is called the main part, or **Principal Member,** of the sentence. The clause *When the day ends* also contains a subject and predicate, but they are of lower rank than the subject and predicate of the principal member. In use, *a clause is always subordinate*, that is, of lower rank, since it does the work of a single part of speech — a noun, an adjective, or an adverb. It usually depends on some other part of the sentence for its meaning.

In the second sentence the principal member is the entire sentence, and the clause forms a part of it — the subject.

THE COMPLEX SENTENCE

To the Teacher. The term *clause* is loosely used in many text-books on Rhetoric and Grammar to name any part of a sentence containing a subject and predicate. In this book the use of the term is restricted to subordinate propositions, and the term **member** is used to name the principal, or coördinate, parts of a sentence.

A sentence containing one principal member and one or more clauses, used either as a part of the principal member or as a modifier, is called a **Complex Sentence.** More briefly,

Definition. A *Complex Sentence* is one that contains one principal member and one or more clauses.

Exercise.

Tell which of the following sentences are simple and which are complex. Give reason for your classification:

1. Perseverance is the road to success.
2. They conquer who believe they can.
3. Demosthenes was a noted man of antiquity.
4. Conduct and courage lead to honor.
5. The water runs smooth where the brook is deep.
6. Knowledge is, in every country, the surest basis of public happiness. — *Washington.*
7. God has made America the schoolhouse of the world.
8. Those who make the worst use of their time complain most of its shortness.
9. A fault which humbles a man is of more use to him than a good action which puffs him up with pride. — *Thomas Wilson.*
10. At the workingman's house, hunger looks in but dares not enter. — *Franklin.*
11. To be happy at home is the ultimate result of all ambition.
    — *Johnson.*
12. (During) These wintry nights, against my window pane, Nature, with busy pencil, draws designs of leaves and blossoms, ferns and vines, which she will make when summer comes again.

52. THE COMPOUND SENTENCE.

1. *A lot was cleared.*
2. *A fence was built.*
3. *The future president split the rails.*

Notice that these sentences are closely related in meaning, the second and the third being a continuation of the thought expressed by the first.

When two or more sentences are closely related in thought they may be united as **Members** of one sentence; as,

A lot was cleared, a fence was built, and the future president split the rails.

[1] *lot* \\ *was cleared*   *(and)*   *fence* \\ *was built*   *and*   *president* \\ *split* | *rails*
     A   *a*   *future*   *the*
                                                                  the

No one of these members depends on another for its meaning; each retains its own subject and predicate; and all are equally important. Hence they are principal members, and are called **coördinate** because they are of equal "order" or rank. *Coördinate* means *equal in rank*.

A sentence made up of coördinate members is called a **Compound Sentence.**

Any or all the members of a compound sentence may contain one or more clauses, thus making the member, or members, *complex;* but the sentence is still compound.

Refer to the illustrative sentence above, and note that each member is a simple sentence.

Sentences 1 and 2 on the next page are compound. Note that in 1 one member is simple and the other complex.

[1] If all the members of a compound sentence can not be diagrammed on one line, the connection may be indicated as follows: *fence* \\ *was built*
     and   *president* \\ *split* | *rails*

THE COMPOUND SENTENCE

Which member is simple, and which complex? How many members has the second sentence? Are these members simple or complex?

1. *A cruel story runs on wheels, and every hand oils the wheels as they run.*

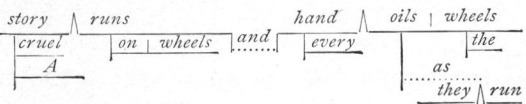

2. *I slept and dreamed that life is beauty;
I woke and found that life is duty.*

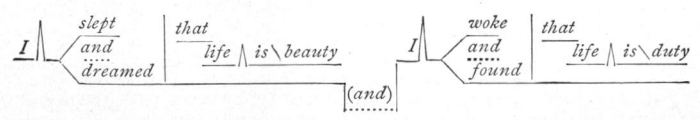

DEFINITION. A *Compound Sentence* is one that is composed of coördinate members. Each of these may be simple or complex.

Exercises.

Ex. I. *Select from Composition* 50, 80 (*pp.* 278, 279, 318), *five simple sentences, five complex sentences, and five compound sentences.*

Ex. II. *Classify the following sentences as to structure (simple, complex, or compound), and give reasons for your classification:*

1. Raindrops and rills have their work to do.
2. We have met the enemy, and they are ours.
3. He who praises everybody praises nobody. — *Johnson*.
4. My father would not go abroad, nor would he allow me to go.
5. Slow are the steps of freedom, but her feet turn never backwards. — *Lowell*.
6. A single grateful thought towards heaven is the most complete prayer. — *Lessing*.

7. If I can't pray, I will not make believe. — *Longfellow.*

8. There is always room for a man of force, and he makes room for many. — *Emerson.*

9. Capital is not what a man has, but what a man is.

10. No fountain is so small that heaven may not be imaged on its bosom. — *Hawthorne.*

11. Even those who do nothing which a reasonable man would call labor imagine themselves to be doing something, and there is no one who would willingly be thought quite an idler in the world.
— *Humboldt.*

12. "Honesty is the best policy," but he who acts on that principle is not an honest man. — *Archbishop Whately.*

13. He is not worthy of the honey-comb who shuns the hive because the bees have stings. — *Shakespeare.*

14.
>The busy world shoves angrily aside
>The man who stands with arms akimbo set,
>Until the occasion tells him what to do;
>And he who waits to have his task marked out
>Shall die and leave his errand unfulfilled.

15.
>The noblest men that live on earth,
> Are men whose hands are brown with toil;
>Who, backed by no ancestral graves,
> Hew down the woods, and till the soil;
>And win thereby a prouder name
>Than follows king's or warrior's fame.

53. COÖRDINATE CONJUNCTIONS.

The members of compound sentences being coördinate (equal in rank), the conjunctions (Gr. 26, p. 43) used to unite them are called **Coördinate Conjunctions.** The coördinate conjunctions in most common use are **and, or, nor,** and **but.**

Many words usually and naturally adverbs are sometimes used to join grammatical structures of equal rank, and therefore become coördinate conjunctions. The most common ones are **also, accordingly,** besides, consequently, else, furthermore, hence, however, likewise, moreover, nevertheless, only, otherwise, still, then, therefore, so, and yet.

When these words are used as conjunctions, *and*, *or*, *nor*, or *but* can be substituted for them or supplied before them without materially changing the meaning ; as,

1. *The day is warm;* **nevertheless** (coörd. conj.) *it is pleasant,* may be changed to

The day is warm, **but nevertheless** (adverb) *it is pleasant.*

2. *Be obedient,* **else** (coörd. conj.) *I will punish you,* may be changed to

Be obedient **or else** (adverb) *I will punish you.*

3. *He was determined,* **yet** (coörd. conj.) *he was quiet,* may be changed to

He was determined, **and yet** (adverb) *he was quiet.*

54. MEMBERS OF COMPOUND SENTENCES RELATED IN THOUGHT.

Care should be taken not to unite unrelated thoughts in forming compound sentences, as has been done in the following :

A lot was cleared, a fence was built, and Lincoln addressed the people from the steps of the Capitol.

The fact stated in the last member of this sentence bears no relation to the part that precedes, and should be stated separately. (Comp. 50, pp. 280, 281.) Other examples of improper sentences are :

1. *We went to cooking school on Friday, and Dewey captured Manila.*
2. *Grandfather lives on a farm; the train went very fast, and the day was pleasant, and Grandfather met us at the station.*
— *From a School Exercise.*

Exercise.

From the following sets of simple sentences form complex sentences, and then change each to a compound sentence. Tell the kind of connective used with each sentence formed.

EXAMPLE. *The Coast Plain has many rivers. They afford good water power.*

Complex: *The Coast Plain has many rivers, which afford good water power.* The connective *which* is a relative pronoun.

Compound: *The Coast Plain has many rivers, and they afford good water power.* The connective *and* is a coördinate conjunction.

1. All these rivers are navigable. They run almost parallel with one another.
2. We visited the great cathedral. There we saw the famous pictures by Rubens.
3. We stood in front of the tomb. The old guide told about the last resting place of the Washingtons.
4. We were in the steel works. We saw sheets of armor plate for the battleship "Pennsylvania."
5. The work is perplexing and difficult. The workmen do it slowly.
6. The cat's away. The mice will play.

TO THE TEACHER. Pupils should be given additional exercises in the analysis and synthesis of sentences, as the need of the class requires. Numbers 13, 29, and 52 of the Composition, pp. 238, 255, 282, and 283, will furnish good material for such drill. The sentences should be analyzed, and the complex and compound sentences resolved into simple sentences. The teacher may select simple sentences for the pupils to combine into complex or compound sentences.

55. SUMMARY OF THE SENTENCE.

STRUCTURE AND USE.

1. **A Sentence** is the complete expression of a thought in words.

In writing, a sentence is marked at its close by a period, an interrogation point, or an exclamation point.

SUMMARY OF THE SENTENCE

2. **The Elements** of the sentence are *Subject, Predicate, Complement, Modifier,* and *Connective.*

Excepting the predicate and the connective, each of these five elements may consist of a word, a phrase, or a clause.

3. **A Phrase** is a group of words that does not contain a predicate and that is used to do the work of a single part of speech. (Gr. 41, p. 69.)

4. **A Clause** is a group of words that contains a predicate and is used to do the work of a single part of speech. (Gr. 41.)

5. According to its **use,** a sentence is *Declarative, Imperative,* or *Interrogative;* also, it may or may not be *Exclamatory.*

6. According to its **structure,** a sentence is *Simple, Complex,* or *Compound.*

7. **A Simple Sentence** is one that contains but *one* subject and *one* predicate. Either or both of these may be compound. (Gr. 50, p. 81.)

8. **A Complex Sentence** is one that contains one principal member and one or more clauses. (Gr. 51.)

9. **A Compound Sentence** is one that is made up of coördinate members. (Gr. 52.) The members, being equal in rank, are connected by coördinate conjunctions, expressed or understood.

10. **A Coördinate Conjunction** connects words or groups of words that are equal in rank, or are in the same grammatical construction.

11. **A Subordinate Conjunction** is one which, placed before a sentence, changes it into a clause, and, if the clause is a modifier, joins it to whatever is modified.

PUNCTUATION.

12. A sentence is **punctuated** according to its structure and use.

13. **A Simple Declarative Sentence** states or declares something, and, if not exclamatory, should be marked at its close by a *period*; if exclamatory, it should be marked by an *exclamation point*. Thus,

1. *Man is a wonderful piece of work.*
2. *He seems to enjoy himself very much.*
3. *What a wonderful piece of work is man!*
4. *How he does enjoy himself!*

14. **A Simple Interrogative Sentence** is one used to ask a question, and, if not exclamatory, should be marked at its close by an *interrogation point*. Thus,

5. *Wasn't that music grand?*
6. *Doesn't he enjoy himself!*

15. **A Simple Imperative Sentence** is used to express a command or an entreaty, and, if not exclamatory, should be marked at its close by a *period*. Thus,

7. *Cling to thy home.*
8. *Cling to thy home!*
9. *Close the door.*
10. *Close the door quick!*
11. *Lead us to some far-off sunny isle.*
12. *Lead us to victory or to death!*
13. *Send for a physician.*
14. *Send for a physician at once!*

16. **A Complex Declarative Sentence** states or declares something. It should be marked at its close by a period, by an exclamation point, or by the terminal mark of a direct quotation closing the sentence. Thus,

15. *The man asked whether your son was at home.*
16. *The man asked, "Is your son at home?"*

SUMMARY OF THE SENTENCE

17. *"Is your son at home?" asked the gentleman.*
18. *The answer was, "Why do you ask?"*
19. *"Who is who?" is the question.*
20. *The query is, "Who is who?"*
21. *We shall soon see who is who.*
22. *The reply came, "It's hard to tell."*
23. *"Charge for the batteries!" shouted the captain.*
24. *The captain shouted, "Charge for the batteries!"*
25. *"Come to see me often," said Col. Smith.*
26. *Mr. Jones replied, "Come back soon, Colonel."*
27. *"What are we?" and "Whither do we tend?" are disputed questions.*
28. *The lecturer attempted to answer the questions, "What are we?" and "Whither do we tend?"*
29. *What we are and whither we tend are disputed questions.*
30. *How he does enjoy himself when he is at home!*

17. **A Complex Interrogative Sentence** is used to ask a question. It should be marked at its close by an interrogation point, by an exclamation point, or by the terminal mark of a quoted question closing the sentence. Thus,

31. *Did the teacher say, "Your answer is wrong, John"?*
32. *Why do you ask, "Where are you going, John?"*
33. *Who wrote, "I would not live alway"?*
34. *Who asked, "Would you like to live always?"*
35. *Does not the Bible command, "Swear not at all"?*
36. *Did the teacher ask, "Did any one hear him swear?"*
37. *Who exclaimed, "Charge for the batteries"?*
38. *Why do you ask, "Did he charge for the batteries?"*
39. *Did the teacher tell you your answer was wrong, John?*
40. *Who wrote that he didn't want to live always?*
41. *Why do you ask where I am going?*
42. *Did the teacher ask whether any one heard him swear?*
43. *Doesn't he enjoy himself when he is at home!*

NOTE. In 31, 33, 35, and 37, the interrogation points belong to the sentences; hence they follow the quotation marks. In 32, 34, 36, and 38, the interrogation points belong to the clauses; hence they are followed by the quotation marks. In 39, 40, 41, and 42, the clauses are indirect quotations; hence no difficulties arise.

18. **A Complex Imperative Sentence** is used to express a command or an entreaty. It should be marked at its close by a period, by an exclamation point, or by the terminal mark of a direct quotation closing the sentence. Thus,

44. *Ask yourself often whether your action is right.*
45. *Stand where you are!*
46. *Ask yourself often, "Is my action right?"*
47. *Read more slowly, "He giveth his beloved sleep."*
48. *Read more forcibly, "Charge for the batteries!"*

19. Only the *members* of **Compound Sentences** are distinguished as to their *use*, and not the sentence as a whole. Thus,

49. *Where are you? and who are you?* (A compound sentence, each of whose members, when standing alone, is a simple interrogative sentence.)

50. *A gaudy verbosity is always eloquence in the opinion of him who writes it; but what is the effect upon the reader?* (A compound sentence, the first of whose members, when standing alone, is a complex declarative sentence; and the second, a simple interrogative sentence.)

51. *Live as though life were earnest, and life will be so.* (A compound sentence, of which the first member, when standing alone, is a complex imperative sentence; and the second member, a simple declarative sentence.

56. REVIEW.

EXERCISE. *From dictation write and punctuate the fifty-one sentences given in* **55**, *and be able to assign a reason for each mark of punctuation used.*

TEST QUESTIONS. 1. What are the elements of a sentence? 2. What is a phrase? 3. How does a phrase differ from a clause?

4. How can you change the sentence "The boy studies" into a clause? 5. What is a subordinate conjunction? 6. Name the different kinds of phrases and clauses according to their use in the sentence. 7. How are adjective clauses connected? 8. What connectives are used with adverbial clauses? 9. Select or compose five sentences that contain subordinate conjunctions, and tell the class of each sentence. 10. Select or compose sentences to show five different uses of the noun clause. 11. According to structure, how are sentences classified? 12. What is the difference between a complex sentence and a compound sentence? 13. Select from Composition 13 and 58 (pp. 238, 293, 294) sentences to illustrate as many of the different kinds of sentences as you can.

PART III.

THE PARTS OF SPEECH. THEIR CLASSIFICATION, INFLECTIONS, AND RELATIONS.

(*To be studied in connection with Part III of the Composition, on pages 308–342.*)

---

57. NOUNS: THEIR CLASSIFICATION.

Point out the nouns in the following:

When Governor Andros asked the people of Hartford, Connecticut, to surrender their charter, a patriot, Captain Wadsworth, seized the document and cleverly hid it in a hollow tree. This tree was afterwards known as the Charter Oak, and the spot where it once stood is now marked by a monument.

Note that some of the nouns in the above differ from the others by beginning with capitals. This is because they are special names given to individual persons, places, or things to distinguish them from others of the same kind. Is the name *Charter Oak* given to all oak trees? Is the name *tree* given to all oak trees? Is the name *Hartford* common to all cities? Is the name *city* common to all cities? The names *Charter Oak* and *Hartford* are given to a particular tree and city to distinguish them from all other trees and cities; or we may say that the names *Charter Oak* and *Hartford* are special names given to individual objects, while the names *tree* and *city* are general names given to any or all objects of their class or kind.

THE NOUN

A special name given to an object to distinguish that object from all others of its kind, is called a **Proper Noun.**

DEFINITION. A *Proper Noun* is a special name belonging to an individual person, people, place, or thing.

All other nouns are **Common Nouns.**

DEFINITION. A *Common Noun* is a general name belonging to each object of its class.

58. CAPITAL LETTERS.

The classification of nouns into common and proper is important because it involves the correct use of capital letters, as is shown in the following parallel sentences:

PROPER.

All proper names and the chief words of such names, whether of animate or inanimate existence, begin with capital letters; as, too, do all words that name the Deity.

I. THE DEITY.

1. "The **Lord** is a great **God** and a great **King** above all gods."

2. The **Governor** of all.

3. Forgive them, **Father**.

II. PERSONS.

4. Yes, **Daniel**, come hither.

5. We called on **President Roosevelt**.

COMMON.

Common nouns begin with small letters; except that personal names, even when used to denote a class, retain their capital letters (see 4 and 6 below).[1]

1. (a) I am the **lord** of this mansion. (b) His **god** is **money**. (c) He is **king**[2] of Spain.

2. The governor[2] of Ohio.

3. Must I stay, **father**?

4. A **Daniel** has come to judgment.

5. We called on Theodore Roosevelt, the **president**.

---

[1] Another exception is that words are sometimes capitalized to give them prominence, especially in treatises; but this use of capitals should not be encouraged in literature.

[2] Words thus used are sometimes begun with capitals.

6. I have heard that **Aunt Mary** admires **Cicero**.

6. My **aunt** admires the **Ciceros** and the **Shakespeares** of every land.

III. COUNTRIES, PLACES, ETC.

7. That man belongs to the **East**.

7. London is situated **east** of Windsor.

8. She located the **Gulf of Mexico**, the **District of Columbia**, and the **Tropic of Cancer**.

8. He defined **gulf, district, tropic, cancer**, and bounded the **state** of Pennsylvania.

IV. FESTIVALS.

9. Will you go on **New Year's Day, Good Friday, Easter, Thanksgiving Day**, or **Memorial Day**?

9. Mary began the work of the new **year** by misspelling **thanksgiving** and **memorial**.

V. MONTHS AND DAYS OF THE WEEK.

10. He was present every **Saturday** and **Sunday** during **January, February**, and **November**.

10. In **spring** and **summer** we live in the North; in **fall** and **winter** we live in the South.

VI. PROMINENT OBJECTS AND EVENTS.

11. We visited the **Capitol** in Washington during the **Civil War**, which occurred long after the **Reformation**.

11. Any **reformation** that will prevent **civil war** will be welcomed by the people of Washington, the **capital** of the United States.

VII. RELIGIOUS DENOMINATIONS AND POLITICAL PARTIES.

12. In England, the **Presbyterians, Methodists, Baptists**, and **Unitarians** are called **Dissenters**.

12. The **dissenters** in our **church** are not numerous.

13. The **Democrats** twice elected Cleveland president.

13. The **democrats** of Russia have little influence in political affairs.

VIII. NAMES OF BOOKS, CHAPTERS, COMPANIES, ETC.

14. Henry Van Dyke wrote "**The Blue Flower**."

14. He plucked a blue **flower**.

15. The **Crucible Steel Company** makes fine grades of steel.

15. This **company** makes crucible steel.

THE NOUN

Exercise.

Use in a sentence each of the following words (1) so that it shall begin with a capital letter (do not use the word to begin the sentence); (2) so that it shall begin with a small letter:

Governor, captain, uncle, king, west, bay, revolution, college, park, republican.

59. GENDER.

Note the indicated nouns in the following sentences:

1. **Mr. Smith** *said that the* **lion** *is the* **king** *of* **beasts.**
2. **Mrs. Smith** *said that the* **lioness** *is the* **queen** *of the* **forest.**

Which of these nouns denote males? Which denote females? Which denotes neither a male nor a female? Which denotes either a male or a female?

The physical difference between the individuals themselves is called **Sex**. The power in their names to make known this difference is called **Gender**.

DEFINITION. *Gender* is the power of a noun or pronoun to denote the sex of the person or thing represented.

Nouns denoting males are of the **Masculine Gender**.
Nouns denoting females are of the **Feminine Gender**.
Nouns denoting neither males nor females are genderless or **Neuter Nouns,** and are said to be of the **Neuter Gender**. *Neuter* means *neither*.
Nouns that may denote either a male or a female are masculine or feminine according to the sex of the particular individual mentioned. When the sex of the individual is unknown or can not be inferred from the context, the noun is said to be in the **Indeterminate** or **Common Gender**.

GRAMMAR

By referring to the two illustrative sentences, it will be seen that the *gender of nouns is shown in three ways:*

	Masculine.	Feminine.
1. By using different prefixes; as,	**Mr.** Smith	**Mrs.** Smith
Other examples are:	**man**servant	**maid**servant
	he-goat	**she**-goat
2. By using different suffixes; as,	lion	lion**ess**
Other examples are:	duke	duch**ess**
	testa**tor**	testa**trix**
3. By using different words; as,	**king**	**queen**
Other examples are:	**monk**	**nun**
	father	**mother**

Exercise.

Arrange the following nouns under three different heads as given above:

Mr. Jones, Miss Jones; husband, wife; administrator, administratrix; emperor, empress; lord, lady; tiger, tigress; tutor, governess; signor, signora; czar, czarina; don, donna or doña; hero, heroine; heir, heiress; beau, belle; nephew, niece; rooster, hen; wizard, witch; stag, hind.

60. THE VALUE OF GENDER.

A knowledge of the gender of nouns is important (1) as a matter of orthography; (2) as it involves the correct use of the pronouns **he, she,** and **it**. Pronouns should be used according to the principles stated below:

Masculine.

1. Nouns that denote males are referred to by the pronoun *he*.

2. Names of animals are often considered as masculine

without regard to the sex, the writer employing *he*, if he fancies the animal to possess masculine characteristics; as, *The grizzly* **bear** *is the most savage of* **his** *race*.

3. Nouns that name something remarkable for strength, power, size, and sublimity, when personified, are considered as masculine, and are referred to by *he;* as, *Death with* **his** *thousand doors*.

4. Singular nouns used so as to stand for persons of both sexes are considered as of the masculine gender, and are referred to by *he;* as, *Every* **person** *has* **his** *faults*.

Feminine.

1. Nouns that denote females are referred to by the pronoun *she*.

2. Names of animals are often considered as feminine without regard to the sex, the writer employing *she* if he fancies the animal to possess feminine characteristics; as, *The* **cat** *steals upon* **her** *prey*.

3. Names of objects remarkable for gentleness, beauty, grace, and peace, when personified, are considered as feminine, and are referred to by the pronoun *she;* as, *The moon unveiled* **her** *peerless light*.

Neuter.

1. Nouns that denote objects without sex are referred to by the pronoun *it*.

2. Names of animals or objects whose sex is disregarded are referred to by the pronoun *it;* as, (1) *The grizzly* **bear** *is the most savage of* **its** *race*. (2) *The* **cat** *steals upon* **its** *prey*.

3. Collective nouns of unity (Gr. **67**, p. 112) are neuter; as, *The* **class** *is large;* **it** *must be divided*.

Common.

1. Singular nouns that may be applied to persons or objects of either sex, such as *parent, pupil, cousin, friend*, etc., may be said to be of the **common gender**; but, since there is *no pronoun* of the *common gender, 3d person, singular*, to represent such nouns, the term *common gender* is practically valueless. Hence, —

2. A singular noun whose gender may be indeterminate is of the **masculine gender** when known to denote a *male;* as, *My* **friend** (John) *brought* **his** *book with* **him.**

3. A singular noun whose gender may be indeterminate is of the **feminine gender** when known to denote a *female;* as, *My* **friend** (Mary) *brought* **her** *books with* **her.**

4. A singular noun whose gender may be indeterminate is of the **masculine gender** when so used that the context *does not denote the sex* of the object; as, *My* **friend** *brought* **his** *books with* **him.** (See "*Masculine*," 4th paragraph.)

Exercise.

Fill the blanks in the following sentences with appropriate pronouns, and tell which of the above principles applies to each:

1. Grandfather sits in _____ easy chair.
2. The savage beast from _____ cavern sprang.
3. Every one has _____ troubles.
4. The doe lifted _____ head with a quick motion.
5. A person's manner not infrequently indicates _____ morals.
6. Everybody should think for _____ self.
7. The elephant is distinguished for _____ strength and sagacity.
8. The child was unconscious of _____ danger.
9. Despair extends _____ raven wings.

10. Truth is fearless, yet _____ is meek and modest.

11. War leaves _____ victims on the field, and homes desolated by _____ mourn over _____ cruelty.

12. Nobody did _____ work better than I.

13. The catamount lies in the boughs to watch _____ prey.

14. The mocking-bird shook from _____ little throat floods of delightful music.

15. The bat is nocturnal in _____ habits.

16. The dog is faithful to _____ master.

17. The woman fell off _____ horse.

18. The fox is noted for _____ cunning.

19. Each member of the class brought _____ books with _____.

20. Summer clothes _____ self in green, and decks _____ self with flowers.

21. Belgium's capital had gathered then _____ beauty and _____ chivalry.

22. Spring hangs _____ infant blossoms on the trees.

23. The administratrix filed _____ account with the court.

24. How does the hen protect _____ brood from the cold?

61. PERSON.

We girls *are going to the* **library.**
Will **you** *go with* **us, Martha?**
Yes, thank **you,** *if* **Helen** *will go.*

Which words in the above sentences are used to denote the persons speaking? Which denote the person spoken to? Which denote a person or a thing spoken of? What part of speech is each of these words?

This distinction of the noun or the pronoun as denoting the speaker, the one spoken to, or the person or thing spoken of, is called **Person.**

DEFINITION. *Person* is the power of a pronoun by its form, and of a noun or pronoun by its context, to distinguish the speaker, the one spoken to, and the person or thing spoken of.

Grammarians have not devised descriptive names for the different distinctions of person, as they have for those of gender. They have simply numbered them **First Person, Second Person,** and **Third Person.**

First Person. A noun is said to be in the first person when it is the name of the person or persons speaking, and is in apposition with a pronoun of the first person; as, *I,* **John,** *will go.* (A *proper* noun in the first person is always set off by the comma.) *We* **girls** *will not go.* (A *common* noun, first person, is not set off unless limited; as, *We, the* **girls** *of No. 10, will not go.*) (Comp. **53.**)

Second Person. A noun is said to be in the second person when it is used in a term of address or in apposition with a pronoun of the second person; as, (1) *When are you going, my* **friends**? (2) **William,** *come here.* (3) *Yes,* **sir,** *I shall.* (4) *Will you* **men** *please leave the room?*

Third Person. All other nouns are said to be in the third person. A noun is in the third person if used as a subject, attribute complement, or object, although it is used by the speaker about himself or in addressing another; as, (1) *The* **subscriber** *gives notice.* (2) *Your* **Excellency** *is very gracious.* (3) *Is this my* **boy**? (4) *I am a* **student.** (5) *I am grateful to your* **Excellency.** (6) *Please notify the* **undersigned.**

REMARK. The distinction of person has importance only in connection with pronouns and verbs. Nouns do not change in form to denote person, but the context makes it known, and for convenience they are said to have person.

62. REVIEW.

TEST QUESTIONS. 1. Which is the largest class of nouns? Why? 2. In what two ways may proper nouns be distinguished? 3. Of

what importance is the classification of nouns as common and proper?
4. What is the difference in the meaning of the terms *sex* and *gender*?
5. What does the word *neuter* mean? 6. How is the word *indeterminate* applied to gender? 7. In what three ways is the gender of nouns and pronouns denoted? 8. Why is it important to know the gender of nouns and pronouns? 9. What is person? 10. Of what importance is a knowledge of person? 11. How is the person of nouns and of pronouns made known?

63. INFLECTION.

Note the difference in form between each indicated word in the first column and the corresponding word in the second column, below.

(1) Point out in each word what letters are added or substituted.

(2) Tell what change in the use or meaning of each word is denoted by the change or variation in its form.

1. *One* **boy**.   *Two* **boys**.
2. *The boys* run.   *The boy* runs.
3. **John** *has a ball*.   **John's** *ball*.
4. **He** *hit the ball*.   *The ball hit* **him**.
5. *The* lion.   *The* lioness.
6. *The* **high** *building*. *The* **highest** *building*.
7. *The birds* sing.   *The birds* sang.

These variations in form do not change the general meaning of the word. The only difference in the meaning of *boy* and *boys* is in the number of objects designated, — *boy* denotes one, *boys* more than one.

In the second example *s* is added to the verb *run* to denote its use or agreement with the subject *boy*, not *boys*.

When the form of a word is varied to denote some change in the use or meaning, the word is said to be **inflected**. *Inflect* means *to turn from a direct course, to vary*.

DEFINITION. *Inflection* is a variation in the form of a word to denote a change in its use or meaning.

The *inflection of nouns and pronouns* is called **Declension** (with the exception of the few inflections of nouns that are made to show gender). The *inflection of verbs* is called **Conjugation**. The *inflection of adjectives and adverbs* is called **Comparison**.

Prepositions, conjunctions, interjections, and expletives are not inflected.

64. NUMBER.

The most common inflection of the noun is that by which we denote **Number**.

With a few exceptions nouns have *two number forms,* the **Singular** and the **Plural**.

DEFINITIONS. The *Singular Number* denotes only one.
The *Plural Number* denotes more than one.

Formation of Plural Number.

GENERAL RULE. **Nearly all nouns are made plural by adding *s* or *es* to the singular form.**

We add *es* when the noun ends in *s*, *x*, *z*, *sh*, or *ch* soft (as in *crutch*). This is because these letters sound so much like *s* that when one of them ends a word we can not pronounce the plural without giving to the word an additional syllable; as, *brush, brush*es; *box, box*es; *witch, witch*es.

Exercise.

Pronounce in the plural number the following nouns; then write their plural forms, observing that they end with **es** *whenever an additional syllable is required:*

THE NOUN

Stamp, chair, tray, peach, tax, wharf, fife, flame, guess, breeze, fez, key, watch, buoy, chief, Indian, gulf, arch, patriarch, ark, topaz, wish, bridge, oak, cuckoo, cameo, cuff, casino, roof, couch, essay, blush, path, hoof, turf.

EXCEPTIONS TO RULE FOR FORMING THE PLURAL OF NOUNS.

The following exceptions to the general rule are important:

I. Eleven nouns form their plurals *without* s *or* es.

These eleven nouns are the only surviving examples of old English inflections forming the plural by the use of en (*ox*, *ox*en) or by a vowel change (*foot*, *feet*). Their plurals are:

Oxen, children, brethren (of a society), kine (pl. of *cow*, used in poetry), feet, teeth, geese, lice, mice, men, women.
Write their singular forms.

II. Twelve nouns ending in **f** and three in **fe** change *f* or *fe* into *ves*; as, *bee***f**, *bee***ves**.

Write the plural of each of the following:
Beef, elf, leaf, self, shelf, wolf, calf, half, loaf, sheaf, thief, wharf, knife, wife, life.

The plurals of all other nouns ending in **f** or **fe** are formed regularly by the addition of *s*.

III. All common nouns ending in **y** preceded by a consonant, change *y* into *i* and add *es*; as, *dais***y**, *dais***ies**. This exception includes nouns ending in **quy**, in which *u* is strictly a consonant: as, *colloq***uy**, *colloq***uies**.

All other nouns ending in **y** are regular, adding only *s*.

To prevent confusion, *the names of persons* usually add only *s* in the plural; as, *the two Cary*s, *the Moody*s.
Write the plurals of the following nouns:
Ally, alley, glory, journey, city, Henry, liberty, money, joy, soliloquy.

IV. Many nouns taken without change from other languages retain their native plurals. In words from Latin and Greek the ending **is** becomes **es** in the plural; the ending **um** or **on** becomes **a**; **ex** or **ix** becomes **ices**; **us** becomes **i**; as,

analysis, analyses	phenomenon, phenomena
basis, bases	appendix, appendices
crisis, crises	vertex, vertices
oasis, oases	alumnus, alumni
aquarium, aquaria	radius, radii

After foreign nouns come to be looked upon as thoroughly English, they often form their plurals in the English way; as,

beau, beaux *or* beaus	bandit, banditti *or* bandits
seraph, seraphim *or* seraphs	stamen, stamina *or* stamens
cherub, cherubim *or* cherubs	radius, radii *or* radiuses

When the English form is in general use it is preferable.

V. Nouns ending in **o** preceded by a vowel form the plural regularly by adding an *s*; as, *cameo*s, *embryo*s, *trio*s.

When the final **o** is preceded by a consonant, some nouns add *es* and others *s* only. These must be learned by observation.

The first sixteen of the following nouns add *es* to form the plural, and the rest add *s* only. Write their plurals and note that many of those adding *s* only are terms used in music:

1. buffalo	9. mulatto	17. alto	24. halo
2. calico	10. negro	18. banjo	25. lasso
3. cargo	11. potato	19. broncho	26. memento
4. echo	12. tomato	20. canto	27. piano
5. embargo	13. tornado	21. contralto	28. solo
6. grotto	14. torpedo	22. domino	29. soprano
7. hero	15. veto	23. flamingo	30. zero
8. motto	16. volcano		

THE NOUN

Test Questions.

1. What is number in grammar? 2. Give the general rule for forming the plural of nouns. 3. How many nouns are included in the first exception to the general rule? 4. How do these form the plural? 5. What nouns does the second exception include? 6. Why do we add *es* to *berry* and only *s* to *turkey* in forming the plural? 7. Tell clearly why we add *es* to *hero* and *s* only to *Nero* to form the plural. 8. How do nouns from a foreign language usually form their plurals? 9. When two plurals are given which is preferable? 10. In forming the plural of nouns ending in *o* how do we determine whether to add *s* or *es*?

Exercise.

Write the plurals of the following nouns and point out those that form their plurals regularly. If irregularly, point out in what way they are exceptions to the general rule:

1. arm	11. cargo	21. lily	31. puppy
2. arch	12. canto	22. leaf	32. pulley
3. axis	13. echo	23. joy	33. radius
4. attorney	14. fairy	24. motto	34. ratio
5. beau	15. folio	25. memento	35. studio
6. beef	16. fife	26. majority	36. survey
7. belief	17. knife	27. Mary	37. stamen
8. chief	18. hero	28. negro	38. tooth
9. charity	19. halo	29. ox	39. vortex
10. chimney	20. half	30. oasis	40. zero

65. SPECIAL RULES OF NUMBER.

I. **Proper Names** preceded by titles, as *Mr. Brown, Miss Brown*, may be made plural in two different ways: (1) By making the title plural; as, **Mr.** *Brown*, **Messrs.** *Brown;* **Miss** *Brown*, **Misses** *Brown*. (2) By making the name plural; as, *the two Mr.* **Browns***; the three Miss* **Browns**.

II. **Compound Nouns** usually form the plural by adding the sign of the plural to the most important part of the compound, that is, to the part which is described by the rest of the word; as, *father-in-law, father*s*-in-law; ox-cart, ox-cart*s; *Knight Templar, Knight*s *Templar.* When the compound is regarded as a whole, the last part is pluralized; as, *forget-me-not*s, *spoonful*s, *English*men, *runaway*s.

A few compounds add the plural sign to both parts; as, *man*servant, **men***servant*s.

CAUTION. *German, talisman, Brahman, Ottoman, Mussulman* are not compounds of *man;* they form their plurals with *s*.

III. **Figures, Letters, Signs**, etc., are made plural by adding 's; as, *Cross your* t's. *Cancel the* 9's. *Make the* +'s *and* —'s *larger. His* I's *and* my's *and* me's, *and his* "I told you so's" *were wearisome.*

Numbers written in words form their plurals regularly; as, *Count by* **twos, fives, tens.**

IV. **Plurals without Inflection.** Some nouns are singular or plural without change of form according to their use; as, *one* **sheep**, *two* **sheep**; *a* **brace** *of ducks, two* **brace** *of ducks; he sold a* **hundredweight** *of sugar; two* **hundredweight** *of sugar.* Similar words are: *pair* (of shoes), *head* (of cattle), *cod, deer, grouse, salmon, swine, trout.* (V., p. 200.)

V. **Plurals of Different Meaning.** Some nouns have two plurals, which differ in meaning. The more important are as follows:

SINGULAR.	PLURAL.	
1. Brother	Brothers	(of a family)
	Brethren	(of a society)
2. Cloth	Cloths	(pieces or kinds of cloth)
	Clothes	(garments)

THE NOUN

3. Die	dies	(coining stamps)
	dice	(for playing games)
4. Fish	fishes	(number)
	fish	(quantity)
5. Genius	geniuses	(human beings)
	genii	(imaginary beings)
6. Head	heads	(belonging to the body)
	head	(of cattle)
7. Index	indexes	(tables of contents)
	indices	(algebraic signs)
8. Pea	peas	(number or quantity)
	pease	(quantity)
9. Penny	pennies	(number of coins)
	pence	(quantity, i.e. value)
10. Shot	shots	(number of discharges)
	shot	(number of balls)
11. Sail	sails	(pieces of canvas)
	sail	(number of vessels)
12. Staff	staffs *or* staves	(sticks or canes)
	staffs	(military term)

Exercises.

Ex. I. *Tell how the meaning of the first sentence in each group differs from the meaning of the second:*

1. He assists his brothers.
    He assists his brethren.
2. The tailor showed some new cloths.
    The tailor showed some new clothes.
3. Teddy's bank contains six pennies.
    Teddy's bank contains six pence.
4. The milkman gave her two cupfuls of milk.
    The milkman gave her two cups full of milk.
5. The prisoner had two dies in his pocket.
    The prisoner had two dice in his pocket.
6. How many shot were there?
    How many shots were there?
7. A story of two genii.
    A story of two geniuses.

Ex. II. *Write the plurals of the following:*

Mr. Andrews	Miss Henry	+
Knight Templar	Major McDowell	½
hanger-on	commander in chief	sheep
four-per-cent	son-in-law	4
countryman	woman-servant	Oh, my
Norman	major-general	why

66. NOUNS THAT DO NOT CHANGE THEIR NUMBER.

Always Singular. Some nouns, from the nature of what they represent, are always singular both in form and in meaning; as, *wisdom, music, courage, pride, patience, gold, platinum.* Others are usually singular; as, *rhetoric, lead, copper, wheat, rye, sugar, wine.*

When used in the plural, *wines, sugars*, etc., mean different kinds of wine, of sugar, etc.; *coppers* are things made of copper.

Always Plural. Some nouns from the nature of what they represent are always or usually plural, both in form and in meaning. The following are examples:

1. ashes
2. annals
3. bitters
4. dregs
5. eaves
6. goods
7. pincers
8. proceeds
9. riches
10. scissors
11. suds
12. tidings
13. tongs
14. thanks
15. trousers
16. victuals
17. vitals
18. mumps

Plural in Form, Singular in Meaning. Some nouns are always plural in form, but are generally singular in meaning; as, *amends, gallows, measles, news, pains* (meaning *care*), *mathematics*, and other nouns ending in *ics*, except *athletics*, which is generally plural.

In the use of some of these nouns custom is divided. When in doubt consult an unabridged dictionary.

THE NOUN

Exercise.

Write the plural, if any, of each given singular, and the singular, if any, of each given plural; note those having no singular and those having no plural:

1. dozen
2. pairs
3. million
4. trout
5. series
6. pride
7. news
8. mumps
9. flax
10. rye
11. oats
12. goods
13. politics
14. mathematics
15. athletics
16. thanks

67. COLLECTIVE NOUNS.

Some nouns in the singular form denote several objects of the same kind taken together; as, *flock, crowd, group, committee.*

What does each of the following nouns represent?

flock	audience	choir	army
crowd	committee	jury	mob
fleet	regiment	class	tribe
group	convention	school	herd

Each of these nouns represents a collection of objects of a certain kind; as, *flock* represents a collection of animals; *crowd*, a collection of people; *group*, a collection of objects. Can the name *flock* be given to any one animal? Can the name *crowd* or *group* be given to any one person or object?

DEFINITION. **A name that represents a collection of objects, but does not apply to any one of the objects, is called a** *Collective Noun.*

Collective Nouns: Singular or Plural. The collective noun at times conveys a singular idea, and at other times a plural idea.

When a collective noun names a number of persons or

things considered as *one whole*, it is called a **Collective Noun of Unity,** and its verb and pronoun are singular in form.

When a collective noun stands for a number of persons or things regarded as *separate individuals*, it is called a **Collective Noun of Plurality,** and its verb and pronoun are plural in form.[1]

Compare the following parallel sentences:

Collective Nouns of Unity.	Collective Nouns of Plurality.
1. The **committee** (as a body) **reports** favorably.	1. The **committee** (as individuals) **differ** on that question.
2. The **jury** will be confined in **its** room. (That is, in a room belonging to the jury as a *body*, not as individuals.)	2. The **jury** will be confined until **they** agree. (That is, until the individuals agree.)
3. A **herd** of cattle **was** in the field.	3. A **herd** of cattle **were** grazing in the field.

When a collective noun is pluralized it loses its collective character and becomes simply a common noun; as, Many *herds* of cattle *were* grazing on the plain.

The noun *herds* in this sentence refers to a number of collections, or groups, and may be applied to any one of the groups, hence it is not a collective noun.

Exercise.

Select appropriate pronouns and verbs, giving your reason for each selection:

1. The army (invades, invade) the country.
2. The army eagerly (pursues, pursue) pleasure as (its, their) chief good.
3. The congregation (attends, attend) to (its, their) duties well.
4. The congregation at Irving Chapel (was, were) large.

[1] A collective noun of unity may name either animate or inanimate objects, but a collective noun of plurality usually names living beings only.

THE NOUN

5. The congregations of Brooklyn (is, are) large.
6. The regiment (consists, consist) of 1000 men.
7. The regiment took off (its, their) knapsacks.
8. The society (meets, meet) in (its, their) hall this evening.
9. The society (differs, differ) on that question.
10. The jury (has, have) been discharged.
11. The jury will be kept together until (it, they) agree.
12. The lowing herd (wind, winds) slowly down the hill.

68. RELATION OF NOUNS.

You have learned that words must be related in order to convey a meaning or form a sentence. Do the following words form a sentence?

Letters the Bruce Grant to gave.

If we form these words into a sentence, as, *Bruce gave the letters to Grant,* by a change of order we bring them into **relation** to one another.

The different relations of the nouns in this sentence are shown by their position or order. The noun *Bruce* occupies the position of subject and has the subject relation; *letters* is used as the object complement, and has the object relation; *Grant* is used as the object of a preposition, and also has the object relation.

Exercise.

Analyze or diagram the following sentences, and give the use and relation of each noun:

1. Our thoughts are heard in heaven. — *Young.*
2. Politeness costs nothing and wins everything. — *Montagu.*
3. Money, says the proverb, makes money. — *Adam Smith.*
4. Men shut their doors against a setting sun. — *Shakespeare.*

5. Our words have wings but fly not where we would.
— *George Eliot.*
6. Never make a defense or apology before you be accused.
— *Charles I.*
7. Roll on, thou deep and dark blue ocean — roll!
Ten thousand fleets sweep over thee in vain;
Man marks the earth with ruin, — his control
Stops with the shore. — *Byron.*

69. INFLECTION TO SHOW RELATION.

Let us again examine this sentence:

Bruce gave the letters to Grant.

Does this sentence tell to whom the letters belonged?

If we wish to say that Bruce gave to Grant the letters *of* Lincoln, or the letters *belonging to* Lincoln, we may express the thought more briefly by using the apostrophe and *s* ('s). Thus,

Bruce gave Lincoln's letters to Grant.

The sign apostrophe and *s* ('s) added to the noun *Lincoln* shows the same relation that is denoted by the word *of* or the words *belonging to*.

This is the only use of nouns in which the relation is shown by an inflection, or a change in the form of the word.[1] In all other uses it is shown by the position of the word in the sentence, or by the use of a preposition.

If we write the above sentence and omit the possessive sign ('s) from the noun *Lincoln*, a different meaning will be conveyed; as,

Bruce gave Lincoln letters to Grant.

[1] Pronouns are inflected to show three different relations.

THE NOUN

This means, Bruce gave to Lincoln letters addressed to Grant.

The inflection apostrophe and *s* ('s) is added to *Lincoln* to show its possessive relation to the noun *letters,* and is an example of **Case Inflection,** or **Case.**

DEFINITION. *Case* **is a variation in the use or form of a noun or pronoun to show its relation to other words.**

The Latin language has more than twenty different inflections, or case endings, to show relation; as, *a, ae, us, u, arum, orum, ibus, ubus,* etc. Nouns in our language once had four inflections, but the ordinary naming form of the noun has taken the place of two of these earlier forms so that nouns now have but two case forms:

1. The **Nominative,** or naming form.
2. The **Possessive,** or form used to express possession.[1]

We speak of a noun, however, as having a third case, the **Objective Case,** to designate its objective use, or relation.

This is because pronouns have an objective form to show the objective relation, and it is, therefore, convenient to use the term *objective case* in parsing nouns.

Note in the following that the noun *man* has the same form in both the nominative and the objective relation:

Man *is to* **man,** *the sorest, surest ill.* — *Young.*

```
    Man  \  is  \  ill
              |  surest
              |  sorest
              |  the
              | to | man
```

If we use the pronoun *he* instead of *man* in the above sentence we must change its form to show the objective relation; as, **He** *is to* **him,** not **He** *is to* **he.**

```
    He  \  is  \  ill
              |  surest
              |  sorest
              |  the
              | to | him
```

---

[1] For other uses of the possessive case see pp. 122, **123.**

70. OUTLINE OF CASE RELATIONS.

According to its use a noun or pronoun may have different relations to other words in sentences. For convenience these relations are grouped in *three cases*, as is shown in the following summary, which may be used for reference:

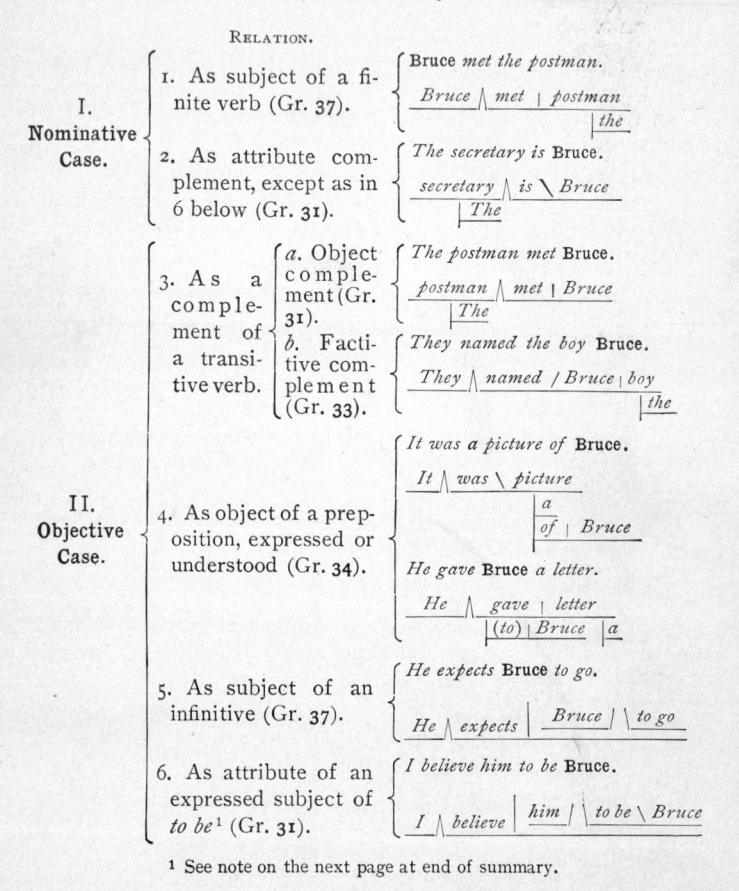

RELATION.

I. Nominative Case.

1. As subject of a finite verb (Gr. 37).

   Bruce met the postman.

   Bruce ∧ met | postman
                | the

2. As attribute complement, except as in 6 below (Gr. 31).

   The secretary is Bruce.

   secretary ∧ is \ Bruce
   | The

II. Objective Case.

3. As a complement of a transitive verb.
   - *a.* Object complement (Gr. 31).

     The postman met Bruce.

     postman ∧ met | Bruce
     | The

   - *b.* Factitive complement (Gr. 33).

     They named the boy Bruce.

     They ∧ named / Bruce | boy
                                 | the

4. As object of a preposition, expressed or understood (Gr. 34).

   It was a picture of Bruce.

   It ∧ was \ picture
              | a
              | of | Bruce

   He gave Bruce a letter.

   He ∧ gave | letter
         | (to) | Bruce | a

5. As subject of an infinitive (Gr. 37).

   He expects Bruce to go.

   He ∧ expects | Bruce | \ to go

6. As attribute of an expressed subject of *to be*[1] (Gr. 31).

   I believe him to be Bruce.

   I ∧ believe | him | \ to be \ Bruce

---

[1] See note on the next page at end of summary.

THE NOUN

III. Possessive Case. { 7. As a possessive modifier (Gr. 20.) {
He received **Bruce's** *letter.*

$$\underline{He \wedge received \mid letter}$$
$$\overline{\mid Bruce's}$$

NOTE. An attribute noun or pronoun is in the nominative case unless attributive to the expressed subject of an infinitive, when it is in the objective case; as,

It is **he.**
It seems to be **he.**
Its being **he** *made no difference.*

They believe me to be **him.**
For me to desire to be **him** *is foolish.*

SPECIAL CASE RELATIONS.

1. When a noun or pronoun is used as an appositive it is in the same case as the noun whose meaning it explains; as,

NOMINATIVE CASE: *The secretary*, **Bruce**, *will write.*
POSSESSIVE CASE: *He went to* **Bruce** *the secretary's desk.*
OBJECTIVE CASE: *We saw the secretary*, **Bruce**.

2. When a noun or pronoun is used without relation to any other part of speech it is said to be in the **Nominative Case.**

   1. By direct address: *Come into the garden*, **Maud.**
   2. By exclamation: *Alas, poor* **Yorick!**
   3. By pleonasm (use of unnecessary words): *The* **boy**, *oh, where was he!* (Oh, where was the boy!)
   4. By specification (titles of books, names of companies, etc., when used alone): **Steps in English; Brown & Bole.**

3. A noun or pronoun used in an absolute phrase is in the **Nominative Case.** (See *Absolute Phrase*, Gr. 47, p. 77.)

   He *being a foreigner, his family was protected.*

4. When a noun is used to express measure of some kind and at the same time is an adverbial modifier it is called an **Adverbial Objective,** and may be said to be in the **Objective Case**; as,

1. *We waited an* **hour.**[1]
2. *The book is worth a* **dollar.**[1]
3. *We walked two* **miles.**[1]

1. $\underline{We \wedge waited}$
   $\overline{\mid hour}$
   $\overline{\mid an}$

[1] In such sentences some prefer to supply a word or words; as,
   1. We waited (for) an hour.
   2. The book is (of the) worth (of) a dollar.
   3. We walked (through) two miles.

By a study of the foregoing the relation and case of nouns and pronouns may be determined.

71. PARSING.

Examine the outline under Grammar 70 and find the different uses of the noun. In what relation is each noun used? In what case?

We are now prepared to *parse* the noun.

To parse means, (1) to classify the word as a part of speech; (2) to point out its inflection, if it has any; and (3) to tell its syntax, or its relation to other words in the sentence.

DEFINITION. *Syntax* treats of the arrangement, relation, and agreement of words in sentences.

72. PARSING THE NOUN.

To parse a noun, give its —

1. Class,
2. Gender,
3. Person,
4. Number,
5. Case,
6. Syntax, or use in the sentence.

EXAMPLES. *The* **groves** *were* **God's** *first* **temples.**

Groves is a common noun — the name of a class; in the neuter gender — it denotes things without sex; 3d person — spoken of; in the plural number — it denotes more than one; in the nominative case — it is the subject of the verb *were*.

God's is a proper noun, masculine gender, 3d person, singular number, possessive case, modifying *temples*.

Temples is a noun, common, neuter, 3d, plural, nominative — the attribute complement of *were*.

TO THE TEACHER. As the pupil becomes familiar with the several distinctions and can readily give the reasons, the shorter forms may be used. After the distinctions are well understood, all the particulars that do not affect the structure of the word may be omitted; as, *Temples* is a noun, attribute of the verb *were*.

Parsing should never be made a mere mouthing of words without thought. This may be avoided by having the pupil parse in writing.

Models for Written Parsing.

groves ∧ *were* \ *temples*
    The   *first*
                            God's

C.N.	C.N.	P.N.
Neut.	Neut.	Masc.
3.	3.	3.
Plur.	Plur.	Sing.
Nom.	Nom.	Poss.
Sub. of *were*.	Att. Comp. *were*.	modifies *temples*.

The Sentence Words.	Class.	Gender.	Person.	Number.	Case.	Syntax or Use.
In	Prep.					
this	Adj.					
place	Com. noun	Neut.	3	Sing.	Obj.	Obj. of Prep. *in*
ran	Verb					
Cassius'	Prop. noun	Masc.	3	Sing.	Poss.	modifies *dagger*
dagger	Com. noun	Neut.	3	Sing.	Nom.	Subj. of *ran*.
through	Adv.					

Exercises.

Ex. I. *Analyze the sentences in the following paragraphs, and then parse orally the nouns in each sentence:*

But all my dreams were soon put to flight by an order from the office to trim the yards, as the wind was getting ahead. I could plainly see, by the looks the sailors occasionally cast to windward and by the dark clouds that were fast coming up, that we had bad weather to prepare for, and had heard the captain say that he expected to be in the Gulf Stream by twelve o'clock. In a few minutes "eight bells" was struck, the watch called, and we went below.

I now began to feel the first discomforts of a sailor's life. The steerage in which I lived was filled with coils of rigging, spare sails, old junk, and ship stores, which had not been stowed away. Moreover, there had been no berths built for us to sleep in, and we were not allowed to drive nails to hang our clothes upon.

Ex. II. *Diagram the following sentences, and parse the nouns according to the model for written parsing:*

1. The South is the land of cotton.
2. Heap high the farmer's wintry hoard.
3. No man's a faithful judge in his own cause.
4. No capital earns such interest as personal culture.
5. Ye mariners, the night is gone!
6. Spenser, the author of the "Faerie Queene," lived in the time of Queen Elizabeth.
7. His friend remained a week.
8. Their work having been finished, the pupils were dismissed.
9. We, the members of the club, have elected Robert president.
10. They believed him to be their friend.
11. The smith, a mighty man was he.

Ex. III. *Select the proper case, giving reason; then diagram the sentences and parse each noun:*

1. The (man, man's) being poor should not make him miserable.
2. The (man, man's) being poor, the boys treat him kindly.
3. The (man, man's), being poor, knew not what to do.
4. We could not prevent (John, John's) going.
5. (Brown, Brown's) being a politician, we were unable to prevent his election.
6. (Brown, Brown's) being a politician aided him very much.
7. No one ever dreamed of that (man, man's) running for office.
8. The (writer, writer's) being a scholar, his conclusions were not doubted.
9. I never thought of (it, its) being (she, her).
10. Much depends on (you, your) studying the foregoing carefully.

THE NOUN

Ex. IV. *Punctuate and diagram the following, telling the case of each appositive* (for punctuation, see *Appositive Expressions*, Gr. 10 and 61, pp. 20, 102 ; also Comp. 53, pp. 284–286) :

1. The wisest of the Jewish kings Solomon became a fool.
2. Mr. McKinley the president sent his message to Congress.
3. A Greek philosopher Diogenes lived in a tub.
4. The Greek philosopher Diogenes lived in a tub.
5. Cotton a fiber is woven into cloth.
6. Have you read the history of Pizarro the conqueror of Peru?
7. The diamond pure carbon is a brilliant gem.
8. The creator of "Robinson Crusoe" Daniel Defoe was the author of more than two hundred works.
9. We the people of the United States do ordain and establish this Constitution.
10. I John was a witness.
11. We girls object.
12. We the older boys protest.

73. THE FORMATION OF THE POSSESSIVE CASE.

NOTE. Case, as applied to nouns, has importance only in connection with the use of the possessive sign. The nominative and objective cases of nouns, being alike in form and not inflected, might be disregarded if it were not for the inflection of pronouns and the convenience of parsing.

Observe the inflection of the nouns in the second column to show the relation denoted by prepositions used with the corresponding noun in the first column:

1. The work **of the pupil** is excellent.	1. The **pupil's** work is excellent.
2. The work **of the pupils** is excellent.	2. The **pupils'** work is excellent.
3. The work **of the children** is excellent.	3. The **children's** work is excellent.

4. The novels **by Dickens** are popular.

4. **Dickens's novels** are popular.

5. The coat **for James** is new.

5. **James's** coat is new.

With which of the nouns is the *s* of the possessive sign omitted?
In the second sentence is the noun *pupils* singular or plural?
In the third sentence is the noun *children* singular or plural?
In the fifth sentence is the noun *James* singular or plural?

It is seen that the possessive case of all the nouns in the above exercise is formed by the addition of the apostrophe and *s* ('s) except the noun *pupils*, which is a plural noun that ends in *s*.

RULE. **Nouns form the possessive case by the addition of an apostrophe and *s* ('s), except plural nouns ending in *s*, to which the apostrophe alone is added.** (Comp. 11, p. 235.)

REMARKS ON THE POSSESSIVE FORM.

1. A few singular nouns that end with an *s* sound are usually written in the possessive by adding the apostrophe alone: especially in the phrases *for appearance' sake, for conscience' sake*, and *for goodness' sake*. But the tendency is to add apostrophe and *s* ('s) even if the singular noun does end with an *s* sound; as, *Charles's* book, *the princess's carriage, her mistress's wishes*.

2. When a compound noun or a group of words treated as one name (a firm-name) denotes possession, the sign of the possessive is added to the last noun only. (See 4 and 9 in the next exercise.)

3. The possessive relation may be expressed by a prepositional objective; as, *a friend of Charles's wife*, instead of *Charles's wife's friend*.

4. The sign of possession should be used with the word immediately preceding the substantive naming the thing possessed; as, *John's book; John and Mary's book; John the student's book; John's books as well as Mary's* (books).

Occasionally the word naming the thing possessed may be omitted (see last example).

THE NOUN

5. As a rule, neuter nouns should not be used in the possessive case. *The beauty of the flower* is better English than *The flower's beauty*.

Exercises.

Ex. I. *Justify the use of each possessive sign in the following:*

PREPOSITIONAL OBJECTIVES.	POSSESSIVES.
1. A house belonging **to the man**.	1. **The man's** house.
2. A dictionary made **by Webster**.	2. **Webster's** dictionary.
3. Shoes designed **for misses**.	3. **Misses'** shoes.
4. The father of both **Henry and John**.	4. **Henry and John's** father.
5. The father **of Henry** and the father **of John**.	5. **Henry's** father and **John's**.

4.
```
        father        
| Henry and John's |
```

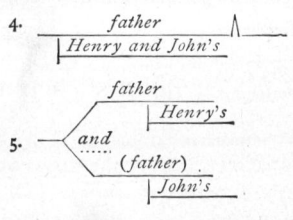

5.
```
         father
       | Henry's |
   and
      (father)
       | John's |
```

6. The administration **of Mayor Hays**.	6. **Mayor Hays's** administration.
7. Books belonging **to Alice**.	7. **Alice's** books.
8. The tub owned **by Diogenes**.	8. **Diogenes's** tub.
9. The store **of Little & Co.**	9. **Little & Co.'s** store.
10. At the home **of Mr. Smith**.	10. At **Mr. Smith's**.
11. At the store **of Weldon the hatter**.	11. At **Weldon the hatter's** store.
12. The reign **of Victoria, queen of England**.	12. **Victoria queen of England's** reign.
13. The work **of one day** for the wages **of three days**.	13. **One day's** work for **three days'** wages.
14. The fault **of somebody else**.	14. **Somebody else's** fault.

NOTES: 1. In the 4th example *Henry and John* is a group of words treated as one name, a firm-name. So also *Little & Co.* in the

9th example. 2. In the 5th example *father* is understood after *John's* because every possessive case is immediately followed by the substantive, expressed or understood, to which it has the possessive relation. This principle also applies to the 10th. 3. As to the 14th, since the adjective *else* always follows the substantive which it limits, and since the possessive must be next to the name of the thing possessed, the sign is, according to idiom (pp. 130, 131), annexed to *else*.

Ex. II. *Change from the prepositional objective to the possessive:*

1. A history of Moses.
2. The barking of the dogs.
3. A picture of William.
4. A picture owned by William.
5. The works of Dickens.
6. The greetings of the Friends.
7. The family of Governor Hastings.
8. Clothing for men and for boys.
9. The home of both Mary and Ann.
10. The home of Mary and that of Ann.
11. The crew of Yale or Harvard.
12. The record of the ball players.
13. The home of his son-in-law.
14. The execution of Mary, Queen of Scots.
15. By the silvery light of the Queen of Night.
16. The death of Grant and of Sheridan.
17. The fault of some one else.
18. The work of five years.
19. The wages of one month.
20. The wishes of the princess.

Ex. III. *Change from the possessive to the prepositional objective, thereby deciding whether or not each is correctly written:*

1. John and Henry's boat.
2. John's boat and Henry's.
3. John and Henry's boats.
4. John's boats and Henry's.

THE NOUN

5. Mason and Dixon's line.
6. Hayes and Wheeler's administration.
7. Hayes's administration and Grant's.
8. Men's and boys' clothing.
9. Men's and boy's clothing.
10. Ned the bootblack's box.
11. Infant's and children's cloaks.
12. Infants' and children's cloaks.
13. A and B's money.
14. A's money and B's.
15. Grant's army and Lee's.
16. Grant's and Lee's armies.
17. Orr and Co.'s store.

Ex. IV. *Insert the apostrophe in its proper place, giving your reason:*

1. That boys hats.
2. Those boys hats.
3. Ciceros oration.
4. The childs illness.
5. My only daughters husbands sister.
6. My two daughters husbands sister.
7. These witnesses statements are very long.
8. This witnesss statements are long.
9. The suns and the fires heat differ.
10. The suns rays are quite warm to-day.
11. The ladys bonnets.
12. Those ladies bonnets.
13. That pupils books.
14. Two years interest.
15. My daughters going need not prevent Anns calling.
16. My daughters friend is going to the city this morning.
17. An honest mans work is noble.
18. A mans foes are often those of his own household.
19. Peters wifes aunt.

Ex. V. *Decide which is the better form, the possessive or the prepositional objective, and change where desirable:*

1. Peter's wife's mother.
2. John's brother's wife's sister is sick.
3. This is my brother's father-in-law's opinion.
4. France's and England's interests differ widely.
5. My brother's wife's sister's drawings have been much admired.
6. The drawings of the sister of the wife of my brother have been much admired.
7. The severity of the sickness of the son of the King caused alarm.
8. Essex's death seemed to haunt Elizabeth's mind.
9. The "Iliad" is Homer the great poet's work.
10. Howard the philanthropist's life was a noble one.

74. REVIEW.

TEST QUESTIONS. 1. What is the difference between a proper noun and a common noun? 2. Of what importance is this classification of nouns? 3. When does a common noun begin with a capital letter? 4. How do the terms *gender* and *sex* differ in meaning? 5. In what three ways is the gender of nouns shown? 6. What is *person* in grammar? 7. Do nouns have special forms to distinguish person? 8. How should a proper noun in the first person be punctuated? 9. How are common nouns in the first person punctuated? 10. What is meant by *inflection?* 11. Illustrate by example. 12. How do nouns generally form the plural? 13. Why should the plural of *enemy* and that of *chimney* be differently formed? 14. What is a collective noun? 15. How are nouns inflected to show relation? 16. How many cases have nouns? 17. How many case forms? 18. Give the rule for forming the possessive case of nouns. 19. How is joint ownership shown by the possessive sign? 20. What substitute for the possessive may be used? 21. How many different uses may a noun have in a sentence? 22. Name them. 23. Write sentences using the noun *James* in eight different constructions.

75. THE PRONOUN.

What is a pronoun? What is the antecedent of a pronoun? What is a relative pronoun? What is person? When is a pronoun in the first person? In the second person? In the third person?

THE PRONOUN

About sixty words in the English language designate persons or objects without mentioning their names. As they are generally used instead of nouns, they are called **Pronouns**. From the various ways in which they are used *pronouns may be divided into four classes*, — **Personal, Relative, Interrogative,** and **Adjective**.

76. PERSONAL PRONOUNS.

Five pronouns, *I, you, he, she,* and *it,* are used, in their various forms, to distinguish, first, **the speaker, I;** second, **the one spoken to, you;** and third, **the person or thing spoken of, he, she,** and **it.** Because these pronouns always show their grammatical person by different forms or words (not because they stand for persons), they are called **Personal Pronouns.**

DEFINITION. A *Personal Pronoun* is one whose form indicates the speaker, the person spoken to, or the person or thing spoken of.

77. THE INFLECTION OF PERSONAL PRONOUNS.

Personal pronouns change their forms by inflection more than do any other words in our language, the different forms of the pronouns *I, you, he, she,* and *it* numbering twenty-eight. Some of these changes are so great that different cases of the same pronoun are entirely different words; note the different cases of the personal pronouns *I, she,* and *he* in the following:

FIRST PERSON: I, my, mine, me, we, our, ours, us.
SECOND PERSON: you, your, yours.

THIRD PERSON:
- *Masc.* he, his, him.
- *Fem.* she, her, hers.
- *Neuter.* it, its.
- they, their, theirs, them.

Some of these changes in form or word, as we have seen, indicate person; as, *I, you, he*: while others indicate gender; as, *he, she*, and *it.* In what person and number do the variations to show gender occur? (See declension in Gr. 78.)

Tell the case, or relation, of the pronouns in the following:

He *laid* him *down and closed* his *eyes.*

Note in this sentence three different forms of the same pronoun to distinguish the *nominative, possessive,* and *objective* cases.

The number of inflections that pronouns have, causes their frequent misuse. To assist in using them properly their inflection is given in tabular form for reference, and rules are added which should be learned and applied.

78. THE DECLENSION OF THE PRONOUN.

Pronouns of the First Person.

	SINGULAR.	PLURAL.
Nominative.	I	we
Possessive.	my *or* mine	our *or* ours
Objective.	me	us

Pronouns of the Second Person.

	Common Form.	Grave Style.	
	SING. AND PLU.	SING.	PLU.
Nominative.	you	thou	ye *or* you
Possessive.	your *or* yours	thy *or* thine	your *or* yours
Objective.	you	thee	you

THE PRONOUN

Pronouns of the Third Person.

	Singular			Plural		
	Masc.	*Fem.*	*Neut.*	*Masc.*	*Fem.*	*Neut.*
Nominative.	he	she	it		they	
Possessive.	his	her *or* hers	its		their *or* theirs	
Objective.	him	her	it		them	

Compound Personal Pronouns are formed by annexing *self* and its plural *selves* to certain forms of the personal pronouns. They are:

Singular. myself   thyself, yourself   himself, herself, itself.
Plural.   ourselves   yourselves   themselves

They have the same form for both nominative and objective, and have no possessive. The place of the possessive is supplied by using for emphasis the definitive adjective (Gr. **117**, p. 193) *own* with the ordinary possessive form; as,

> *I have my* **own** *seat.*
> *Take your* **own** *seats.*
> *He has a home of his* **own.**

In the last sentence the emphatic form of the pronoun *his own,* is used substantively as the object of the preposition *of.* (See page 130, *This book of mine.*)

79. USES OF PRONOUNS.

RULE 1. A pronoun used as the subject of a *finite* verb or as a nominative absolute, is in the nominative case and should have the nominative form.

RULE 2. A pronoun used as the subject of an infinitive or as the object of a verb or preposition, is in the objective case and should have the objective form.

RULE 3. A pronoun used as an attribute is in the nominative case unless attributive to the expressed subject of an infinitive, when it is in the objective case.

Why did we not need these rules when learning about the noun? What rule have you learned for writing the possessive case of nouns? How do we form the possessive case of pronouns? Give the possessive case singular and plural of the personal pronouns. Is an apostrophe (') used with these forms?

CAUTION. Never use an apostrophe with the words *ours*, *yours*, *his*, *hers*, *its*, *theirs*. Remember that *it's* means *it is*.

Two Forms of the Possessive. The possessive form of the pronoun has the power of an adjective and modifies a noun expressed or understood. When the noun is expressed, the first of the two possessive forms is used; when the noun is not present or the possessive is used as a complement, the second is used. For example:

1. *Your book is new but mine is old.*

Mine may be parsed as a personal pronoun, possessive form, but used in the subject relation; the subject of the verb *is*.

```
  book  \  is  \  new        mine \ is \ old
 | Your |         | but |
```

2. *The book is yours.*   3. *This book of mine is old.*

```
  book \ is \ yours              book \ is \ old
 | The |                        | This |
                                | of | mine |
```

Some grammarians would dispose of these possessive forms by substituting a word modified by the possessive, as,

This book of **my books** *is old,*

and then parse the pronoun as in the possessive case, modifying the noun. But one may properly speak of *this book of mine* even if there is but the one book. Also, the explanation involves ambiguity in such expressions as *He is a friend of mine*. *A friend of* **mine** might not be *a friend of* **my** friends. We may either parse *mine* as possessive in form, but used idiomatically in the objective relation, as the object of the preposition *of*, or we may say it is an idiomatic expression;

THE PRONOUN 131

i.e., an expression established by usage, but not governed by the ordinary rules of grammar. The expressions *meseems* and *methinks* are idiomatic and are equivalent to *it seems to me*.

REMARK. The longer forms *mine* and *thine* were once the only forms, and were used until the seventeenth century, when they dropped the *n* sound before nouns beginning with a consonant, and became *my* and *thy*; as,

   1. *Look upon* **my** *son for he is* **mine** *only child.* — Luke ix. 38.
   2. *Lend* **thy** *hand. Wipe thou* **thine** *eyes.* — Shakespeare.

These forms are now used only when they are not followed by the nouns they modify.

Uses of Compound Personal Pronouns. The compound personal pronouns are used for the most part reflexively [1] in the objective case, or they are added for emphasis in either the nominative or the objective to the nouns or pronouns which they represent; as,

USED REFLEXIVELY.
1. *I hurt myself.*
2. *The house is divided against itself.*

USED FOR EMPHASIS.
3a. *He himself is sick.*
3b. *He is sick himself.*
4. *They saw the president himself.*

Grave Style. The grave style of the pronoun of the second person, — including the singular forms *thou, thy, thine,* and *thee,* and the plural nominative form *ye,* — is used now by the Friends, or Quakers, and also in poetry and in sacred services. The common forms *you,*

[1] A pronoun is called **reflexive** when it is the object in a sentence and refers back (reflects) to the subject as its antecedent. Formerly the reflexive pronoun was often used without the *self* or *selves*; as, *I do repent me.* — Shakespeare. *Now I lay me down to sleep.* — Child's Prayer.

your, and *yours* are used in all other cases. Remember, however, that *you* singular is followed by the same form of the verb as *you* plural, and use this form of the verb with it, as, *you were, you are*, etc., even when speaking to only one person.

Exercises.

Ex. I. *Analyze and diagram the following numbered sentences; parse the personal pronouns, and explain why each case form is used. Thus:*

They expect him to come.

They	\	expect	him	/	to come
P.P.			P.P.		
3.			3.		
Com.			Masc.		
Plur.			Sing.		
Nom.			Obj.		
Sub. of			Sub. of		
expect.			*to come*.		

ORAL. *They* is a personal pronoun, third person, common gender, plural number; it is in the nominative case as the subject of the finite verb *expect* (Rule 1).

Him is a personal pronoun; it is in the objective case, being used as the subject of the infinitive *to come* (Rule 2).

They knew it was she.

They \ knew | it /\ was \ she

P.P.
3d.
Fem.
Sing.
Nom.
Attrib. referring to
the Sub. *it*.

ORAL. *She* is a personal pronoun, third person, feminine gender, singular number; it is in the nominative form, because it is used as an attribute referring to the pronoun *it*, which is in the nominative case as the subject of the finite verb *was* (Rule 3).

1. We expect him to do his part.
2. You know he will do right.
3. They thought it was she.
4. Second thoughts, they say, are best. — *Dryden*.
5. At last they steal us from ourselves away. — *Pope*.
6. A dream itself is but the shadow. — *Shakespeare*.
7. Then like fire he meets the foe,
   And strikes him dead for thine and thee. — *Tennyson*.
8. Nature designed us to be of good cheer. — *Jerrold*.

9. Methinks, with his heavy heart and weary brain, Time should himself be glad to die.

10. Pilgrim, I greet thee; silver and gold have I none, but such as I have, give I unto thee.

11. The sun veils himself in his own rays to blind the gaze of the too curious starer. — *Alcott*.

12. Give me[1] the erect and manly foe
That I may return blow for blow.

13. He cast off his friends, as a huntsman his pack,
For he knew, when he chose, he could whistle them back.
— *Goldsmith*.

14. You hear that boy laughing? You think he's all fun;
But the angels laugh, too, at the good he has done;
The children laugh loud as they troop to his call,
And the poor man who knows him laughs loudest of all.
— *O. W. Holmes*.

15. Chancing to raise her eyes as the elder lady was regarding her, she playfully put back her hair, which was simply braided upon her forehead, and threw into her beaming look such an expression of affection and artless loveliness, that blessed spirits might have smiled to look upon her. — *Charles Dickens*.

Ex. II. *Select two personal pronouns that may be used in each of the following blanks, and justify their case forms:*

1. William and _____ shall take a walk to-day.
2. Shall _____ go with _____?
3. _____ shall walk through the meadow near where _____ grandfather lives.
4. Get a book at the library for Elizabeth and _____.
5. They awarded the prize to _____ who wrote the composition entitled "Bird Life."
6. No one expected _____ to win the prize offered by _____ great-uncle.

---

[1] In expressions like *Give me the book, Write me an excuse*, etc., the pronouns are in the old dative case; that is, they are in a case which is no longer used, but which, in the early history of our language, was used and recognized. Modern writers, however, prefer to say that such words are in the objective case, being indirect objects or being governed by prepositions understood.

7. He is a better writer than _____.
8. _____ are younger than either Harry or _____.
9. Neither you nor _____ can perform the task.
10. I fear that it is _____.
11. I know it to be _____.
12. If I were _____ I should go to school.
13. _____ girls are happy.
14. He would not believe _____ girls.
15. It was _____ whom you thought to be _____.
16. I respect you more than _____.
17. This book is _____ not _____.

80. PERSONAL PRONOUNS: CAUTIONS.

1. The simple personal pronoun and its antecedent should not be used as subjects of the same predicate.

Ex. I. *Determine which of the following forms is correct:*

1. Papa he (*or* Papa) bought me a sled.
2. George and Thomas (*or* George and Thomas they) went home.
3. And the ball it (*or* And the ball) rolled into the sewer.
4. The clock it (*or* The clock) was twenty minutes fast.
5. The mouse and the cat they (*or* The mouse and the cat) ran a race.

2. Seldom use *myself* as a substitute for the simple personal pronoun.

Ex. II. *Determine which of the following is correct:*

1. She invited Sarah and (myself *or* me) to go with her.
2. James and (I *or* myself) are in the same society.
3. That is between you and (I, *or* myself, *or* me).
4. He told you and (myself, *or* I, *or* me) to bring the ferns.
5. The invitation is for you and (myself *or* me).

3. Never use the personal pronoun *them* when the adjective *those* is required.

THE PRONOUN

Ex. III. *Determine which of the following is correct:*

1. (Them *or* Those) are mine; the others are yours.
2. Will you lend me (them *or* those) books?
3. He told (them *or* those) to be there at 9 o'clock.
4. Give me a peck of (those *or* them) potatoes.
5. (Those *or* Them) boys are old enough to have more judgment.

4. Never use the forms *hisself, theirself, theirselves, your'n* (your own), *her'n,* or *his'n.*

Ex. IV. *In the blanks insert the proper emphatic compound personal pronoun or the proper emphatic form of the possessive* (**my own,** etc.):

1. The victim _____ declared that he was not the criminal.
2. The books on that shelf are _____.
3. Preachers _____ do not always practice what they preach.
4. Do it _____.
5. We _____ will look after her.
6. It belongs to me _____.
7. My father gave it to us to be _____.
8. The teacher _____ could have done no better.
9. I know that it is _____ even though you do claim it.
10. The boys _____ paid for the broken glass.

5. The common and the grave forms of the pronouns of the second person should not occur in the same sentence.

Ex. V. *Correct the following:*

1. Thou art sad; have you heard bad news?
2. Bestow thou upon us your blessing.
3. You can't always have thy wish realized.
4. Love thyself last, and others will love you.
5. Thy smile is a benediction and your words a delight.

6. Do not use *he, it, they,* or any other pronoun when its reference to an antecedent is not clear. Avoid ambiguity

by repeating the antecedent or by changing indirect discourse to direct discourse.

AMBIGUOUS.	CLEAR.
The boy can not leave his father, for if he should leave him he would die. (Not clear which would die.)	The boy can not leave his father, for if he should leave him his father would die. (Antecedent repeated.)
Harry promised his father never to abandon his friends (said to his father that he would never abandon his friends). (Whose friends?)	Harry gave his father this promise (said to his father): "I will never abandon my friends." *Or* "I will never abandon your friends." (Direct discourse.)

Ex. VI. *Change the following, making each express a clear meaning:*

1. Arthur tried to see Ben in the crowd, but could not because he was so short.

2. The girl asked her mother how old she was.

3. He said to his friend that, if he did not get better soon, he thought he'd better go home. (Give four different meanings.)

4. The man told the boy that his dog had killed his chickens, and that it was but fair that he should pay him for his loss.

5. This farmer went to his neighbor and told him that his cattle were in his fields.

81. RELATIVE PRONOUNS.

(Review Gr. 44, pp. 72, 73.)

1. *We know not* **what** *lies beyond.*

2. *We know not that* **which** *lies beyond.*

Notice that in the first sentence the pronoun *what* introduces the noun clause *what lies beyond;* but in the second sentence the pronoun *which* relates to its antecedent *that*, to which it connects the adjective clause *which lies beyond*.

These pronouns are called **Relative Pronouns**.

DEFINITION. A *Relative Pronoun* is one which introduces an adjective clause or a noun clause that is not directly interrogative.[1]

The chief relative pronouns are **who, which, that,** and **what.** *Who* is thus declined, the singular and the plural being the same:

Nominative . . . who
Possessive . . . . whose
Objective . . . . whom

The other relative pronouns are not declined, except that *whose* is sometimes used as the possessive form of *which*, a usage that many writers feel is seldom warranted.

Exercise.

Tell whether each of the relative pronouns in the following sentences introduces a noun clause or connects an adjective clause with an antecedent:

1. Who steals my purse steals trash.
2. He that getteth wisdom loveth his own soul.
3. Cherish patriotism, which is each citizen's birthright.
4. I have learned what true liberty is.
5. He that plods will reach the goal.
6. The service of a friend is to make us do what we can.
7. Who seeks for aid must faithful be to friend.
8. Truth is the highest thing that man may keep.
9. Men who are ennobled by study are more numerous than they who are ennobled by nature.

[1] In such expressions as *I know who went*, the word *who*, because it introduces an indirect question, is considered by some grammarians an interrogative pronoun (Gr. 84, pp. 141, 142). The treatment here given seems simpler.

82. USES OF THE RELATIVE PRONOUNS.

Who (**whose, whom**) should usually have an antecedent that designates persons.

Which should have as its antecedent a word designating animals or things.

Who and **which** are known as the **Coördinate Relatives.** Ordinarily they should be used only to introduce a clause that adds a new idea. This clause is not necessary in order to make known the author's primary thought; its relative always has the force of a connective and a personal pronoun. For example, in the sentence "Cherish patriotism, which is each citizen's birthright," the relative clause adds a new thought; the author's primary thought is *Cherish patriotism;* and the relative *which* is equal to the connective and pronoun *because it,* or *for it.*

RULE OF PUNCTUATION. **Clauses containing** *who* **or** *which* **used coördinately should be set off by a comma or by commas.** (Comp. 53, pp. 284–286.)

That may have as its antecedent a word designating persons, animals, or things. It should be used whenever the antecedent includes both persons and things. (See sentence 16 in next exercise.)

That is known as the **Restrictive Relative.** It should be used whenever a relative clause is necessary in order to make clear the author's primary meaning, unless the use of *who* or *which* adds decidedly to the pleasing sound of the sentence. For example, in the sentence "He that plods will reach the goal" the clause *that plods* is necessary in order to make clear the author's primary meaning; and the relative *that* is not equal to a connective and a personal pronoun.

THE PRONOUN

Rule of Punctuation. **Clauses containing the restrictive relative *that* should not be set off by a comma or by commas.** (Comp. 53.)

This rule applies also to clauses introduced by *who* or *which* used restrictively.

What (relative pronoun) seldom refers to persons. It always introduces a substantive clause, and always carries its antecedent within itself; that is, it is equivalent to the adjective pronoun *that* plus the relative pronoun *which*. For example, *He receives* **what** *he asks for*, is equivalent to *He receives* **that** *for* **which** *he asks*.

Note. **As** is a relative pronoun when used after *such, same, so much, so great*, etc.; as, *He is such a man* **as** *I admire*.

But is sometimes a relative pronoun after a negative, being equal to *who not;* as, *There is no boy* **but** *will help his mother*.

Note. To the relative pronouns **who, which,** and **what** the suffixes -ever, -so, or -soever may be added, forming the **Compound Relative Pronouns**; as, *whoever, whoso, whosoever*.

Exercise.

Insert the proper relative pronoun and the necessary punctuation, if any (Comp. 53):

1. I know the man ———— you met last night.
2. Mr. Williams ———— is the general's secretary has moved to the city.
3. He claimed to hate music ———— is merely popular in its nature.
4. Pittsburg ———— is a very busy city is known everywhere for its wealth of manufactures.
5. He asked me a question ———— I could not answer.
6. The smile ———— lit up her face was a revelation to me.
7. A smile ———— I am sure was infrequent with her lit up her face.
8. He says that the horse ———— you rode is unable to go farther. (Why *which* instead of *that*?)

9. He says my horse ——— is a Kentucky thoroughbred is worth $800.

10. Stop at the house ——— is next to the mill.

11. My house ——— is near the river stands in a large yard.

12. Her hair ——— was dark and glossy hung in ringlets.

13. People ——— live in glass houses should not throw stones.

14. I *whom* am your friend tell you this.

15. Gen. Warren ——— fell at Bunker Hill was a hero.

16. My memory clings to the dear friends and country ——— I left.

17. Our only dog *which* was called Fido went mad.

18. She was the finest actress *which* I ever saw.

19. The settlers of Plymouth ——— are known as the "Pilgrim Fathers" laid the foundations of religious liberty in America.

20. She is the same person ——— I met at your home.

21. He is a man in ——— I have little faith.

22. Columbus ——— was a Genoese discovered America.

23. The wisest man ——— lives is liable to err.

24. The earth is enveloped by an ocean of air ——— is composed chiefly of oxygen and nitrogen.

25. It is the book ——— I had yesterday.

26. The men and the tools ——— you sent for have arrived.

27. The lady and her dog ——— just passed, walk out together every day.

28. Cotton ——— is a fiber is woven into cloth.

29. She is the lady to ——— you wrote.

30. This is a task ——— is without end.

31. You ——— know better are most at fault.

32. Washington was the man ——— the colonies needed.

33. No beast so fierce ——— knows some touch of pity.

83. THE RELATIVE PRONOUN: CAUTIONS.

1. To avoid ambiguity place the relative clause as near as possible to the word that it limits.

Ex. I. *Make a relative clause of the second sentence of each of the following pairs of sentences, placing it as near*

THE PRONOUN

as possible to the modified word, and punctuating correctly (Comp. **53**):

1. A dog was found in the street. It wore a brass collar.
2. The figs were in small wooden boxes. We ate these figs.
3. A purse was picked up by a boy. It was made of leather.
4. I will tell my father. He is waiting at the gate.
5. I will tell the lady. I mean the lady waiting at the gate.
6. The love of money causes untold suffering. It is the root of all evil.
7. A poor child was found in the street by a wealthy and benevolent gentleman. The child was suffering from cold and hunger.
8. A mad dog bit a horse on the leg. The dog has since died.
9. A gentleman going abroad for the summer will rent his house to a small family. It contains all modern improvements.
10. The picture represents a dark little maid. It hangs on the wall.

2. Several connected relative clauses relating to the same antecedent require the same relative pronoun.

Ex. II. *Insert the proper relatives, and diagram:*

A seal _____ was carried by Washington and _____ was probably shot from his watch-chain, was found in a field after a lapse of eighty years.

84. INTERROGATIVE PRONOUNS.

DEFINITION. **An Interrogative pronoun is one that is used to ask a question.**

Its so-called antecedent is the important word in the expected answer.

The interrogative pronouns are **who, which,** and **what.** The old interrogative **whether** is not now in use.

Who is declined just as the relative pronoun *who* is declined (Gr. **81**). **Which** and **what** have the same form in the objective as in the nominative.

Uses of Interrogative Pronouns.

Who refers to persons only; as, **Who** *is president?* **To whom** *was the property given?* **Whose** *property do you mean?*

Which asks for one out of a number and may apply to either persons or things; as, **Which** *is your book?* **Which** *is your cousin?*

What refers to animals and things; as, **What** *is that on the table?* **What** *moves so rapidly over the floor?*

NOTE. Which and what are often interrogative adjectives (see Gr. 117, p. 194); as, **Which** *man do you mean?* **What** *manner of man is this?*

85. ADJECTIVE PRONOUNS.

An Adjective Pronoun is a word that is usually a definitive adjective (Gr. 117, p. 193), but that does not modify any expressed noun; as, *The* **first** *shall be the* **last**. **None** *know it better than I. Is* **this** *your book?*

Of the adjective pronouns, **one** is the best example. It refers in a general way to any person, and is preferable to *you* used in a similar way. Say, *As one enters, one sees*, rather than *As you enter, you see*. **One** has a possessive form, **one's**, and a plural form, **ones**; as, **One** *prefers the largest for* **one's** *private collection. The smaller* **ones** *are less interesting.*

None has no possessive and no plural form, but is sometimes used with a plural verb; as, **None** *of us were there.*

Other adjective pronouns are **this, that, these, those, former, latter, few, many, some, other, any, all,** and **such.**

86. WHAT AND THAT: CAUTION.

Use **but that** to introduce a noun clause; do not use **but what**: as, *Who knows* **but that** (not **but what**) *he will go?*

THE PRONOUN

```
            │  but that
            │  ........
 Who ∧ knows │  he ∧ will go
```

The pronoun *what* is correctly used after the preposition *but* (meaning *except*) as an element in an objective clause, the clause being the object of the preposition; as, *He took nothing* **but what** *I gave.*

```
 He ∧ took │ nothing
           │ but │ I ∧ gave │ what
```

Exercise.

Insert **what** *or* **that**:

1. I can not believe but _____ I shall see him.
2. He knows nothing but _____ you told him.
3. I did not know but _____ it might be done.
4. I believe all but _____ John told me.

87. REVIEW.

Ex. I. *Insert the proper pronoun:*

1. _____ do you think I met in Paris?
2. Let you and _____ go fishing.
3. The jury rendered _____ verdict.
4. It is hard to fight those _____ you know are right.
5. It is the same book _____ I lent her.
6. People _____ know him respect him.
7. Boys _____ study hard and _____ study wisely make progress.
8. I met a lady _____ all agree is handsome.
9. He is no better than _____.
10. Between you and _____, that man did not deserve it.

Ex. II. *Analyze or diagram the following sentences, and parse all the pronouns:*

1. One can not always have one's choice.
2. Do you know who that is?
3. I do not care for either of them.
4. The fault is yours, not mine.
5. Who he is can not be ascertained.
6. We should have a care for others' comfort.
7. This medicine is what you need.
8. What strange contrasts this world of ours presents!
9. We shall soon see who is going.
10. We think we know what they will do.
11. This watch of mine runs too fast.
12. Ask for whatever you want.
13. Theirs have increased, ours have decreased.
14. Give it to whoever wants it.

TEST QUESTIONS. 1. Which pronouns change their forms to denote person? 2. What is a reflexive pronoun? 3. In what relation, or case, is it used? 4. In what cases may compound personal pronouns be used? 5. Name four pronouns that have three case forms. 6. When or in what constructions must the nominative case form be used? 7. What two uses have relative pronouns? 8. How does the relative *what* differ from other relatives? 9. When are *as* and *but* used as relative pronouns? 10. When does a singular pronoun represent a collective noun? 11. With what kind of clauses is the relative pronoun *that*, and not *who* or *which*, used? 12. What is an adjective pronoun? 13. What is an interrogative pronoun? 14. Do interrogative pronouns have case forms? 15. Which relative pronoun has case forms?

88. THE VERB.

What part of speech must every sentence contain? Why? Of what use is the verb in a sentence? What is meant by a verb of complete predication? How does a finite verb differ from an infinitive? In what respect are infinitives and participles alike?

We have learned that the **verb** is the most important part of speech in the sentence. It is *the word*, or the part of the sentence by which an assertion is made, and no

THE VERB

sentence can be formed without it. It is therefore important that we study its various forms, in order that we may use them correctly. We shall first consider the various **Classes of Verbs.**

89. TRANSITIVE AND INTRANSITIVE VERBS.

1. *The boy hit the ball.*
2. *The ball was hit by the boy.*

Observe that the verb in each of these sentences expresses action. What word in the first sentence names the object that receives the action or is affected by it?

Notice that the subject of thought *boy* performs an act, and that the verb *hit* asserts that act as going over from the subject to the object *ball*.

Has the second sentence an object? What part of the sentence represents the receiver of the action expressed by the verb?

A verb that expresses action which goes over to a receiver of the act is called a **Transitive Verb.** Transitive means *going over.*

DEFINITION. **A** *Transitive Verb* **is one whose action goes over to a receiver of the action.**

NOTE. Some verbs, like *have, own, inherit*, etc., do not express action, yet take an object to denote that which is possessed or affected by them, and hence are transitive. Any verb that has an object is transitive.

All verbs that are *not* transitive are **Intransitive.**

DEFINITION. **An** *Intransitive Verb* **is one whose action does not go over to a receiver.**

An intransitive verb may have an attribute complement, but it never has an object complement.

Exercises.

Ex. I. *Study the following sentences, and tell why the verbs in the first group are intransitive and those in the second group are transitive:*

INTRANSITIVE.	TRANSITIVE.
The children play.	They play games.
The children are playing.	Games are played by them.
The pupils are singing.	They are singing "America."
The pupils sang well.	"America" was sung well.
The book lies there.	She lays the book there.
The gentleman spoke to me.	He speaks German.
He can not see well.	He did not see me there.
Strike while the iron is hot.	Strike the hot iron.
The farmer plows around the field.	The farmer plows the field.
Millet was a great artist.	He painted the "Angelus."

Turn to the lessons on Complements, Gr. **31** and **35**, pp. **51, 52, 57, 58**, *and determine whether the verbs in the exercises are transitive or intransitive.*

Point out the verbs in "*Oliver Horn,*" pp. **241, 242**, *and tell whether they are transitive or intransitive.*

Ex. II. *Make short sentences using each of the following verbs first transitively and then intransitively:*

Awake, blew, dissolve, fly, grind, hear, keep, pay, survive, shake, sounds, follow, read, shoot, spell, struck, wear, writes, tasted.

90. ERRORS IN THE USE OF TRANSITIVE AND INTRANSITIVE VERBS.

1. Verbs are either transitive or intransitive, according to their use. A few, however, are always transitive, and a few are always intransitive. Of these, the verbs *lie* and

THE VERB

lay, rise and *raise*, in their various forms, are frequently misused, as are also the verbs *sit* and *set*.

The following forms are:

INTRANSITIVE.	TRANSITIVE.
Have no object.	*Must have an object.*
Lie, lying, lain. (Reclining.)	Laying, laid. (Placing something.)
Rise, rose, rising, risen. (Getting up.)	Raise, raised, raising. (Lifting something.)
Sit, sat, sitting.[1] (Taking a seat, or remaining seated.)	Set, setting. (Placing something.)

2. The form *lay* is used either transitively or intransitively according to its meaning. When it means *to rest*, *lay* is intransitive, and is used to denote action *in the past;* as, *We* **lay** *down yesterday.* (Not *We* **laid** *down yesterday.*) When *lay* means *to place something*, it is transitive, and is used to denote action *in the present;* as, *We* **lay** *the book down now.*

The forms *set* and *setting* are used intransitively when they mean *going below the horizon* or *beginning a journey*.

Exercises.

Ex. I. *Write ten sentences showing how* **lay**, **set**, *and* **setting** *may be used either transitively or intransitively.*

Ex. II. *Use the proper forms of* **lie** *and* **lay**:

1. I _____ in bed till 7 o'clock every morning.
2. He always _____ his books just where he shouldn't _____ them.
3. I _____ on the lounge last night a long time.
4. She generally _____ abed until she is called.

---

[1] The forms of *sit* may be used transitively, as in the sentence, *They sat them down to weep.* — Milton.

GRAMMAR

5. Mary has not _____ the paper where I told her to _____ it.
6. This morning I _____ in bed till 9 o'clock.
7. That book has _____ on the desk too long.
8. Fred _____ on the sofa most of his time.
9. "Now I _____ me down to sleep."
10. Harry, _____ down and take a nap.
11. Harry _____ down and took a nap.
12. When we are weary, we _____ down.
13. James, _____ your ruler on the desk.
14. He could not _____ on his right side.
15. Have you _____ my books away?
16. John, have you _____ there long?
17. He told me to _____ down, and I _____ down.
18. Samuel was _____ on the floor, and Willie was _____ bricks in rows.
19. He _____ it there yesterday.
20. She told me to _____ the slate down, and I _____ it down.

Ex. III. *Use the proper forms of* **rise** *and* **raise**:

1. I _____ at 6:20 every morning.
2. The balloon had _____ before I came.
3. The curtain will _____ at 8 to-night.
4. The sun _____ at 7.
5. Freddie, _____ the window, please.
6. The moon _____ an hour before I _____.
7. Uncle was just _____ from dinner as I came in.
8. When you saw us, we were _____ the boat.
9. I _____ earlier this morning than I had _____ for a long time.
10. The boy _____ and read.
11. The boy _____ and reads.
12. She _____ more money than I.
13. The allies _____ the blockade.
14. Do you like to see a balloon _____?
15. Mother put the bread by the stove to _____.
16. They entered just as the curtain was _____.
17. The river is _____ very rapidly.
18. The river _____ two feet last night.
19. Shall I _____ or lower the picture?

THE VERB

Ex. IV. *Use the proper forms of* **sit** *and* **set**:

1. I _____ alone all day yesterday.
2. The sun _____ in the west.
3. Harry _____ down and talked to me.
4. Harry, _____ down and talk to me.
5. They _____ out for New York yesterday.
6. Kate, your dress _____ well.
7. The bird is _____ on her eggs.
8. The little girl is _____ the table.
9. She and I usually _____ together.
10. John _____ there and reads.
11. John, _____ there and read.
12. Go and _____ down somewhere!
13. She told me to _____ there, and I _____ down.
14. _____ the lamp on the table, and _____ by the window.
15. Has she _____ on those steps long?
16. She has _____ there for at least an hour.
17. The boy had been out _____ traps for quail, but was now quietly _____ by the fireside.
18. The table has been _____ for some time.
19. I laid my book away, and _____ by the window.

Ex. V. *Use the proper forms of* **lie, lay, rise, raise, sit,** *or* **set**:

1. The shower has _____ the dust.
2. My watch _____ on the bureau all day yesterday.
3. It was reported that the boy had _____ four dollars.
4. I am so weary that I must _____ down.
5. Why have you _____ here so long?
6. You have _____ your coat on my new hat.
7. Shall I _____ down for a little while?
8. I _____ late this morning.
9. You may _____ here.
10. Shall we now _____ ?
11. It was reported that the river had _____ four feet.
12.   A good man should and must
    _____ rather down with loss, than _____ unjust.

91. PRINCIPAL VERBS AND AUXILIARY VERBS.

Note the uses of the verbs *has* and *lost* in the following sentence:

The boy **has lost** *his ball.*

Which verb may be omitted with but slight change of meaning in the sentence?

If we omit the word *lost* the sentence would convey an entirely different meaning:

The boy **has** *his ball.*

It will be seen that *lost* is the principal verb used in making the predication, and that *has* is merely combined with it as an **Auxiliary,** or as a help in expressing its meaning.

DEFINITION. **A verb that is used to help express the meaning of another verb is called an** *Auxiliary Verb.*

The auxiliaries are do (does), did; be (with all its different forms); have (has), had; shall, should; will, would; may, might; can, could; and must.

Exercise.

Turn to Composition 52, *pp.* 282, 283, *and point out the auxiliary and the principal verbs.*

92. VERBAL INFLECTIONS.

Like nouns and pronouns, verbs have different forms (made partly by inflection and partly by auxiliaries) to show their different uses in the sentence.

93. VOICE.

Let us observe again the two sentences:

1. *The boy hit the ball.*

   ```
   boy  \  hit  |  ball
   | The        | the
   ```

2. *The ball was hit by the boy.*

   ```
   ball  \  was hit
   | The  | by | boy
   |           | the
   ```

Do these sentences express the same thought? Wherein do they differ? In the first sentence what word is the subject? How is this same word used in the second sentence? What receives the action expressed by the verb in the second sentence?

Notice that the object of the first sentence becomes the subject of the second, and the simple verb *hit* is changed to *was hit*. This change in the form of a transitive verb helps to give variety of expression, and is called **Voice**.

DEFINITIONS. *Voice* is the variation in the use and form of a *transitive verb* that shows whether the subject is the doer or the receiver of the action.

The *Active Voice* represents the subject as the doer of the action.
The *Passive Voice* represents the subject as the receiver of the action. *Passive* means *receiving* or *enduring*.

The Active Voice is used when we wish to *direct attention to the actor*.	1. **Mr. Logan** *sent the messenger.* 2. **Who** *stole the goods?*
The Passive Voice is used (1) when we wish *to direct attention to the act;* (2) when we wish *to conceal the actor* (see 2); (3) in speaking of *the act when the actor is unknown* (see 3).	1. *The messenger* **was sent** *by Mr. Logan.* 2. *The messenger* **has been sent.** 3. *The goods* **were stolen.**

Only transitive verbs have voice. Some intransitive verbs followed by an attribute resemble the passive form; as, *He is gone.* They are *come*. *Gone* and *come* are here used as attribute complements to denote a condition of the subject, and are not verbs in the passive voice expressing an action received by the subject. These forms are generally used when speaking of inanimate objects; as, *The melancholy days* **are come**. *The flowers* **are gone**. But they should not, as a rule, be used to predicate anything of sentient beings, when their own volition is to be expressed; as, *Our friends* **have** (not *are*) **come**. *Robert* **has** (not *is*) **gone** *to school*.

94. ACTIVE AND PASSIVE FORMS.

When a verb in a sentence is changed from the active to the passive voice, the object of the sentence becomes the subject, and the subject becomes the object of a preposition; as,

Active Voice.

1. *The children loved Longfellow.*

Passive Voice.

2. *Longfellow was loved by the children.*

If the verb has both a direct and an indirect object, the indirect object remains unchanged; as,

1. *The children gave him a chair.*

2. *A chair was given him by the children.*

```
  children  | gave | chair          chair  | was given
  | The     | (to) | him  | a       | A    | (to) | him
                                            | by  | children
                                                   | the
```

Sometimes the indirect object is made the subject of the passive verb; as,

3. *He was given a chair by the children.*

```
  He | was given  | chair
     | by | children | a
     | the
```

THE VERB

In this construction the direct object remains unchanged, and for convenience may be called a **Retained Object**. The broken line of the diagram shows that it is not a real object.

An objective complement of a verb in the active voice becomes an attribute in the passive voice; as,

1. *They named the city Rome.*　　2. *The city was named Rome by them.*

Since an intransitive verb never has an object, it can not be used in the passive voice. However, an intransitive verb and a preposition may sometimes assume the office of a transitive verb. In this case the object becomes the subject, and the preposition becomes a part of the verb; as,

1. *My uncle laughed at him.*[1]　　2. *He was laughed at by my uncle.*

Exercise.

Determine the voice of each verb in the following sentences; rewrite each sentence, changing the verbs in the active voice to the passive and those in the passive to the active:

1. Autumn leaves were gathered by the girls.
2. They gave the teacher the leaves.
3. The dog drew the cart.
4. The child was bitten by the dog.
5. We saw a wild duck.
6. Does the farmer sell corn?

[1] Another way of disposing of the active form is the following:

7. The Southern States export cotton.
8. The book was read by the teacher.
9. We were taught French by Miss Stone.
10. French was taught by Miss Stone.
11. The man does his work well.
12. Rip Van Winkle entered the house.
13. Did the servant break the vase?
14. The way across the mountains was known by the travelers.
15. The travelers saw the snow-capped Alps in the distance.
16. The American flag was raised by the captain.
17. We informed our friends of our arrival.
18. William Penn founded Philadelphia.
19. This composition was written by James.
20. Helen set the dish on the first shelf.
21. Did she lay the letter on the desk?
22. The Pilgrims settled Boston.
23. The English called these people Puritans.
24. We were elected officers by the society.
25. Whittier wrote many poems against slavery.
26. A breeze sets every leaf in motion.

95. MODE.

We use verbs in different ways and give them several forms, in order to show the manner, or *mode*, in which a thought is asserted.

In the following, note the different forms, or modes, of the verb *be* used to assert our thoughts about James:

1. *James* is *here*.
2. *I wish that James* were *here!*
3. *James* may be *here*.
4. *James*, be *here to-morrow*.

The verbs in these sentences show by their forms four different manners of asserting thought. *Is* asserts it as a fact; *were* asserts it as contrary to fact (James is *not* here); *may be* asserts it as possible; and *be* expresses it as a command.

THE VERB

Not only the **form** of a verb, but also its *use*, which is sometimes shown by its position in the sentence, may make known the manner of assertion.

We **study** *diligently*. **Study** *diligently*. The dropping of the subject changes the *assertion of a fact* into a *command*.

DEFINITION. *Mode* is that form or use of a verb that shows the manner of assertion.

Exercise.

Study the following sentences and tell whether each verb asserts a thought — (1) *as a* **fact**; (2) *as a* **wish or condition implying the contrary to be true**; (3) *as* **possible**; (4) *as a* **command**:

1. Emma studies her lesson.
2. Emma, study your lesson.
3. If Emma be sick (I don't believe she is) she need not study.
4. If Emma is sick (she may be sick) she should not study.
5. Emma can study.
6. Dare to do right.
7. If the earth is round men can sail around it.
8. If the earth be flat men can not sail around it.
9. If he have not a friend he may quit the stage. — *Bacon.*
10. Great truths are portions of the soul of man. — *Lowell.*

96. TENSE.

I come *now.*
I came *yesterday.*
I shall come *to-morrow.*

Observe that the different forms of the verb *come* in the above sentences denote an action as taking place at three different times.

Which denotes present time? Which denotes past time? Which, future time?

This variation in the form of the verb to denote the time of the action is called **Tense**. *Tense* is an old French word for *time*.

DEFINITION. *Tense* is a variation in the form of a verb to denote the time of an action or event.

A verb denoting present action is in the **Present Tense**; as, *They go*.

A verb denoting past action is in the **Past Tense**; as, *They went*.

A verb denoting future action is in the **Future Tense**; as, *They shall go*, or *will go*.

These three tenses mark the three great divisions of time, and are called **Primary Tenses**. The indicative mode has three additional tense forms called **Secondary Tenses** to denote completed or perfected action. They are the *present perfect*, the *past perfect*, and the *future perfect*.

The **Present Perfect Tense** is formed by putting *have* (*has*) before the past participle (Gr. 39, p. 66); as, *They* **have gone**.

The **Past Perfect Tense** is formed by putting *had* before the past participle; as, *They* **had gone**.

The **Future Perfect Tense** is formed by putting *shall have* or *will have* before the past participle; as, *They* **will have** *gone*.

Exercise.

The following verbs are in the past tense. Write each in the future tense with the subject **I** *or* **we**, *and also with some other subject. Use the auxiliary* **shall** *with* **I** *or* **we**, *and* **will** *with any other subject;* as, "I (or we) shall go;" "You (or he, they, the boy, etc.) will go."

began	blew	brought	caught
chose	crept	cut	drank
drove	bid	found	froze
went	hit	hid	laid
said	sold	shone	wrote
struck	threw	wore	won
hoped	lived	stopped	tried

97. NUMBER AND PERSON OF THE SUBJECT, AND THE S-FORM OF THE VERB.

We have learned that *simple word subjects* are either nouns or pronouns, and that these two parts of speech may be inflected (changed in form) to indicate difference in *number*.

Number, therefore, is a property of nouns and pronouns, and is that form or use by which they denote one or more than one.

Although verbs do not possess the "property of number," they regularly change some forms because of the number of the subject. Note the following verbs used in the present tense and in the present perfect

PRESENT.

I walk.   *He walks.*
You walk.   *The man walks.*
We walk.   *A dog walks.*
They walk.

PRESENT PERFECT.

I have walked.   *She has walked.*
You have walked.   *The girl has walked.*
We have walked.   *The cat has walked.*
The people have walked.

In what person is each of the subjects in the first column? In what number?

In what person and number is each of the subjects in the second column?

In the present tense how do the verbs in the first column differ from the verbs in the second?

In the present perfect tense how do the auxiliary verbs in the first column differ from those in the second?

These sentences suggest the following principle:

All subjects in the third person, singular number, when used with verbs in the present tense, are followed by the *s*-form of the

verb, and when used with verbs in the present perfect tense, are followed by the *s*-form of the auxiliary.

In making the *s*-form of verbs the same rules generally apply as in adding *s* to nouns to form the plural; thus,

*Catch, catch*es ; *lie, lie*s ; *marry, marri*es ; *journey, journey*s.

98. USE OF THE VERB WITH SINGULAR AND WITH PLURAL SUBJECTS.

In determining whether to use or to reject the *s*-form of the verb, everything depends upon the number of its subject. To decide whether a subject is in the singular or in the plural number, one must look beyond the mere form of the word to the character of the thought expressed by it. The following examples may prove helpful:

SINGULAR SUBJECTS.

1. *The secretary has arrived.*

3. *The secretary and treasurer was seen.*

The article[1] *the* not being repeated, *secretary and treasurer* is the name or title of but one person.

5. *A red and white flag has been sent.*

The article *a* not being repeated, the adjectives *red* and *white* refer to the same flag.

7. *My friend and neighbor* (one person) *has just died.*

9. *The "Pleasures of Memory" was published in 1792.*

"*Pleasures of Memory*" is a noun, the name or title of a book.

PLURAL SUBJECTS.

2. *The secretaries have arrived.*

4. *The secretary and the treasurer were seen.*

The article *the* being repeated, *secretary* and *treasurer* refer to different persons.

6. *A red and a white flag have been sent.*

The article *a* being repeated, the adjectives *red* and *white* refer to different flags, the noun *flag* being understood after *red*.

8. *My friend and my neighbor* (different persons) *have just died.*

10. *The pleasures of memory are delightful.*

Pleasures is the subject; a plural noun.

[1] The adjectives *a*, *an*, and *the* are called **Articles**. See Gr. 117, p. 194.

THE VERB

SINGULAR SUBJECTS.

11. *John and Will's sled is broken.*

The meaning of this sentence is that the two boys own a sled together, and therefore the verb is singular. Note also that the possessive sign comes at the end of the firm-name.

PLURAL SUBJECTS.

12. *John and Will's sleds are broken.*

The "firm" John and Will has more than one sled.

13. *John's sled and Will's are broken.*

Each boy owns one sled, the noun *sled* being understood after *Will's*.

14. *John's sleds and Will's are broken.*

Each owns more than one sled.

15. *Bread and milk is wholesome food.*

Bread and milk is a noun, the name of a kind of food.

16. *Bread and milk are plentiful.*

Bread and *milk* are spoken of as different objects, not "considered as a whole."

17. *Nine tenths of the soil is sand.*

18. *Nine tenths of the words are misspelled.*

When the subject is a partitive word (a word meaning a part), and is followed by *of*, its number is determined by the number of the noun or pronoun following *of*. In 17 the noun *soil* is singular; in 18 the noun *words* is plural.

19. *A variety of music charms the ear.*

20. *A variety of beautiful objects please the eye.*

Nouns like *variety, abundance, plenty*, etc., which are not plural, nor strictly collective nouns, are treated as partitive words and must be regarded as plural in effect when they are followed by a plural modifier to which the verb makes direct reference; as, *Plenty of oranges are brought from Florida.* This is true, however, only in sentences similar to 17 to 20 inclusive.

21. *The choir sings its selections well.*

The *choir*, as a body, as one whole, sings. Therefore, *choir* is a collective noun of unity; that is, singular number.

22. *The choir respect their leader.*

The *choir*, not as a whole but as individuals, respect their leader. In this sentence, *choir* is a collective noun of plurality.

SINGULAR SUBJECTS.

23. *Three times one is three.*

In this sentence the meaning is "One (unit or thing) taken three times is three." The subject *one* is an adjective pronoun, singular number.

25. *The number of deserters arrested was small.*

The word *number* when preceded by *the*, is singular.

PLURAL SUBJECTS.

24. *Three times two are six.*

In this sentence the meaning is "Two (units or things) taken three times are six." The subject *two* is an adjective pronoun, plural number.

26. *A number of deserters were arrested.*

(See 19 and 20, and the remark following them.)

Great care must be taken not to mistake an apparent subject for the true one. Thus,

27. *An examination of his affairs shows him to be a bankrupt.*

The real subject being *examination*, the form *shows* is correct. By mistaking *affairs* for the real subject, one is liable to say *show*.

28. *There are more than one error in his work.*

This sentence being introduced by the expletive *there*, the subject follows its verb. The real subject is *more* (meaning *more errors*), hence *are* is correct. By mistaking *error* for the real subject, *is* would be the verb. A better form, however, is, "There are more errors than one in his work."

29. *This is the only one of the books that is valuable.*

One, and not *books*, is the antecedent of the relative pronoun *that*. *That* is, therefore, in the singular number.

30. *This is one of the best books that have been published.*

Books, and not *one*, is the antecedent. The relative pronoun *that* is, therefore, plural.

In negative expressions great care must be taken to avoid the very general error of rejecting the *s*-form of the verb with singular subjects. This is often true before the contraction *n't* for *not:*

He doesn't (not *He don't*). *She doesn't* (not *She don't*). *It doesn't* (not *It don't*). (Comp. **20**, pp. 247, 248.)

THE VERB

He (She or It) isn't (not "*ain't*").
He (She or It) hasn't (not "*hain't*").
I'm not; You aren't, or *You're not; We aren't,* or *We're not* (not "*ain't*").
I (You or We) haven't (not "*hain't*"). (Comp. 51, p. 281.)

Exercise.

Decide which of the verbs in parentheses, in the following sentences, is the correct one, and give your reason for your decision:

1. Books (is, ~~are~~) a noun.
2. A ball and socket (forms, ~~form~~) a universal joint.
3. The committee (is, are) at variance on some points.
4. What sounds (has, have) each of the vowels?
5. Three fourths of the men (~~was~~, were) discharged.
6. Each of the three (brings, bring) a different excuse.
7. John, when (was, were) you in the city?
8. The end and aim of his life (is, are) to get money.
9. Part of the crop (was, were) injured.
10. He (doesn't, don't) like it.
11. The power and influence of his work (is, are) well known.
12. To relieve the wretched (was, were) his pride.
13. One of you (is, are) mistaken.
14. Nine tenths of our happiness (depends, depend) on this.
15. The able scholar and critic (has, have) a fine library.
16. Why (is, are) dust and ashes proud?
17. Young's "Night Thoughts" (is, are) his greatest poetical work.
18. There (comes, come) the boys.
19. There (is, are) several reasons for this.
20. A number of boys (was, were) present.
21. The number of pupils absent (was, were) small.
22. His hope and ambition (was, were) to be a lawyer.
23. The story of his adventures, which (was, were) recently published, (is, are) probably truthful.
24. A new class of words (is, are) explained in this lesson.
25. (Was, were) either of these men considered honest?
26. Hence (arises, arise) the six forms for expressing time.

27. There (is, are) no data by which it can be estimated.

28. There (seems, seem) to be no others included.

29. In piety and virtue (consists, consist) man's happiness.

30. Ambition is one of those passions that (is, are) never satisfied.

31. There (was, were) no memoranda kept.

32. In the savage mind, there (seems, seem) to be hardly any ideas but those which enter by the senses.

33. With him, to will and to do (is, are) the same.

34. Neither of the letters (was, were) received.

35. In all her movements there (is, are) grace and dignity.

36. One of the cities which (was, were) built still (remains, remain).

37. One regiment (is, are) waiting for the order to march.

38. A black and white horse (was, were) sold for $100.

39. To profess regard and to act differently (marks, mark) a base mind.

40. Enough of his original energy and power (was, were) left to render his enemies uneasy.

41. The Society of Friends (was, were) founded by George Fox.

99. USE OF THE VERB WITH SINGULAR AND WITH PLURAL SUBJECTS (*Continued*).

1. Two or more singular subjects connected by *or, nor, and also, and too, and not, but not, if not,* or *as well as,* may be said to form a compound subject whose meaning is singular; as,

   1. *John or James attends.*
   2. *Neither John nor James attends.*
   3. *John, and also James, attends.*
   4. *John, and James too, attends.*
   5. *John, and not James, attends.*
   6. *John, but not James, attends.*
   7. *John, if not James, attends.*
   8. *John, as well as James, attends.*

Notice the commas.

Although these subjects are, for convenience, called "compound," the fact is that they are simple subjects belonging to different propositions, or statements. Thus,

1. `John ∧ (attends)   or   James ∧ attends`

The verb *attends* in the 1st and 2d sentences, agrees with *James*, and is understood with *John*. In the 3d to 8th inclusive, the verb *attends* agrees with *John*, and is understood with *James*.

The thoughts in 3, 4, 7, and 8, however, should usually be expressed in some less confusing form.

2. When two or more singular subjects connected by *and* are preceded by *each*, *every*, or *no*, they are said to form a compound subject whose meaning is singular, and which requires a singular verb; as,

> 1. *Each book and paper was in its place.*
> 2. *Every leaf and every twig teems with life.*
> 3. *No oppressor and no tyrant triumphs here.*

These so-called compound subjects are really simple subjects belonging to different propositions. That is to say, the verbs agree with the subjects next them and are understood with the other subjects. Thus,

1. `Each | book ∧ (was, etc.)   and   paper (each) ∧ was | in | place | its`

3. When two or more subjects requiring different number forms are connected by *or* or *nor*, the verb should agree with the one nearest it; as,

> 1. *Either you or I am expected at the meeting.*
>   (You are expected at the meeting, or I am.)
> 2. *Neither you nor he is allowed to go in.*
>   (You are not allowed to go in, nor is he.)
> 3. *Either the captain or the sailors are to blame.*
>   (Either the captain is to blame, or the sailors are.)
> 4. *Either the sailors or the captain is to blame.*
>   (Either the sailors are to blame, or the captain is.)

Each of these four sentences is an example of a *contracted sentence*, one verb being omitted. This construction should not, as a rule, be used unless the subjects require the same number form. Either the predicate should be completed with the first subject, or the form of the sentence should be changed. (See sentences in parentheses.)

1.
Either
you ∧ (are, etc.) | or | I ∧ am expected | at | meeting | the

4. A singular nominative followed by *with* and an object should have a verb in the singular; as,

The museum, with all its treasures, was burned.

It is better, generally, to use *and*, if the sense allows, and to put the verb in the plural number; as, *The museum and all its treasures were burned.*

Exercise.

Select the proper form of the verbs, and give the reason for your selection:

1. Neither John nor James (is, are) there.
2. Every boy and girl (was, were) invited.
3. The pupils, as well as the teacher, (was, were) pleased.
4. The teacher, but not the pupils, (was, were) pleased.
5. The teacher, as well as the pupils, (were, was) pleased.
6. Neither he nor I (is, am) going.
7. One or more lives (was, were) lost.
8. The Carnegie Institute, with all its wonders, (is, are) free to the public.
9. Question after question (was, were) asked by the child.
10. The population of Pittsburg and Allegheny, with their surrounding boroughs, (was, were) almost half a million in 1900.

100. REGULAR AND IRREGULAR VERBS.

Most of the verbs of our language regularly form the past tense and the past participle (Gr. **39,** p. 66) by adding *ed* (or *d*) to the simplest form of the verb; thus:

THE VERB

REGULAR VERBS.

SIMPLEST FORM.	PAST TENSE.	PAST PARTICIPLE.
Play	Played	Played
Glide	Glided	Glided
Wish	Wished	Wished
Love	Loved	Loved
Cry	Cried	Cried

Some verbs, however, form their past tense and past participle irregularly; thus:

IRREGULAR VERBS.

SIMPLEST FORM.	PAST TENSE.	PAST PARTICIPLE.
Slay	Slew	Slain
Ride	Rode	Ridden
Wear	Wore	Worn
Go	Went	Gone

DEFINITIONS. A verb that forms its past tense and past participle by adding *d* or *ed* to its simplest form, is called a *Regular Verb*.

A verb that forms its past tense and past participle in any other way than by adding *d* or *ed* to its simplest form, is called an *Irregular Verb*.[1]

The simplest form of the verb is the present infinitive (Gr. **105**, p. 172), without *to*. In all verbs except *be* the present indicative (Gr. **101**), the form without *s*, is the same as the present infinitive (if any).

Principal Parts of the Verb. The present indicative (without *s*), the past tense, and the past participle are the **Principal Parts** of the verb, because from them we can make all the other forms or parts.

The present participle is sometimes given as one of the principal parts. To give it seems unnecessary, however, as it is always formed by adding *ing* to the present infinitive.

---

[1] By some grammarians another classification is made, dividing verbs into *strong* and *weak* verbs. Those which form the past tense by a change of the vowel are called **Strong Verbs**; as, *drive, drove*. All others, whether regular or irregular, are called **Weak Verbs**.

GRAMMAR

NOTES. A verb having more than one form for either the past tense or the past participle, or for both, is called a **Redundant Verb**; as, present, *dare;* past tense, *dared* or *durst;* present, *show;* past participle, *showed* or *shown.*

If any one of the principal parts of a verb is wanting, the verb is called **Defective**. For example, *beware* has only the present tense. *Can, may, must, shall,* and *ought* have no past participle.

Therefore the expression *had ought* is incorrect, and should never be used.

A few verbs take as their subject the pronoun *it* without a definite antecedent: as, *It rains; It is cold,* etc. Verbs thus used are called **Impersonal Verbs**.

Exercise.

Tell of each of these verbs whether it is regular, irregular, defective, or redundant; then use some form of each to fill the following blanks (if the verb is transitive, use the pronoun **it** *or some other appropriate object after the verb):*

I _____ now. I _____ yesterday. I have _____.

I eat the apple now. I ate the apple yesterday. I have eaten the apple.

PRESENT.	PAST.	PAST PARTICIPLE.
Am	Was	Been
Begin	Began	Begun
Cleave (*to split*)	Cleft	Cleft, cloven, cleaved
Cleave (*to adhere*)	Cleaved	Cleaved
Do	Did	Done
Dare (*to venture*)	Durst, dared	Dared
Dare (*to challenge*)	Dared	Dared
Eat	Ate	Eaten
Fly (*to take wing*)	Flew	Flown
Flee (*to run away*)	Fled	Fled
Flow, overflow	Flowed, over-	Flowed, over-
Go	Went	Gone
Hang (*to suspend*)	Hung	Hung
Hang (*to take life*)	Hanged	Hanged
Have	Had	Had
Lose	Lost	Lost

THE VERB

Present.	Past.	Past Participle.
Loose	Loosed	Loosed
Lay (*to place*)	Laid	Laid
Lie (*to recline*)	Lay	Lain
Lie (*to deceive*)	Lied	Lied
Rise (*to get up*)	Rose	Risen
Raise (*to lift up*)	Raised	Raised
Sit (*to be seated*)	Sat	Sat
Set (*to place*, etc.)	Set	Set
Dream	Dreamed, dreamt	Dreamed, dreamt
Drink	Drank	Drunk, drank
Ring	Rang, rung	Rung
Run	Ran	Run
See	Saw	Seen
Sing	Sang, sung	Sung
Spring	Sprang, sprung	Sprung
Sink	Sunk, sank	Sunk
Shrink	Shrank, shrunk	Shrunk
Dive	Dived	Dived
Beware	———	———
Ought	Ought	———
Shall	Should	———
Can	Could	———
May	Might	———
Will	Would	———
Must	Must	———
———	Quoth[1]	———

To the Teacher. Pupils should have practice in using the above forms in sentences until they can use them correctly. For a complete list of irregular verbs see Gr. 116, pp. 190–192.

101. THE INDICATIVE MODE AND ITS TENSES.

Definition. The *Indicative Mode* is that form of the verb used to assert something as a fact. It is also used to state conditions or suppositions thought of as facts. It is used:

1. To make an *affirmation : The earth* **is** *round. The boy's coat* **was made** *of silk. It* **rains**.

[1] Rarely used. " *Quoth* the raven, ' Nevermore.' "

2. To ask a *question :* **Is** *the earth round?* **Was** *the coat* **made** *of silk?* **Will** *it* **rain** *to-day ?*

3. In *clauses* when the supposition is not necessarily contrary to the fact: *If the earth* **is** *round* (it is), *men can sail around it. Though the boy's coat* **was made** *of silk* (it was), *it did not look well. If it* **rains** *to-day* (it may or may not), *I shall not go to the picnic.* (See Subjunctive Mode, Gr. 102.)

The tenses of the indicative mode are the *present*, the *past*, the *future*, the *present perfect*, the *past perfect*, and the *future perfect*.

The Present Indicative is used to express:
1. What is actually present; as, *That custom* **is** *quite popular now.*
2. What is true at all times; as, *The sun* **gives** *light. They proved that the earth* **is** *round* (not *was round*).
3. What occurs frequently or habitually; as, *He* **writes** *for the press.*
4. What is to occur in the future; as, *Mr. Jones* **lectures** *next week.*

The Past Indicative denotes time wholly past, having no relation to any other past time and not including present time; as,

1. *That custom* **was** *quite popular formerly.*
2. *She* **visited** *the place often last year.*

The Future Indicative expresses indefinite future action or being; as,

1. *That custom* **will be** *quite popular.*
2. *She* **will visit** *the place while recovering.*

The Present Perfect Indicative expresses action or being as completed in a period of time — an hour, a year, etc. — of which the present is a part; as,

1. *That custom* **has been** *quite popular this year.*
2. *She* **has visited** *the place often this summer.*

The Past Perfect Indicative expresses action or being as completed at or before some definite past time; as,

1. *That custom* **had been** *quite popular, but it ceased at once when John died.*
2. *She never went to Gowanda after her son's death, though she* **had visited** *the place often before that.*

The Future Perfect Indicative expresses action or being that will have been completed at or before some definite future time; as,

1. *Charles* **will have been** *captain just two years next Christmas.*
2. *She* **will have visited** *the place three times if she goes there to-morrow.*

102. THE SUBJUNCTIVE MODE AND ITS TENSES.

DEFINITION. The *Subjunctive Mode* is a form or use of the verb that expresses something that is not a fact, but merely thought of as a possibility.

This mode is used to imply that the contrary is true; as,

If the earth **were** *flat* (it is not), *men could not sail around it.*
If I **were** *you* (I am not), *I should try to understand the lesson.*

This mode may also express *a wish*, implying either the contrary to be true, or an intention unfulfilled; as,

O that I **were** *a child again!*
The sentence is, that you **be hanged.**

The subjunctive is so called because it is usually subjoined, or added, to another statement. When so used it is generally preceded by a subordinate conjunction, — *if, lest, though,* etc. The conjunction is omitted when the verb stands before the subject; as,

Were *I in your place, I should not go.*
If I **were** *in your place, I should not go.*

The forms peculiar to the subjunctive mode are found in the present tense of active verbs, and in the present and past tenses of the verb *be.* Thus:

1. **Subjunctive Form** (without *s*). *If water* **run** *up hill, two threes are seven.*

Notice that the supposition "If water run up hill" is contrary to fact.

2. **Indicative Form** (with *s*). *If water* **runs** *down hill, two threes are six.*

Notice that "If water runs down hill" is not contrary to fact.

Notice further illustrations:

PRESENT TENSE (expressing present or future time).

Subjunctive Form (no *s*). *If he* be *honest* (he is not), *he will pay me.*

Indicative Form (*s*). *If he* is *honest* (he may or may not be), *he will pay me.*

PAST TENSE.

Subjunctive Form (no *s*), expressing present time. *If he* **were** *honest* (he is not), *he would pay me.*

Indicative Form (*s*), expressing past time. *If he* **was** *honest* (which you admit), *why was he discharged?*

Exercise.

Choose the correct form:

1. If he (was, were) near enough, I should speak to him.
2. I wish I (was, were) wealthy.
3. If I (was, were) he, I should accept.
4. O that he (was, were) my brother!
5. Though he (was, were) very industrious, he continued very poor.
6. Though he (was, were) an angel, I should not believe him.
7. If he (is, be) there, ask him to come in.
8. If it (snows, snow) next week, I can't leave.
9. If your father (comes, come), let me know.
10. If your father (was, were) here, you would act differently.
11. Unless some sweetness at the bottom (lies, lie),
    Who cares for all the crinkling of the pie?

103. THE POTENTIAL MODE AND ITS TENSES.

DEFINITION. The *Potential Mode* is that form of the verb used to assert permission, power, necessity, determination, or obligation, by means of the auxiliaries *may, can, must, might, could, would,* and *should.*

	DECLARATIVE.	INTERROGATIVE.
1. To express *permission;* as,	*He* **may** *or* **might** *go.*	**May** *or* **might** *he go?*

THE VERB

	DECLARATIVE.	INTERROGATIVE.
2. To express *power;* as,	*He* **can** *or* **could** *go.*	**Can** *or* **could** *he go?*
3. To express *necessity;* as,	*He* **must** *go.*	**Must** *he go?*
4. To express *obligation;* as,	*He* **should** *go.*	**Should** *he go?*
5. To express *willingness* or *determination;* as,	*He* **would** *go.*	**Would** *he go?*

The Potential Mode makes the assertion chiefly with the *auxiliary* verb; as, *He* **can** *go.*

The Indicative Mode makes the assertion chiefly with the *principal* verb; as, *He* **has** *gone.*

The Tenses of the Potential Mode are the *present*, the *present perfect*, the *past*, and the *past perfect*. These "tenses," however, in no way denote the time indicated by their names.

The Present Potential may denote either *present* or *future* time. Its auxiliaries are *may, can,* and *must.* As,

I can sing (present).
I may go to-morrow (future).

The Present Perfect Potential denotes *past* time. Its auxiliaries are *may have, can have, must have.* As,

I must have read the book.

The Past Potential may denote *present* or *future* time. Its auxiliaries are *might, could, would, should.* As,

I should go to-day (present).
We hoped that she would sing (future to time of hoping).

NOTE. As the last example shows, the time of the past potential in a subordinate clause is either the same as the time of the principal verb or subsequent (future) to it.

The Past Perfect Potential denotes *past* time. Its auxiliaries are *might have, could have, would have, should have.* As,

This poem should have appeared yesterday.

NOTE. As the last example shows, the past perfect potential implies that the act referred to *did not take place*.

104. THE IMPERATIVE MODE AND ITS TENSE.

DEFINITION. The *Imperative Mode* is that form of the verb used to express a command or a request; as,

1. **Come** *hither, my little daughter.*
2. "**Leave** *me not thus, sir,*" *she said.*
3. *John,* **lend** *me your knife, please.*
4. **Hear** *me for my cause, and* **be** *silent.*

The subject of a verb in this mode being always *thou, you,* or *ye* (generally understood), the verb can be used only in the *second person*.

The imperative mode has but one tense, the *present*. The command is present, but implies a future act.

105. THE INFINITIVE AND ITS TENSES.

DEFINITION. The *Infinitive* is the form of the verb (usually preceded by *to*) which assumes or expresses in a general way some action or state, but does not directly assert it of a subject.

The infinitive can not be used as the predicate of a sentence, as its predication is merely assumed or implied.

The infinitive is usually preceded by the sign *to*. In some cases *to* is omitted; as,

I saw him **do** *the work* (I saw him to do the work).

The infinitive has two tenses,—the *present* and the *present perfect*.

The Present Infinitive may denote *present, past,* or *future* time; as,

He ought **to go** *now.*
He was obliged **to go** *yesterday.*
I asked him **to go** *to-morrow.*

The Present Perfect Infinitive denotes past time only; as,

He ought **to have gone** *yesterday.* (Every present perfect infinitive begins with *to have*.)

THE VERB

The time expressed by the infinitive may be:

1. After that expressed by the finite verb; as,

    FINITE. INFINITIVE.
   He **intended** **to see** *you*.
  (The seeing follows the intending.)

2. The same as that expressed by the finite verb; as,

    FINITE. INFINITIVE.
   He **appeared** **to enjoy** *himself*.
 (The enjoying is at the same time as the appearing.)

3. Before that expressed by the finite verb; as,

    FINITE. INFINITIVE.
   I **was proud** **to have been born** *in France*.
 (Time of being born is before time of being proud.)

The Present Infinitive should be used:

1. In order to make known an action occurring after that made known by the finite verb.
2. In order to make known an action occurring at the same time as that made known by the finite verb.

The two uses are shown in the following sentences:

1. *This poem ought* **to appear** (not *to have appeared*) *to-day or to-morrow*.
2. *I should have liked* **to see** (not *to have seen*) *him*. (The seeing is after the liking.)
3. *I should not have let you* **eat** (not *have eaten*) *it*. (The eating is after the letting.)
4. *He seemed* **to enjoy** (not *to have enjoyed*) *it*. (The enjoying is at the same time as the seeming.)

The Present Perfect Infinitive should be used in order to make known an action occurring before that made known by the finite verb; as,

1. *This poem ought* **to have appeared** (not *to appear*) *yesterday*.
2. *He is reported* **to have rescued** (not *to rescue*) *the man from drowning*. (The rescuing was before the reporting.)
3. *We believed the box* **to have been opened** (not *to be opened*) *by the wrong person*. (The opening was before the believing.)

4. *He appeared* **to have seen** (not *to see*) *better days*. (The seeing was before the appearing.)

CAUTION. Avoid the use of *and* instead of *to*; as,
1. *Come* **to** *see me often* (not *Come* **and** *see me often*).
2. *Try* **to** *come early* (not *Try* **and** *come early*).

106. THE PARTICIPLE AND ITS TENSES.

DEFINITION. **The *Participle* is an inflected form of the verb which, like the infinitive, assumes or expresses in a general way some action or state, but does not directly assert it of a subject.** The participle, therefore, can not be used as a predicate. It merely assumes its predication.

Any combination of a participle with its modifiers and complements is called a **Participial Phrase.**

A substantive used only as the subject of a participle is the principal word of an absolute phrase. (See Gr. 47, p. 77.)

The participle has three tenses, — the *present*, the *past*, and the *past perfect*.

The Present Participle denotes action or being continuing at the time indicated by the finite verb; as,

John, **driving** *through the park*, **met** *his uncle*.

The Past Participle denotes action or being completed at the time indicated by the finite verb; as,

John, **driven** *through the park*, **met** *his uncle*.

The Past Perfect Participle denotes action or being completed before the time indicated by the finite verb; as,

John, **having driven** *through the park*, **met** *his uncle*.

107. CONJUGATION.

The orderly arrangement of all the different forms of the verb for the purpose of showing *voice*, *mode*, *tense*, *person*, and *number* is called Conjugation.

108. CONJUGATION OF THE VERB *BE*.

Present.	Past.	Past Participle.
Am	Was	Been.

Indicative Mode.

Present Tense.

Person.   *Singular Number.*   *Plural Number.*

1. (I) am.   (We) are.
2. (You) are, *or* (Thou) art.   (You *or* Ye) are.
3. (He) is.   (They) are.

Present Perfect Tense.

(*Have*, combined with the past participle.)

1. (I) have been.   (We) have been.
2. (You) have been, *or* (Thou) hast been.   (You *or* Ye) have been.
3. (He) has been, *or* hath been.   (They) have been.

Past Tense.

1. (I) was.   (We) were.
2. (You) were, *or* (Thou) wast *or* wert.   (You *or* Ye) were.
3. (He) was.   (They) were.

Past Perfect Tense.

(*Had*, combined with the past participle.)

1. (I) had been.   (We) had been.
2. (You) had been, *or* (Thou) hadst been.   (You *or* Ye) had been.
3. (He) had been.   (They) had been.

Future Tense.

(*Shall* or *will*, combined with the present infinitive.)

Simple futurity; expectation.

1. (I) shall be.   (We) shall be.
2. (You) will be, *or* (Thou) wilt be. (You *or* Ye) will be.
3. (He) will be.   (They) will be.

Determination.

Person.	Singular Number.	Plural Number.
1.	(I) will be.	(We) will be.
2.	(You) shall be, *or* (Thou) shalt be.	(You *or* Ye) shall be.
3.	(He) shall be.	(They) shall be.

FUTURE PERFECT TENSE.

(*Shall* or *will*, combined with the present perfect infinitive *have been*.)

1. (I) shall have been.   (We) shall have been.
2. (You) will have been, *or* (Thou) wilt have been.   (You *or* Ye) will have been.
3. (He) will have been.   (They) will have been.

Subjunctive Mode.[1]
(Usually follows *if*, *though*, *lest*, etc.)

PRESENT TENSE.

1. (If I) **be**.   (If we) **be**.
2. (If you *or* If thou) **be**.   (If you *or* If ye) **be**.
3. (If he) **be**.   (If they) **be**.

PRESENT PERFECT TENSE.

1. (If I) have been.   (If we) have been.
2. (If you *or* If thou) have been.   (If you *or* If ye) have been.
3. (If he) have been.   (If they) have been.

PAST TENSE.

1. (If I) **were**.   (If we) were.
2. (If you) were, *or* (If thou) **wert**.   (If you *or* If ye) were.
3. (If he) **were**.   (If they) were.

PAST PERFECT TENSE.

1. (If I) had been.   (If we) had been.
2. (If you *or* If thou) had been.   (If you *or* If ye) had been.
3. (If he) had been.   (If they) had been.

[1] The forms of the subjunctive mode different from those of the indicative in the present and past tenses are shown by full-face type.

THE VERB

Potential Mode.

Present Tense.

(May, can, or *must,* combined with the present infinitive.)

Person.	Singular Number.	Plural Number.
1.	(I) may, can, *or* must be.	(We) may, can, *or* must be.
2.	(You) may, can, *or* must be, *or* (Thou) mayst, canst, *or* must be.	(You *or* Ye) may, can, *or* must be.
3.	(He) may, can, *or* must be.	(They) may, can, *or* must be.

Present Perfect Tense.

(May, can, or *must,* combined with the present perfect infinitive *have been.*)

1. (I) may, can, *or* must have been.   (We) may, can, *or* must have been.
2. (You) may, can, *or* must have been, *or* (Thou) mayst, canst, *or* must have been.   (You *or* Ye) may, can, *or* must have been.
3. (He) may, can, *or* must have been.   (They) may, can, *or* must have been.

Past Tense.

(Might, could, would, or *should,* combined with the present infinitive.)

1. (I) might, could, would, *or* should be.   (We) might, could, would, *or* should be.
2. (You) might, could, would, *or* should be, *or* (Thou) mightst, couldst, wouldst, *or* shouldst be.   (You *or* Ye) might, could, would, *or* should be.
3. (He) might, could, would, *or* should be.   (They) might, could, would, *or* should be.

Past Perfect Tense.

(Might, could, would, or *should,* combined with the present perfect infinitive *have been.*)

1. (I) might, could, would, *or* should have been.   (We) might, could, would, *or* should have been.
2. (You) might, could, would, *or* should have been, *or* (Thou) mightst, couldst, wouldst, *or* shouldst have been.   (You *or* ye) might, could, would, *or* should have been.
3. (He) might, could, would, *or* should have been.   (They) might, could, would, *or* should have been.

Imperative Mode.

PRESENT TENSE.

Person.	Singular Number.	Plural Number.
2.	Be (you *or* thou).	Be (you *or* ye).

Infinitives.

PRESENT.	PRESENT PERFECT.
To be.	To have been.

Participles.

PRESENT.	PAST.	PERFECT.
Being.	Been.	Having been.

109. CONJUGATION OF THE VERB *LOVE*.

ACTIVE VOICE.

Indicative Mode.

PRESENT TENSE.

Person.	Singular Number.	Plural Number.
1.	(I) love.	(We) love.
2.	(You) love, *or* (Thou) lovest.	(You *or* Ye) love.
3.	(He) loves, *or* loveth.	(They) love.

PRESENT PERFECT TENSE.

1.	(I) have loved.	(We) have loved.
2.	(You) have loved, *or* (Thou) hast loved.	(You *or* Ye) have loved.
3.	(He) has loved, *or* hath loved.	(They) have loved.

PAST TENSE.

1.	(I) loved.	(We) loved.
2.	(You) loved, *or* (Thou) lovedst.	(You *or* Ye) loved.
3.	(He) loved.	(They) loved.

PAST PERFECT TENSE.

1.	(I) had loved.	(We) had loved.
2.	(You) had loved, *or* (Thou) hadst loved.	(You *or* Ye) had loved.
3.	(He) had loved.	(They) had loved.

THE VERB

Future Tense.

Simple futurity; expectation.

Person.	Singular Number.	Plural Number.
1.	(I) shall love.	(We) shall love.
2.	(You) will love, *or* (Thou) wilt love.	(You *or* Ye) will love.
3.	(He) will love.	(They) will love.

Determination.

1. (I) will love. (We) will love.
2. (You) shall love, *or* (Thou) shalt love. (You *or* Ye) shall love.
3. (He) shall love. (They) shall love.

Future Perfect Tense.

1. (I) shall have loved. (We) shall have loved.
2. (You) will have loved, *or* (Thou) wilt have loved. (You *or* Ye) will have loved.
3. (He) will have loved. (They) will have loved.

Subjunctive Mode.

Present Tense.

1. (If I) love. (If we) love.
2. (If you *or* If thou) **love.** (If you *or* If ye) love.
3. (If he) **love.** (If they) love.

Present Perfect Tense.

1. (If I) have loved. (If we) have loved.
2. (If you *or* If thou) **have** loved. (If you *or* If ye) have loved.
3. (If he) **have** loved. (If they) have loved.

Past Tense.

1. (If I) loved. (If we) loved.
2. (If you *or* If thou) **loved.** (If you *or* If ye) loved.
3. (If he) loved. (If they) loved.

Past Perfect Tense.

1. (If I) had loved. (If we) had loved.
2. (If you *or* If thou) **had** loved. (If you *or* If ye) had loved.
3. (If he) had loved. (If they) had loved.

Potential Mode.

PRESENT TENSE.

Person. Singular Number. / Plural Number.
1. (I) may, can, *or* must love.
2. (You) may, can, *or* must love, *or* (Thou) mayst, canst, *or* must love.
3. (He) may, can, *or* must love.

1. (We) may, can, *or* must love.
2. (You *or* Ye) may, can, *or* must love.
3. (They) may, can, *or* must love.

PRESENT PERFECT TENSE.

1. (I) may, can, *or* must have loved.
2. (You) may, can, *or* must have loved, *or* (Thou) mayst, canst, *or* must have loved.
3. (He) may, can, *or* must have loved.

1. (We) may, can, *or* must have loved.
2. (You *or* Ye) may, can, *or* must have loved.
3. (They) may, can, *or* must have loved.

PAST TENSE.

1. (I) might, could, would, *or* should love.
2. (You) might, could, would, *or* should love, *or* (Thou) mightst, couldst, wouldst, *or* shouldst love.
3. (He) might, could, would, *or* should love.

1. (We) might, could, would, *or* should love.
2. (You *or* Ye) might, could, would, *or* should love.
3. (They) might, could, would, *or* should love.

PAST PERFECT TENSE.

1. (I) might, could, would, *or* should have loved.
2. (You) might, could, would, *or* should have loved, *or* (Thou) mightst, couldst, wouldst, *or* shouldst have loved.
3. (He) might, could, would, *or* should have loved.

1. (We) might, could, would, *or* should have loved.
2. (You *or* Ye) might, could, would, *or* should have loved.
3. (They) might, could, would, *or* should have loved.

Imperative Mode.

PRESENT TENSE.

Person.	Singular Number.	Plural Number.
2.	Love (you *or* thou).	Love (you *or* ye).

Infinitives.

PRESENT.	PRESENT PERFECT.
To love.	To have loved.

Participles.

PRESENT.	PAST.	PERFECT.
Loving.	Loved.	Having loved.

110. PASSIVE VOICE.

The tenses of the passive voice are the same as those of the active. They are made by adding the past participle of a transitive verb to the various forms of the verb *be;* thus,

INDICATIVE, PRESENT.

Person.	Singular Number.	Plural Number.
1.	(I) am loved.	(We) are loved.
2.	(You) are loved, *or* (Thou) art loved.	(You *or* Ye) are loved.
3.	(He) is loved.	(They) are loved.

Exercises.

Ex. I. *Complete the passive conjugation of the verb* **love** *in all the modes and tenses.*

Ex. II. *Write a synopsis of the verb* **see** *in the third person, singular number, passive conjugation; that is, write the third person singular of the verb* **see** *in all the modes and tenses of the passive voice.*

111. PROGRESSIVE CONJUGATION.

The simplest form of the verb is used to express what is habitual or customary; as, *She* **sings**. *He* **plays** *the violin;* but to represent an action as still going on (in progress), another form, called the **Progressive,** is used; as, *She* **is singing**. *He* **is playing** *the violin.*

The progressive form in the active voice is made by adding the present participle of any verb to the different forms of the verb *be,* in all the modes and tenses [1]; thus,

INDICATIVE, PRESENT.

Person.	Singular Number.	Plural Number.
1.	(I) am loving.	(We) are loving.
2.	(You) are loving, *or* (Thou) art loving.	(You *or* Ye) are loving.
3.	(He) is loving.	(They) are loving.

Exercise.

Write a synopsis of the verb **call** *in the first person, singular, progressive form, active and passive.*

112. EMPHATIC CONJUGATION.

The Emphatic Form is made by placing the auxiliary *do, does,* or *did (dost, doth,* or *didst),* before the present infinitive, that is, the simplest form, of the principal verb. This applies to the present and past tenses of the indicative and of the subjunctive, and to the imperative, all in the active voice; thus (Indic.), *I do love, I did love;* (Subj.), *If I do love, If I did love;* (Imp.), *Do (you) love.*

---

[1] In the passive voice there are progressive forms in the present and past indicative, and past subjunctive; thus, *I am being loved, I was being loved, If I were being loved.*

These forms are called the *emphatic form*, because in speaking the auxiliary is emphasized; as, *I* **do** *know; They* **did** *come.*

They are commonly used, however, without emphasis in negative and interrogative sentences; as, *I do not know. Did they come?*

Do as a principal verb is conjugated regularly; that is, its conjugation may be written out by substituting, in Gr. **109**, *do* for *love; did* for the past tense *loved;* and *done* for the participle *loved* (see Gr. **100**, Exercise, p. 166).

When *do* is an auxiliary, parse it and its principal verb together as one verb.

Exercises.

Ex. I. *Tell whether the form of* **do** *in each of the following sentences is an auxiliary or a principal verb:*

1. Do noble things.
2. Do not envy another.
3. Dost thou love life? Then do not squander time.
4. Alfred did his work well, but Howard did not do anything at all.
5. After all, the joy of success does not equal that which attends the patient working.

Ex. II. *Write the following forms of the verbs* **call** *and* **see**:

1. First person, plural, present, indicative, active.
2. Second person, singular, present perfect, indicative, passive.
3. Third person, singular, present, subjunctive, active.
4. Singular, imperative, active.
5. First person, plural, future perfect, active.
6. Third person, plural, past, potential, active.
7. Third person, singular, past perfect, potential, passive.
8. The present infinitive, passive.
9. The present perfect infinitive, active.
10. The past participle, passive.

113. USE OF SHALL AND WILL.

The auxiliaries *shall* and *will* used in forming the future tense have somewhat different meanings. Which of these words should be used depends upon the meaning that the speaker wishes to express; as,

> *I* shall *go*. (Speaker expects to go.)
> *I* will *go*. (Speaker determines to go.)
> *You* shall *go*. (Speaker determines that you shall go.)
> *He* will *go*. (Speaker expects him to go.)

The following sentences convey different meanings according to whether *shall* or *will* is used. Try to explain the difference in meaning between each sentence as it stands and the same with the other auxiliary substituted:

1. I shall (will) not see you.
2. We will (shall) not come.
3. He shall (will) not go alone.
4. They shall (will) meet us at the station.
5. You will (shall) be in Europe then.
6. They shall (will) be punished.
7. My friends shall (will) be present.
8. The estate will (shall) be divided.
9. The admission shall (will) be free.
10. He says that the admission shall (will) be free.

The uses of **shall** and **will** are summarized in the following: (Gr. **108, 109,** Indic. Fut.)

Simple Future with Idea of Expectation.	Future with Idea of Determination.
I (*or* we) shall go.	I (*or* we) will go.
You (he, they, *etc*.) will go.	You (he, they, *etc*.) shall go.

RULE. **To express simple futurity or expectation on the part of the speaker, use** *shall* **with the subjects** *I* **and** *we,* **and** *will* **with all other subjects.**

To express determination on the part of the speaker, use *will* **with the subjects** *I* **and** *we,* **and use** *shall* **with all other subjects.**

THE VERB

In questions *shall* is always used with the subjects *I* and *we*. With other subjects use the auxiliary that is expected in the reply. Thus,

> **Shall** *I meet you to-morrow?*
> **Will** *you keep this pledge?* (*I* will.)
> **Shall** *you be able to come to-morrow?* (*I* shall.)

Should and **would** are in origin the past tenses of *shall* and *will,* and in corresponding uses follow the same rules. **Should**, however, has also a special meaning equivalent to *ought,* and is used in that sense with all subjects alike.

Exercises.

Ex. I. *Justify the use of* **shall, will, should,** *and* **would** *in the following sentences:*

1. I think it will rain soon.
2. We shall be disappointed.
3. We will do our duty.
4. Shall I have permission to go?
5. I should be pleased to assist you at any time.
6. If I did need help, I would not ask for it.
7. "You should see it in Fair week, sir," said Jackanapes.
8. "And what sort of a figure shall I cut, at the court of King Pelias!"
9. "You will get a handsomer pair of sandals by and by," said the old woman. "Only let King Pelias get a glimpse of that bare foot, and you shall see him turn pale as ashes, I promise you."
10. For whosoever will save his life shall lose it: and whosoever will lose his life for my sake shall find it.

11. You may break, you may shatter
        The vase if you will;
     But the scent of the roses
        Will hang round it still.

12. I would study, I would know, I would admire forever.
                                                                    — *Emerson.*

13. And so the active breath of life
        Should stir our dull and sluggard wills.

Ex. II. *Fill the following blanks with* **shall, will, should,** *or* **would.**

1. _____ I go or not?
2. I _____ never see him again! Never!
3. Alas, alas! I _____ never see him again.
4. I _____ be obliged if you _____ do me this favor.
5. If you _____ call, I _____ accompany you.
6. I think we _____ have rain to-day.
7. Where _____ I meet you?
8. I _____ suffer if I do not do as I am requested.
9. _____ we be there in time?
10. Help me, or I _____ drown.
11. _____ you be of age this year?
12. _____ you go this evening or to-morrow?
13. _____ we go with you to the station?
14. I _____ be pleased to hear from you.
15. When _____ we see you again?
16. In spite of all I could do he _____ not remain.
17. The teacher said we _____ remain.
18. Every boy and girl _____ read "Hiawatha."
19. At first I didn't think you _____ enjoy this visit.
20. I _____ think you _____ have known better.

114. HOW TO PARSE VERBS.

A finite verb is parsed by stating:

1. The class as to **form**, — regular or irregular, giving its principal parts if irregular.

2. The class as to **use**, — transitive or intransitive, giving its voice (active or passive) if it is transitive.

3. The mode, — indicative, subjunctive, potential, or imperative.

4. The tense.

5. The subject, person, and number.

THE VERB

An infinitive or a participle is parsed by stating:

1. Its tense.
2. Whether it is transitive or intransitive, active or passive.
3. How it (or the phrase of which it is a part) is used.

MODELS FOR ORAL PARSING.

As it lies *in the earth, iron ore* is *in veins or pockets,* walled *about with rock.*

Lies is a verb; the principal parts are *lie, lay, lain,* hence it is irregular; it expresses an action that does not pass to a receiver, and is therefore intransitive; it asserts a fact, and therefore is in the indicative mode; it denotes present time, and therefore is in the present tense. It is in the third person and singular number, to agree with its subject *it*.

Abbreviated form. Is is an irregular, intransitive verb, indicative mode, present tense, third person, singular number, to agree with its subject *ore*.

Walled is a past participle, passive, from the verb *wall*. It is used as an adjective to modify *veins or pockets*.

WRITTEN PARSING.

Nature \ *teaches*	*beasts* / \ *to know* \ *friends.* | *their*
Ir. V.	Inf.
Tr.	Pres.
Act.	Tr.
Ind.	Act.
Pres.	Assum. Pred.
3.	of *beasts*
Sing.	
to agree	
with *Nature*.	

Exercises.

Ex. I. *Parse orally all the verbs in the selection on pages* 293, 294.

Ex. II. *Parse in writing all the verbs in the following, according to the model given:*

1. Knowledge wanes, but wisdom lingers. — *Tennyson.*
2. Wealth may seek us, but wisdom must be sought. — *Young.*
3. Act well your part; there all the honor lies.
4. We, by our sufferings, learn to prize our bliss. — *Dryden.*
5. Suffer that you may be wise; labor that you may have.
6. If a man empty his purse into his head, no one can take it from him. — *Franklin.*
7. Never put off till to-morrow what you can do to-day.
8. The reason I beat the Austrians is, they did not know the value of five minutes. — *Napoleon.*
9. No man has learned anything rightly, until he know that every day is Doomsday. — *Emerson.*
10. Men but like visions are, time all doth claim;
    He lives, who dies to win a lasting name. — *Drummond.*

115. REVIEW.

EXERCISE. *Tell which of the forms in parentheses is correct, and give the reason for your answer:*

1. I (saw, seen) my duty and I (done, did) it.
2. The land was (overflown, overflowed) after the river had (raised, risen).
3. He had (gone, went) home before the storm had (began, begun).
4. The murderer was (hung, hanged) at daylight.
5. Our fathers held that all men (were, are) created equal.
6. I expected he (will, would) come.
7. It was his intention (to introduce, to have introduced) the bill.
8. "(Can, May) I use your knife a moment?" asked she.
9. "You (may, can) have it longer, if you wish," answered he.
10. (Will, Shall) I put some coal on the fire?
11. I vow I (shall, will) never go there again.
12. If I (should, would) say so, I (should, would) be guilty of falsehood.
13. "Eight bells" (was, were) struck.

14. Each day and each hour (brings, bring) (their, its) own trials.

15. If he (were, was) here he could see for (his self, himself).

16. If my friend (was, were) here I (should, would) be happier.

17. Neither you nor I (am, are) to blame.

18. Thou who (are, art) the author of life, (can, canst) restore it.

19. Every one of you (have, has) the wrong answer.

20. Money, as well as provisions, (was, were) needed.

21. He (lived, has lived) there several years before he died.

22. The prisoner says that he (will, shall) try (and, to) keep his promise.

23. And if I (was, were) a fairy, what (should, would) I give to quiet thine earnest prayer?

TEST QUESTIONS. 1. Into what two great classes are verbs divided? 2. Define an intransitive verb. 3. Choose a verb that may be either transitive or intransitive, and illustrate both uses. 4. Select three verbs used only intransitively. 5. Why are auxiliaries necessary? 6. Make a list of auxiliary verbs. 7. What kind of verbs can not be used in the passive voice? 8. Why? 9. How is the passive voice formed? 10. In changing a sentence from the active to the passive form what does the object complement become? 11. The indirect object? 12. The objective complement? 13. What properties of the verb are shown by inflection? Illustrate.

14. What is mode? 15. What mode is formed by the use of auxiliaries? 16. Give the mode auxiliaries. 17. What are the primary tenses of the verb? 18. The secondary tenses? 19. Mention the tense auxiliaries. 20. Which auxiliary is used with the subjects *I* and *we* to express simple futurity? 21. Which to express determination? 22. When is the *s*-form of the verb used? 23. Upon what does the use of the *s*-form of the verb depend? 24. When may a singular noun or pronoun be used as the subject of *were*? 25. Why are some verbs said to be irregular?

26. What is meant by the conjugation of a verb? 27. By the synopsis of a verb? 28. How are the tenses of the passive voice formed? 29. How does the progressive form of the verb differ in meaning from the ordinary form? 30. What is a redundant verb? 31. A defective verb? 32. An impersonal verb? 33. What is the difference in meaning between *May I go?* and *Can I go?* 34. When is the verb *set* used intransitively? Illustrate. 35. What is the rule for the use of *shall* and *will?*

116. LIST OF IRREGULAR VERBS.

The following list contains most of the irregular verbs in the language. The forms in italics are now but little used. An R means that the regular form may also be used; and when the **R** is in full-face type it indicates that the regular form is preferable. The present participle is here omitted, as it is always formed by adding *ing* to the present infinitive (Gr. 100).

Present.	Past.	Past P.	Present.	Past.	Past P.
Abide	abode	abode	Burn	burnt, R.	burnt, **R.**
Am, be	was	been	Burst	burst	burst
Arise	arose	arisen	Buy	bought	bought
Awake	awoke, R.	awaked	Cast	cast	cast
Bear, *for-*	bore, *bare*	borne / born[1]	Catch	caught	caught
Beat	beat	beaten / beat	Chide	chid, R.	chidden / chid, R.
Begin	began	begun	Choose	chose	chosen
Bend	bent, R.	bent, R.	Cleave[2] (*to split*)	cleft, R.	cleft, R. / cloven
Bereave	bereft, R.	bereft, R.	Cling	clung	clung
Beseech	besought	besought	Clothe	clad, **R.**	clad, **R.**
Bet	bet, R.	bet, R.	Come, *be-*	came	come
Bid	bade / bid	bidden / bid	Cost	cost	cost
Bind	bound	bound	Creep	crept	crept
Bite	bit	bitten / bit	Crow	crew, **R.**	crowed
Bleed	bled	bled	Curse	curst, **R.**	curst, **R.**
Blend	blent, **R.**	blent, **R.**	Cut	cut	cut
Bless	blest, **R.**	blest, **R.**	Dare[3]	durst, R.	dared
Blow	blew	blown	Deal	dealt	dealt
Break	broke	broken	Dig	dug, R.	dug, R.
Breed	bred	bred	Dive	dove, **R.**	dived
Bring	brought	brought	Do	did	done
Build	built, R.	built, R.	Draw	drew	drawn
			Dream	dreamt, **R.**	dreamt, **R.**
			Dress	drest, **R.**	drest, **R.**

[1] Born is passive only, in sense of *brought forth*.

[2] Cleave, *to adhere*, is regular.

[3] Dare, *to challenge*, is regular.

THE VERB

Present.	Past.	Past P.	Present.	Past.	Past P.
Drink	drank	drunk	Lade	laded	laden, **R.**
Drive	drove	driven	Lay	laid	laid
Dwell	dwelt, **R.**	dwelt, **R.**	Lead, *mis-*	led	led
Eat	ate	eaten	Lean	leant, **R.**	leant, **R.**
Fall, *be-*	fell	fallen	Leap	leapt, **R.**	leapt, **R.**
Feed	fed	fed	Learn	learnt, **R.**	learnt, **R.**
Feel	felt	felt	Leave	left	left
Fight	fought	fought	Lend	lent	lent
Find	found	found	Let	let	let
Flee	fled	fled	Lie *(recline)*	lay	lain
Fling	flung	flung	Light	lit, **R.**	lit, **R.**
Fly	flew	flown	Lose	lost	lost
Forget	forgot	{ forgotten { forgot	Make	made	made
			Mean	meant	meant
Forsake	forsook	forsaken	Meet	met	met
Freeze	froze	frozen	Mow	mowed	mown, **R.**
Get	got	{ got { gotten	Pay, *re-*	paid	paid
			Pen	pent, **R.**	pent, **R.**
Gild	gilt, **R.**	gilt, **R.**	Put	put	put
Gird	girt, **R.**	girt, **R.**	Quit	quit, **R.**	quit, **R.**
Give, *for-*	gave	given	Rap	rapt, **R.**	rapt, **R.**
Go, *under-*	went	gone	Read	rĕad	rĕad
Grave [1]	graved	graven, **R.**	Rend	rent	rent
Grind	ground	ground	Rid	rid, **R.**	rid, **R.**
Grow	grew	grown	Ride	rode	ridden
Hang [2]	hung	hung	Ring	rang, rung	rung
Have	had	had	Rise	rose	risen
Hear	heard	heard	Rive	rived	riven, **R.**
Heave	hove, **R.**	hove, **R.**	Run	ran, *run*	run
Hew	hewed	hewn, **R.**	Saw	sawed	sawn, **R.**
Hide	hid	{ hidden { hid	Say	said	said
			See	saw	seen
Hit	hit	hit	Seek	sought	sought
Hold, *be-*	held	held	Sell	sold	sold
Hurt	hurt	hurt	Send	sent	sent
Keep	kept	kept	Set	set	set
Kneel	knelt, **R.**	knelt, **R.**	Shake	shook	shaken
Knit	knit, **R.**	knit, **R.**	Shape	shaped	shapen, **R.**
Know	knew	known	Shave	shaved	shaven, **R.**

[1] Engrave is regular.   [2] Hang, *to take life*, is regular.

Present.	Past.	Past P.	Present.	Past.	Past P.
Shear	shore, R.	shorn, R.	Steal	stole	stolen
Shed	shed	shed	Stick	stuck	stuck
Shine	shone, R.	shone, R.	Sting	stung	stung
Shoe	shod	shod	Strew	strewed	strewn, R.
Shoot	shot	shot	Stride	strode	stridden
Show	showed	shown, R.	Strike	struck	struck / *stricken*
Shred	shred, R.	shred, R.	String	strung	strung
Shrink	shrank / shrunk	shrunk	Strive	strove	striven
Shrive	shrove, R.	shriven, R.	Strow	strowed	strown, R.
Shut	shut	shut	Swear	swore	sworn
Sing	sang, sung	sung	Sweat	sweat, R.	sweat, R.
Sink	sank, sunk	sunk	Sweep	swept	swept
Sit	sat	sat	Swell	swelled	swollen, R.
Slay	slew	slain	Swim	swam / *swum*	swum
Sleep	slept	slept	Swing	swung	swung
Slide	slid	slidden / slid	Take	took	taken
Sling	slung	slung	Teach	taught	taught
Slink	slunk	slunk	Tear	tore	torn
Slit	slit	slit	Tell	told	told
Smell	smelt, R.	smelt, R.	Think	thought	thought
Smite	smote	smitten	Thrive	throve, R.	thriven, R.
Sow	sowed	sown, R.	Throw	threw	thrown
Speak	spoke	spoken	Thrust	thrust	thrust
Speed	sped, R.	sped, R.	Tread	trod	trodden / trod
Spell	spelt, R.	spelt, R.	Wake	woke, R.	woke, R.
Spend	spent	spent	Wear	wore	worn
Spill	spilt, R.	spilt, R.	Weave	wove	woven
Spin	spun	spun	Wed	wedded	wed, R.
Spit	spit	spit	Weep	wept	wept
Split	split	split	Wet	wet, R.	wet, R.
Spoil	spoilt, R.	spoilt, R.	Win	won	won
Spread	spread	spread	Wind	wound	wound
Spring	sprang / sprung	sprung	Work	wrought, R.	wrought, R.
Stand	stood	stood	Wrap	wrapt, R.	wrapt, R.
Stave	stove, R.	stove, R.	Wring	wrung	wrung
Stay	staid, R.	staid, R.	Write	wrote	written

117. THE ADJECTIVE.

An adjective is a word used to modify the meaning of a noun or pronoun (Gr. 20 and 21, pp. 33, 34). This modification may be made in two ways:

1. It may be made by pointing out or describing some property or quality in the person or thing named by the substantive; as,

> **Unselfish** *boys become* **noble** *men.*
> *A* **pleasant** *word on a* **rainy** *day is a ray of* **golden** *sunshine.*
> *The* **best** *love is a* **helping** *hand.*

The adjective *unselfish* tells what kind or quality of boys, *noble* tells what kind of men, *golden* tells the quality of sunshine.

DEFINITION. **An adjective used to describe or tell the kind or quality of the person or thing named is called a** *Descriptive Adjective.*

The great majority of adjectives are descriptive. They include, as a small part of their number, **Proper Adjectives**, or those derived from proper names; as, *The* **American** *flag; The* **Spanish** *fleet.*

2. An adjective may modify the meaning of a substantive by defining or pointing out that which is named; as, **this** *boy*, **that** *word*; or by limiting or indicating the number or quantity of that which is named; as, **two** *boys*, *the* **first** *word*, **much** *sunshine*, **enough** *rain*.

DEFINITION. **An adjective that defines or limits a noun without describing is called a** *Definitive Adjective.*[1]

As compared with adjectives that describe, there are very few definitive adjectives. The principal ones are:

one	third, *etc.*	each	this
two, *etc.*	a	every	that
first	an	either	these
second	the	neither	those

[1] Sometimes called a **Limiting Adjective.**

former	other	such	no	more
latter	any	both	many	most
last	one	same	few	enough
some	all	another	much	

Which and **what** when used as adjectives, either in asking questions (sometimes called **Interrogative Adjectives**) or in exclamations, are definitives; as,

> **Which** *boy played truant?*
> **What** *boy would play truant?*
> **What** *shadows we are,* **what** *shadows we pursue! — Burke.*

NOTE. **Which** asks for *one* of a number of persons or things.

What is applied to persons or things indefinitely.

Which (whichever) and **what** (whatever) sometimes introduce a noun clause and modify like an adjective. In such use also they are definitives; as,

> *I know* **which** *boy played truant.*
> *Give me* **whatever** *information you have.*

This, these, that, those, and **yonder** are definitives used to point out objects and are called **Demonstrative Adjectives**; as,

> **This**[1] *apple is sweet.*[1] **Those**[1] *grapes are sour.*[1]

The adjectives **a, an,** and **the** are called **Articles**.

A (an) is the **Indefinite Article** because it denotes any one of a number of persons or things.

The is the **Definite Article** because it points out some particular person or thing.

---

[1] An adjective may exert its influence over a noun in two ways:

First, it may stand near the word it modifies, either before or after, influencing it directly; as,

> **Gentle** *words were spoken.*
> *His words,* **gentle** *and* **helpful,** *were often heard wherever trouble was.*

Second, it may complete an assertion, following a copulative verb (Gr. **32,** p. 52). In this use it modifies the subject, exerting its influence indirectly; as,

> *His words were* **gentle** *and* **helpful.**
> **Gentle** *and* **helpful** *was he.*
> *To help others is* **pleasant.**

Adjectives used in the second way are sometimes called **Predicate Adjectives**.

THE ADJECTIVE

Exercise.

Point out and classify the adjectives in the following sentences:

1. There is a pleasure in the pathless woods.
2. Every man is odd.
3. Then the sea I found calm as a cradled child in dreamless slumber bound.
4. Much wit he had, but little wisdom.
5. Loss of sincerity is loss of vital power.
6. See yonder maker of the dead man's bed.
7. Great sins make great sufferers.
8. Each man is the servant of all men, and all men of each.
9. Rough winds do shake the darling buds of May.
10. To some men are given ten talents.
11. The noblest mind the best contentment has.
12. He did not know which profession to choose.
13. The snowy lands are springing, in clover green and soft.
14. Far in a wild, unknown to public view,
    From youth to age a reverend hermit grew.
15. Delightful is this loneliness.
16. Constant quiet fills my peaceful breast
    With unmixed joy, uninterrupted rest.
17. Certain winds will make men's temper bad.
18. Write it on your heart that every day is the best day in the year.
19. Considerable genius is shown in a few of his short poems.
20. The former books were printed in England in the seventeenth century; the latter in America in the twentieth.

118. COMPARISON.

Notice the adjectives in the following sentences:

1. *George is tall, Frank is taller, but Luther is the tallest of the three.*
2. *Jane is studious, Mary is more studious, but Ruth is the most studious girl in school.*

3. *Apples are good, oranges are better, and peaches best of all.*

What quality of the three boys is compared by the adjectives in the first sentence? How are the different degrees of this quality denoted? Notice that Frank possesses the quality of tallness in a greater degree than George. Which boy possesses it in the greatest degree? How are these different degrees shown? How is comparison shown by the adjectives in the second sentence? In the third sentence?

We see, then, that an adjective has the power to make us know that objects possess a quality in different degrees. This is done either by an inflection (pp. 103, 104) or by the use of an additional word, and is called **Comparison.**

DEFINITION. *Comparison* **of adjectives is a modification, by inflection or otherwise, to show degrees of quality.**

Three degrees of comparison may be shown by the adjective, and to the forms making known these three degrees are given the names **Positive, Comparative,** and **Superlative.**

The Positive Form is the ordinary form of the adjective, and merely indicates the presence of the quality; as, *tall, studious, good,* etc.

The Comparative Form indicates that one of two objects contains more of the given quality than the other; as, *taller, more studious, better* (*than another*).

The Superlative Form indicates that one of three or more objects contains more of a given quality than any one of the others; as, *tallest, most studious, best* (*of all*).

Adjectives are compared in three ways:

1. Adjectives of one syllable and many adjectives of two syllables [1] are compared by adding *-er* to form the comparative and *-est* to form the superlative; as, *tall, taller, tallest; noble, nobler, noblest; happy, happier, happiest.*

2. Some adjectives of two syllables [1] and all longer adjectives are compared by using *more* to form the comparative and *most* to form

---

[1] In the case of a regular adjective of two syllables *sound* ordinarily determines whether to use the forms in *-er* and *-est* or to place *more* and *most* before the positive form. Use whichever seems more euphonious.

the superlative; as, *more pleasant, most pleasant; more studious, most studious.*

In **Descending Comparison** the comparative is formed by using *less*, and the superlative by using *least*, before the positive; as, *less happy, least happy.*

3. Some adjectives are compared irregularly; as, *good, better, best; bad, worse, worst.*

119. IRREGULAR ADJECTIVES.

Irregular and partly irregular adjectives, few in number but of very frequent use, are thus compared:

Positive.	Comparative.	Superlative.
bad / ill / evil	worse	worst
far	farther / further	farthest / furthest
fore	former	foremost / first
good / well	better	best
hind	hinder	hindmost
in (*infrequent as adjective*)	inner	inmost / innermost
late	later / latter	latest / last
little	less	least
many	more	most
much	more	most
———	nether	nethermost
nigh	nigher	nighest / next
old	older / elder	oldest / eldest
out (*infrequent as adjective*)	outer / utter	outmost, outermost / utmost, uttermost
top	———	topmost
up (*infrequent as adjective*)	upper	upmost / uppermost

120. THE ADJECTIVE: IMPORTANT FACTS.

The adjective is important as involving:

I. PUNCTUATION.

1. " Two honest young men were chosen." In this sentence *young* tells the kind of *men*, *honest* tells the kind of *young men*, and *two* tells the number of *honest young men*. Hence these adjectives are of unequal rank, and are therefore not separated by the comma (Comp. 56, note, p. 291).

2. "A tall, straight, and dignified man entered." In this sentence *tall*, *straight*, and *dignified* modify *man* independently: the man is *tall* and *straight* and *dignified;* hence these adjectives are of the same (equal) rank, and are therefore separated by the comma.

II. THE USE OF *OTHER* IN COMPARISON.

1. In making comparisons when the adjective used is in the positive or the comparative degree, neither of the terms compared must include the other. Thus,

   1. *John* was as active as *any of his companions*.
   2. *John* was more active than *any of his companions*.
   3. *Iron* is harder than *lead*.

In these sentences notice that *John* is not included in *any of his companions*, and that *iron* is not a kind of *lead*. In such sentences the word **other** should never be used.

2. **Other** should be inserted in making comparisons with adjectives in the positive or comparative degree when its presence is necessary to prevent one of the terms compared from including the other. Thus,

   1. *No* **other** *metal* is so useful as *iron*.
   2. *Iron* is more useful than *any* **other** *metal*.
   3. *John* is taller than *any* **other** *boy in his class*.

In these sentences *other* is necessary because *iron* is a *metal*, and *John* is a *boy in his class*.

3. Since the superlative denotes an object possessing a quality in the highest or lowest degree of all that are considered, the term compared must be included in the term with which it is compared; and as a rule, therefore, **other** is not used with this degree. Thus,

Iron is the most useful *of all metals*.

III. The Comparison of Adjectives Whose Meaning Does Not Admit of Increase or Diminution.

Because of their meaning some adjectives do not admit of comparison; for example, *wooden, horizontal, true, perfect.*

It is of course incorrect to compare such adjectives. Say, " This line is *more nearly horizontal* than that," etc., when wishing to make a comparison between two objects approaching perfection.

IV. The Correct Use of *A*, *An*, and *The*.

1. A or an is used to limit a noun to one thing of a class — to any one; as, *A* man = *any one* man. *An* earl = *any one* earl.

2. A or an is not used to limit a noun denoting the whole of a class; as, **Man** (not *a man*) *is mortal. He received the title of* **earl** (not *an earl*).

3. **A,** when used before *few*, changes the meaning from *not many* to *some. A,* when used before *little*, changes the meaning from *not much* to *some.* Thus, *few* men = *not many* men ; *a few* men = *some* men. *Little* cause = *not much* cause ; *a little* cause = *some* cause.

4. **The** is used:

(*a.*) To refer to some particular thing or things already known or to be described; as, **The** sun *rises.* **The** house *that my brother built was destroyed.*

(*b.*) Before a noun, in the singular, to particularize the class without designating any individual; as, **The** horse *is a useful animal.* **The** oak *is valuable.*

5. The article is omitted before names used in such general or unlimited sense as not to require it; as, **Truth** (not *The truth*) *is mighty.* **Astronomy** (not *The astronomy*) *is a difficult science. He made some sort of* **excuse** (not *an excuse*). **One third of 6** *is 2* (not *the one third of 6*). *He was appointed* **chairman** (not *the chairman*). *He has* **pneumonia** (not *the pneumonia*).

6. When adjectives of equal rank refer to the same object the article is used only with the first; as, *I have* **a** *red, white, and blue flag* (one flag). But,

When adjectives of equal rank refer to different objects the article **is** repeated with each adjective; as, *I have* **a** *red,* **a** *white, and* **a** *blue flag* (three flags).

7. When several connected nouns stand for the same object the article is used only with the first; as, *Webster* **the** *orator and statesman* (one person). But,

When several connected nouns stand for different objects the article is repeated with each noun, if necessary to avoid ambiguity; as, *Webster*, **the** *orator, and* **the** *governor were in the first carriage* (two persons). *I have just sold* **a** *house and* **a** *lot* (separate property); but, **The** *men, women, and children walked over the bridge* (neither obscure nor ambiguous).

8. When several connected nouns stand for different objects, if the first takes the article it must be repeated when the same form of the article is not applicable to all; as, **A** *cow,* **an** *ox, and* **a** *horse* (not *A cow, ox, and horse*).

V. The Agreement with the Noun.

1. Adjectives denoting one agree with nouns in the singular; as, *One eye; That basis; This memorandum.* Adjectives denoting more than one agree with nouns in the plural; as, *Two eyes; Those bases; These memoranda.*

2. If an adjective is necessarily plural, the noun to agree with it must be plural; as, *Five tons* (not *five ton*); *Five pounds* (not *five pound*).

NOTE. *Brace, dozen, score, yoke, hundred, thousand*, etc., have the same form in both numbers when used with numerals.

VI. The Use of *Either* and *Neither*.

1. *Either* and *neither* are used to designate one of two objects only. When more than two objects are referred to, use *any, any one, none, no one;* as, **Neither** *of these* (two) *houses is for sale.* *You may have* **any one** *of those* (three or more) *which you wish.*

2. To express reciprocal relation the terms *each other* and *one another* are often used; as, *Those* **two** *people help* **each other**; *Those* **three** (or more) *persons help* **one another**.

(*Each other* is used of two only; *one another* is used of more than two.)

VII. Errors in Comparison and Arrangement.

1. Avoid double comparisons; as, *more unkinder; most unkindest.*

2. Place adjectives where there can be no doubt as to what they are intended to modify; as, *A dish of fried bacon* (not *A fried dish of bacon*).

121. REVIEW.

Ex. I. *Rewrite the following, arranging the adjectives in better order when possible, and punctuate:*

1. I like little pretty flowers.
2. He sold a black blind old horse.
3. A wooden rickety large building.
4. An energetic brave restless people.
5. He was a young agreeable man.
6. That noble brave patriotic leader.
7. Mary found a silk lady's black glove.
8. That poor industrious old blind man.
9. A Newfoundland handsome large dog.
10. That was a mournful sad tale.
11. An enlightened civilized nation.
12. We erected a marble costly new fountain.
13. Red beautiful large apples covered the ground.

Ex. II. *Correct the errors in the following, giving reasons:*

1. Texas is larger than any state in the Union. 2. Texas is the largest of all other states in the Union. 3. No state in the Union is so large as Texas.

4. Of all the other American cities, New York is the largest.
5. He was the wisest of all his brothers.
6. Eve was the fairest of all her daughters.

7. Grant was greater than any American general. 8. No American general was so great as General Grant. 9. Grant was the most distinguished of any of his generals. 10. Grant was more distinguished than any of his other generals.

11. John was the tallest of his playmates.
12. That form is more preferable.
13. All the metals are less useful than iron.
14. Washington is more beloved than any man that ever lived.
15. A more healthier location can not be found.
16. He was the most active of all his companions.
17. He did more to accomplish this result than any other man that preceded or followed him.

18. This opinion is becoming more universal.
19. He was of all others most trustworthy.
20. Joseph's lesson was more perfect than that of any pupil in his class.
21. That boy is the brightest of all his playmates.
22. There is no metal so useful as iron.
23. Nothing delights me so much as a sail on the lakes.
24. Time ought, above all kinds of property, to be free from invasion.
25. This was the most satisfactory of any preceding effort.
26. He was more active than any other of his companions.
27. The most principal point was overlooked.
28. Which was the greatest man, Napoleon or Cæsar?

Ex. III. *Insert or omit* **the, an,** *or* **a,** *in the following, giving reasons:*

1. What kind of a house do you want?
2. He died of the pleurisy.
3. There are a few pleasant days in March, because it is a stormy month.
4. Few men live to be a hundred years old, but not many.
5. Where did you get that kind of a hat?
6. This girl has an active and an energetic mind.
7. He carried a large and small basket.
8. The secretary and treasurer were absent.
9. The secretary and the treasurer was absent.
10. An oak, pine, and ash shade the lawn.
11. What kind of an adjective is *happy?*
12. Little can be done, but not much.
13. He saved a little from the fire, as it broke out in the night, when all were asleep.
14. Jones was the captain of our company.
15. The four fifths of ten equals eight.
16. *Congeal* contains a long and short vowel sound.
17. The farmer sold the large and small potatoes.
18. We have learned about the definite and indefinite article.
19. I saw a hot and cold spring twenty feet apart.
20. What sort of a man is he who never needs a friend?
21. Charles is suffering from an attack of the rheumatism.

THE ADJECTIVE

Ex. IV. *Use* **this, these, that,** *and* **those** *properly in the following, giving reason for each selection:*

1. I like ———— kind of apples.
2. I have not seen him ———— twenty years.
3. I dislike ———— sort of berries.
4. "Thank you for ———— molasses."
5. Why should we be annoyed by ———— sort of men?
6. ———— memoranda are correct.
7. "I have no use for ———— kind of people."
8. ———— phenomenon, the northern lights, is very beautiful.
9. I never admired ———— sort of hats.

Ex. V. *Correct the errors in the following, and give reasons:*

1. Churchill received the title of a duke.
2. Both the boy and girl came to see us.
3. Neither the man nor woman was seen.
4. Distinguish between the nominative and objective.
5. I bought a Webster's and Worcester's dictionary.
6. I exchanged two yokes of oxen for five barrel of wine.
7. Neither of the three men could swim.
8. Of those four books, I don't want either.
9. The boy and girl help one another.
10. Those three boys resemble each other.
11. It was a blue soft beautiful sky.
12. They sang the three last verses of the 23d Psalm.
13. I like the sweet and sour grapes.
14. The woman is the equal of man.
15. I never saw a sight so beautiful as this one.
16. I never saw any one so well pleased as he.
17. It is a better poem than ever was written.
18. Sing the third and fifth verse, please.
19. Sing the third and the fifth verses, please.
20. What kind of a phrase is *in town?*
21. Those two boys are very kind to one another.
22. A noun and pronoun are alike in office.
23. He was appointed the secretary.

24. An eel is a sort of a fish.

25. I know the pond is nine foot deep, for I measured it with a ten-feet pole.

26. Draw the lines more perpendicular.

27. I expected some kind of a reward for having got the most correct answer to the problem.

28. Some of the boys are helping each other.

122. HOW TO PARSE ADJECTIVES.

To parse an adjective give:
1. Its class, — descriptive or definitive.
2. Its degree of comparison, if compared.
3. Its use, — what it modifies.

MODEL FOR ORAL AND WRITTEN PARSING.

That *man is never* **alone** *who has* **noble** *thoughts.*

That points out which man without describing; it is therefore a definitive adjective, and modifies *man*.

Alone describes the condition (quality) of the man; it is therefore a descriptive adjective; it is used to complete the predicate and to modify the noun *man*, to which it relates.

Noble describes the quality of thoughts; it is therefore a descriptive adjective; it is in the positive degree, and is used to modify the noun *thoughts*.

Abbreviated Form: *Noble* is a descriptive adjective, positive degree, and is used to modify the noun *thoughts*.

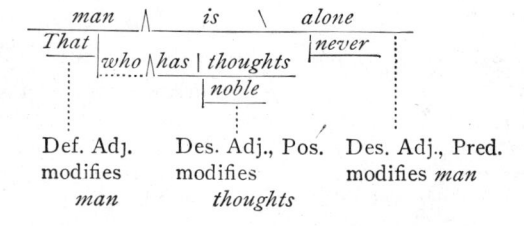

```
        man   \     is    \  alone
    That       |who \has | thoughts  |never
               :         | noble
```

Def. Adj.   Des. Adj., Pos.   Des. Adj., Pred.
modifies   modifies   modifies *man*
man   *thoughts*

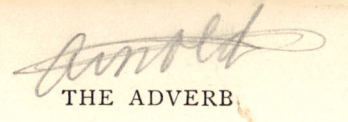

Exercise.

Parse the adjectives in the following:

But if one principal character of Italian landscape is melancholy another is elevation. We have no simple rusticity of scene, no cowslip and buttercup humility of seclusion. Tall mulberry trees, with festoons of the luxuriant vine, purple with ponderous clusters, trailed and trellised between and over them, shade the wide fields of stately Indian corn. . . . In a country of this pomp of natural glory, tempered with melancholy memory of departed pride, what are we to wish for, what are we naturally to expect, in the character of her most humble of edifices; those which are most connected with present life, least with the past?—*John Ruskin in "The Poetry of Architecture."*

123. THE ADVERB.

You have already learned that adverbs modify the meaning of verbs, adjectives, or adverbs ; as,

1. *He walked* rapidly.
2. *The rose is* very *beautiful.*
3. *He answered* very *quietly.*

Which words in the following sentences both modify verbs **and** connect clauses?

1. *This is the place where Cæsar crossed the Rubicon.*
2. *We came when we heard you were here.*
3. *You must start to school before the bell rings.*

Adverbs have two different *uses*. They may merely modify, or they may both modify and connect. These classes are known respectively as **Simple Adverbs** and **Conjunctive Adverbs.**

The principal **Conjunctive Adverbs** are **as, after, before, when, since** (meaning time), **till, until, where, while,** and **why.**

NOTE. **When, where, why,** and **how** when used to ask questions are called **Interrogative Adverbs**; as,

> **When** *did the general arrive?*
> **Where** *is Bunker Hill?*

In meaning, adverbs are of several kinds:

1. **Adverbs of Time.**

    > *He is going* **soon.**
    > *I will see you* **by and by.**
    > *Go* **now.**

Others are *yet, lately, ever, then, hereafter, sometimes,* and *always.*

2. **Adverbs of Place.**

    > *John found it* **there.**
    > *Flames fly* **upward.**

Others are *here, hither, thither, hence,* and *thence.*

3. **Adverbs of Manner.**

    > *He recited* **well.**
    > *She is* **better** *dressed than her sisters.*
    > *He answered* **thus.**

Others are *quickly, pleasantly, worse, ill,* and *slowly.*

4. **Adverbs of Degree.**

    > *I am* **almost** *frozen.*
    > *He is* **nearly** *done.*
    > *She is* **very** *studious.*

Others are *little, quite, all, wholly, so, partly,* and *enough.*

NOTE. A few adverbs modify a whole sentence, and are sometimes called **Modal Adverbs**; as,

> **Perhaps** *I shall go to-morrow evening.*

Others are *surely, probably,* and *possibly.*

NOTE. **Yes** and **no**, with like words, are often called adverbs of **assertion**. If they are adverbs at all they are *modal* in nature. Really, however, they are sentence equivalents; for example: "Will you go with me?" "*Yes.*" Here *Yes* is the equivalent of "I will go with you."

THE ADVERB

NOTE. Adverbs often modify an adjective or an adverbial phrase, instead of a single word; as, *He went* **quite** *to the top.* *He sailed* **nearly** *around the world.*

NOTE. Two or more words taken together may convey a single adverbial idea. In this case they are called **Phrase Adverbs;** as, *Here and there, ever and anon, again and again,* etc.

124. COMPARISON OF ADVERBS.

Adverbs, like adjectives, admit of comparison. They are compared in three different ways:

1. Some adverbs are compared by adding *-er* and *-est* to the simple form; as,

Positive.	Comparative.	Superlative.
fast	faster	fastest
rough	rougher	roughest
slow	slower	slowest
soon	sooner	soonest
early	earlier	earliest

NOTE. Poetry often demands the use of the comparative and the superlative in *-er* and *-est* when they would not be used in prose.

2. Adverbs ending in *-ly* are usually compared by prefixing *more* and *most*, or *less* and *least*, to the simple forms; as,

Positive.	Comparative.	Superlative.
wisely	more wisely	most wisely
firmly	less firmly	least firmly
earnestly	more earnestly	most earnestly

3. Some adverbs are compared irregularly; as,

Positive.	Comparative.	Superlative.
badly } ill }	worse	worst
far	farther	farthest
forth	further	furthest
little	less	least

Positive.	Comparative.	Superlative.
much	more	most
well	better	best

NOTE. The forms given above, with the exception of *badly* and *forth*, are also used as adjectives.

125. HOW TO PARSE ADVERBS.

To parse an adverb give:

1. Its class, — simple, conjunctive, interrogative, modal.
2. If simple, its kind.
3. Its degree of comparison, if compared.
4. Its use — the word, phrase, or sentence whose meaning it modifies.

Examples of Parsing.

He walked **rapidly.**

Rapidly is a simple adverb of manner. It is in the positive degree, and modifies *walked*.

This is the place **where** *Cæsar crossed the Rubicon.*

Where is a conjunctive adverb; it modifies *crossed* and connects the clause *Cæsar crossed the Rubicon* with *place*.

He answered **very** *quietly.*

Very is a simple adverb of degree; it modifies *quietly*.

Why *did Cæsar cross the Rubicon?*

Why is an interrogative adverb, and modifies *did cross*.

Exercise.

Analyze the following sentences and parse the adverbs:

1. He was already at the door, but he dared not go out.
2. Raleigh had spent so much money already that he was forced to give up the attempt to plant a colony in America.

ADJECTIVES AND ADVERBS

3.   To live with them is far less sweet
       Than to remember thee.

4. To live long it is necessary to live slowly.
5. When did Washington take command of the Continental army?
6. When a fool makes up his mind, the market has gone by.
7. Where liberty dwells, there is my country.
8. How are the mighty fallen!
9. The noblest principle in education is to teach how to live for one's country. — *Balch.*
10. Nothing is politically right that is morally wrong. — *O'Connor.*
11. The family is practically a little state in itself.
12. Let us have faith that right makes might; and in that faith let us dare to do our duty as we understand it. — *Lincoln.*

13.   Mont Blanc is the monarch of mountains,
       They crowned him long ago
       On a throne of rocks, in a robe of clouds,
       With a diadem of snow. — *Byron.*

14.   This little rill, that from the springs
       Of yonder grove its current brings,
       Plays on the slope awhile, and then
       Goes prattling into groves again,
       Oft to its warbling waters drew
       My little feet, when life was new. — *Bryant.*

126. SIMILAR ADJECTIVES AND ADVERBS.

Many words are used both as adjectives and as adverbs without a change of form. Their use determines the part of speech to which they belong.

Exercises.

Ex. I. *Distinguish the adverbs and the adjectives in the following sentences:*

1. Is he the best scholar who behaves the best?
2. Is he well when he is able to do the work well?

3. Drink deep or taste not the Pierian spring.
4. A company of soldiers marched six files deep.
5. He is entirely wrong in holding out so long.
6. He was sick, nigh unto death.
7. The tumult shows the battle nigh.
8. There's some ill planet reigns.
9. How ill this taper burns!
10. All left the world much as they found it.
11. Much learning doth make thee mad.

Ex. II. *How does the first sentence in each of the following pairs differ in meaning from the second?*

1. The river ran smooth.
   The engine ran smoothly.

2. The lady looked cold as she passed by.
   The lady looked coldly at me as she passed.

3. The moon looks calm and peaceful.
   The moon looks down calmly and peacefully upon the battle-field.

4. The soldiers are careful with their guns.
   They load their guns carefully.

Ex. III. *Choose the proper adjective or adverb and give reason for your choice:*

1. The sky looks (beautiful, beautifully).
2. You behaved very (proper, properly).
3. The man acted (wild, wildly).
4. The ship sailed (smooth, smoothly).
5. The dead Indian looked (fierce, fiercely).
6. The machinery works (good, well).
7. The bird sang (sweet, sweetly).
8. The fire burns (bright, brightly).
9. (Sure, surely) he is a fine gentleman.
10. The man writes (plain, plainly).
11. The tone of his language was (decided, decidedly) harsh.
12. She is a (remarkable, remarkably) beautiful person.
13. He is (remarkable, remarkably) bright.
14. I stayed at home yesterday because I felt (bad, badly).

127. THE PREPOSITION.

It has been shown (Gr. 25, pp. 39–41) that a preposition connects a substantive to some other word, and indicates a relation between them.

The preposition, although having little meaning in itself, is a very useful word in the sentence, as by it both variety and precision of statement may be obtained.

To obtain this precision of statement care must be taken to use the preposition that expresses the exact shade of meaning desired. This skill in the use of prepositions is acquired by practice. Certain words, however, having the prefixes *ab* (meaning *from*), *ad* (meaning *to* or *for*), and *com* (meaning *with*), are followed by prepositions having the meaning of the prefixes; for example:

ab: abduct from; absent from; absorb from; abstain from; abstract from.
ad: adapt to *or* for; addicted to; address to; adhere to; adjacent to.
com: combat with; combine with; communicate with; compare with; comply with.

NOTE. The final letter of each of these prefixes sometimes changes in order to harmonize with the next letter in the word in which it is used:

ab: *ab*-duct from; *a*-vert from.
ad: *ad*-mit to; *a*-spire to; *al*-lude to; *an*-nex to; *an*-nounce to.
com: *com*-pound with; *con*-tract with; *col*-laborate with; *co*-equal with.

As a rule, then, after words having these prefixes use a preposition having the same meaning as the prefix.

Many words, however, require a special preposition after them, and in a few instances the same word has widely differing meanings when followed by different prepositions. Some of these words are noted in the following list:

Abhorrence *for*.
Accord *with*.
Acquit *of*.
Adapted *to* (by plan).
Adapted *for* (by nature).
Agree *with* (a person).
Agree *to* (a statement).
Confer *on* (to give to).
Confer *with* (to talk with).
Confide *in* (to trust in).
Confide *to* (to intrust to).
Congenial *to*.
Congratulate *on* or *upon*.
Convenient *to* (a person or place).
Convenient *for* (a purpose).
Correspond *with* (a person).
Correspond *to* (a thing).
Deliver *from, out of, of, to* (a person).
Deliver *at* (a place).
Differ *from* (in likeness).
Differ *with* (in opinion).
Involve *in*.
Part *from* (a person).
Part *with* (a thing).
Profit *by*.
Prohibit *from*.
Reconcile *to* (a person).
Reconcile *with* (a statement).
Taste *of* (food).
Taste *for* (art, or something desired).
Wait *on, upon, for, at*.

ADDITIONAL RULES. Use *in, on, at*, and *by* as a rule to show *rest;* as, *He stays* in *the house;* on *the porch;* at *the seaside;* by *the spring.*

Use *to, into, unto, toward*, and *from* as a rule to show *motion together with direction;* as, *He was going* to *the store;* into *the house.*

Use *between* when speaking of two; *among* when speaking of more than two; as, *He divided the apple* between *the two boys, and the orange* among *the three girls.*

Use *by* to indicate the actor, and *with* to indicate the instrument; as, *The boy was hit* with *a stone* by *his companion.*

Use *in* when speaking of large cities, *at* when speaking of villages and hotels.

Avoid the use of *of* in such phrases as *the capture of the colonel, the fear of wild animals, the love of God,* etc. What two meanings may each of these phrases have? Such ambiguity may be avoided by the use of the possessive case or the use of a verb or participle; as, *God's love; the fear shown by wild animals; the soldier whom the colonel captured.*

Avoid the use of *onto* and *off of*. Although frequently heard,

THE PREPOSITION

these expressions are not warranted. Say "He got *off* the car and stepped *on* a slowly moving train." Say "I took it *from* him," not "I took it *off of* him."

In Parsing Prepositions we need only to state that the word is a preposition, and to point out the words between which it shows relation.

Exercises.

Ex. I. *Use correctly in sentences the various prepositions mentioned on the preceding page.*

Ex. II. *Fill the blanks with appropriate prepositions:*

1. He poured ink _____ the jug.
2. The wheat was cut _____ a reaper.
3. My book is different _____ yours.
4. He divided his property _____ his four sons.
5. She divided her estate _____ her two daughters.
6. He died _____ thirst.
7. I put the knife _____ my pocket.
8. The man died _____ smallpox.
9. I differ _____ you on that question.
10. You may rely _____ what I say, and confide _____ his honesty.
11. I am tall in comparison _____ you.
12. We remained _____ the South _____ a little village.
13. We visited _____ London _____ a week.
14. The boy was admitted _____ school.
15. He _____ three others was commended.
16. He was absent _____ school.

Ex. III. *How does the first sentence of each of the following pairs differ in meaning from the second?*

1. { The boys jumped into the water.
   { The boys jumped in the water.
2. { The children were running in the hall.
   { The children were running into the hall.

3. { They divided the money among them.
   { They divided the money between them.

4. { Two boys beside the man.
   { Two boys besides the man.

Ex. IV. *Parse all the prepositions in the poem "Seadrift," pages* 330, 331.

128. THE CONJUNCTION.

There are four kinds of words that, besides their primary use in the sentence, serve as connectives; namely, *copulative verbs, relative pronouns, conjunctive adverbs*, and *prepositions.*

In addition to these connective words, there is also the **Conjunction,** a word that is *used chiefly to connect.* (Gr. **26,** pp. 42, 43.)

Conjunctions are used to connect (1) words and phrases of equal rank, (2) the members of compound sentences, (3) clauses to the elements they modify.

According to their use, conjunctions are divided into two classes, — *coördinate* and *subordinate*. (Gr. **53, 46.**)

Coördinate Conjunctions connect the parts of a sentence so that they remain equal in rank; **Subordinate Conjunctions** connect the parts so that one becomes dependent upon the other. For example, if we connect the two sentences

(1) *He is industrious* and (2) *He succeeds* with the coördinate conjunction *and*, we form a compound sentence the members of which are of equal rank; thus,

$$\underline{He \wedge is \setminus industrious} \quad \underline{he \wedge succeeds.}$$
$$\qquad\qquad |\; and\; |$$

But if we connect these sentences with the subordinate conjunction *because* we change their rank so that one becomes an adverbial clause dependent upon the other; thus,

```
He /\ succeeds
        | because
           he /\ is \ industrious.
```

The word *that* when used to introduce a noun clause is sometimes classed as a subordinate conjunction. It seems, however, to be used to give euphony to the sentence rather than to connect its parts, and may be classed as an *Expletive*. Thus,

```
                that
I /\ know  |    he /\ is \ industrious.
```

Correlative Conjunctions. Conjunctions often occur in pairs, the first one preparing the way for the second, and having no connecting power by itself.

Omit *and* from the first of the following sentences and *as* from the second, and note the loss of connection and of meaning:

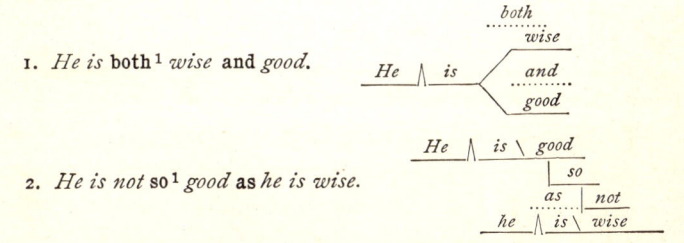

1. *He is* **both**[1] *wise* **and** *good.*

```
               both
                wise
He /\ is  <    and
                good
```

2. *He is not* **so**[1] *good* **as** *he is wise.*

```
He /\ is \ good
        | so
      as   | not
      he /\ is \ wise
```

These words *taken together* are called **Correlatives,** a word that means *having mutual relation*.

[1] In the first sentence notice that *both . . . and* are coördinate correlatives, and that *both* may be omitted without changing the meaning, being merely introductory; but in the second *so . . . as* are subordinate correlatives, and *so* is an adverb and can not be omitted without changing the meaning.

The most common correlative conjunctions are "both . . . and," "either . . . or," "neither . . . nor," "whether . . . or," "as . . . as," "so . . . as," and "not only . . . but also."

CAUTIONS. 1. Correlatives should be so placed that they will indicate clearly what expressions the author wishes to connect. As a rule the word after the first correlative should be the same part of speech as the word after the second ; as,

   1. *He gave* **both** *advice* **and** *money ;*
  not *He* **both** *gave advice* **and** *money.*

   2. *He may give the book* **either** *to you* **or** *to me ;*
  not *He may* **either** *give the book to you* **or** *to me.*

   3. *She dresses* **not only** *richly* **but also** *tastefully ;*
  not *She* **not only** *dresses richly* **but** *tastefully.*

2. Do not use "*neither . . . or*" for "*neither . . . nor*."

   4. *He was discouraged by* **neither** *danger* **nor** *misfortune ;*
  not *He was discouraged by* **neither** *danger* **or** *misfortune.*

3. "*As . . . as*" is used in making equal comparisons; "*so . . . as*" is used in making unequal comparisons.

   5. *He is* **as** *good* **as** *he is wise.*
   6. *He is not* **so** *good* **as** *he is wise.*

NOTE. Two or more words may be taken together and used as a single conjunction : as if, as though, as long as, as soon as, as sure as, except that, in case that, in order that, forasmuch as, provided that.

Parsing Conjunctions. In parsing a conjunction we need only to tell its kind and its use, or what it connects.

Test Questions.

1. How does a preposition differ from a conjunction? 2. What prepositions should be used after words having the prefixes **ad, ab, con**? 3. How do *in* and *into, among* and *between*, differ in use? (Give examples.) 4. What five kinds of connective words are there? 5. Illustrate and explain the use of each kind of connective. 6. Explain the difference in use between a coördinate and a subordinate conjunction. 7. What is the meaning of the term *correlative?* 8. What part of speech should follow the second term of a correlative conjunction?

9. How do *as . . . as* and *so . . . as* differ in use? 10. Write five sentences to illustrate the correct use of *either . . . or* and *neither . . . nor*.

Exercises.

Ex. I. *Write or select from your reader five sentences, using different correlative conjunctions in each sentence.*

Ex. II. *Point out the conjunctions in the selections on pages* 226, 265, 304, *and tell the kind and use of each.*

129. INTERJECTIONS AND EXPLETIVES.

Interjections, being independent elements, have no syntax. (See Gr. 27, pp. 44, 45.)

The expletives *there, for, that,* and *as* are each used in only one construction, as shown on pp. 19, 62, 85, 219–221.

130. WORDS VARIOUSLY USED.

The part of speech to which a word belongs, is determined solely by its use. If the word *run* is spoken, it is impossible to tell its part of speech without having the speaker's idea. If he is thinking of a small stream or of a path followed by wild animals, or of any one of several other things, it is a noun; but if he is thinking of moving swiftly on the feet, or of any one of more than forty other acts (see "Webster's International Dictionary"), it is a verb.

Many words may be thus used as several different parts

of speech. It is therefore never safe to say that a word is of any given part of speech until its use, that is, its relation to the other words of a sentence, has been carefully studied.

The following list of words variously used is given primarily to emphasize the necessity of careful examination before stating that a word belongs to any given class. Occasionally, also, it may be useful for reference.

A . . . *Article* or *Adj.* A wise son maketh a glad father.
  Prep. I go a-fishing. I set it a-going. This use is now infrequent in literature. It means *to* or *for*.
About . *Adv.* It came about[1] in this way. About ten were injured.
  Prep. He went about his work. Have you much money about you?
Above . *Adj.* The above remarks may be safely quoted.
  Adv. O Father that rulest above!
  Noun. Every good gift cometh from above.
  Prep. Above the clouds is the sun still shining.
After . . *Adj.* After ages will record his good deeds.
  Adv. He went forth soon after.
  Conj. Adv. I started after it had become dark.
  Prep. After an unselfish deed the heart is light.
Alike . . *Adj.* They look alike.
  Adv. All should be alike anxious to do deeds of kindness.
All . . . *Adj.* Pleasant words are all remembered.
  Adj. Pronoun. All should determine to succeed.
  Adv. A young man should live all for success rather than all for pleasure.
  Noun. To her country she gave her all, ten noble sons.
Any . . *Adj.* Will any man forget his mother?
  Adj. Pronoun. Any who deserve it, may achieve honor.
  Adv. Is he any better? (With comparative adj.; colloquial.)

[1] As *came about* means the same as *happened*, the two words may be taken together as the verb.

WORDS VARIOUSLY USED

As . . .   *Adv.* (the first of the correlatives *as . . . as*). He will do the work as well as it can be done.

Conj. (the second of the correlatives *as . . . as*). He is as honest as you say.

Conj. Adv. He came as he had promised.

Expletive (as sign of apposition). He went out as mate. Booth often appeared as Hamlet.

Relative Pronoun (after *such, same, many*). As many as I saw were ready.

Before .   *Adv.* He had been there before.

Conj. Adv. Before he crossed the Hellespont, Alexander had dreamed of conquering the world.

Prep. He stood before the inn.

Below .   *Adj.* Looking forth, he saw the plain below.

Adv. Go below, quickly!

Noun. A frightened voice came from below.

Prep. The spring is a few rods below the old elm.

Both . .   *Adj.* We heard both sides of the argument.

Adj. Pronoun. Both helped to win the victory.

Conj. (the first of the correlatives *both . . . and*). He is both famous and honest.

But . .   *Adj.* Men are but children of a larger growth.

Adv. If they kill us, we shall but die.

Conj. There is little hope, but I shall try.

Prep. All but the determined fail in the race of life.

Relative Pro. (after negative expressions, with the meaning *that not*). There is no lad but honors his mother.

By . . .   *Adv.* He walked by[1] without speaking.

Prep. He went by rail, not by steamer.

Either. .   *Adj.* The word is pronounced either way.

Adj. Pronoun. Either will prove a good investment.

Conj. (first of correlatives *either . . . or*). Every boy should receive an education either in school or in shop.

Each . .   *Adj.* Each warrior drew his battle blade.

Adj. Pronoun. Each took off his hat.

Else . .   *Adj.* This is no one else's[2] business. No one else can earn a man's success for him.

Adv. How else can I do it?

Conj. Thou desirest not sacrifice, else would I give it.

---

[1] Perhaps the verb is *walk by*.

[2] Note that the possessive sign is idiomatically transferred to the adjective.

Enough . *Adj.* We have lunch enough for all.
Adj. Pronoun. We have enough for all.
Adv. I know you well enough.
Interjection. Enough![1] Say no more!

Except . *Conj.* Except the Lord build the house, they labor in vain that build it.
Prep. I will pay for everything except the luxuries.
Verb. We except to the testimony of the first witness.

For . . *Conj.* We did not wait longer, for it was becoming dark.
Expletive. For[2] boys to forget their honor is fatal.
Prep. He gave up all for honor.

Full . . *Adj.* The path of life is full of thorns.
Adv. Full many a flower is born to blush unseen.
Noun. The moon shone at its full.
Verb. Manufacturers sometimes full woolen fabrics.

Hard . . *Adj.* The lessons are too long and hard.
Adv. The boy worked so hard that he became ill.

However . *Conj.* He may not come; however, I shall tell him if he does.
Adv. However hard he works, he fails to succeed.

Ill . . . *Adj.* There's some ill planet reigns.
Adv. Ill fares the land ... where men decay.
Noun. O'er all the ills of life victorious.

Late . . *Adj.* Late pupils are usually careless.
Adv. Some girls study early and late.

Like . . *Adj.* The staff of his spear was like[3] a weaver's beam.
Adv. She sings like[3] a nightingale. (This should not be confused with the conjunctive adverb *as* in "She sings as a nightingale sings." *Like* is an adverb modifying *sings*. *Nightingale* is the object of the preposition *to* or *unto*, understood, the phrase *unto a nightingale* being adverbial and modifying *like*. When used in comparing objects *like* is an adjective; when used in comparing acts it is an adverb. Notice

---

[1] This may be called an adjective used for a noun: "You have said enough." See page 45.

[2] To call *for* thus used an expletive gives the term a wider meaning than it has when applied to *there* introductory (Gr. 9). The word is used thus by idiom; it is certainly not a preposition, as it shows no relation between words; it is therefore perhaps wise to widen the meaning of *expletive* enough to include it.

[3] Some authors consider *like* thus used to be equivalent to a preposition.

WORDS VARIOUSLY USED

Like . . that when the second verb is expressed, *as* and not *like* should be used: "He runs like a deer;" but, "He runs as a deer runs; He runs as a deer does.")
Noun. Like produces like. We shall not look upon his like again.
Verb. Employers like punctuality.

Low . . *Adj.* The land lies low. Keep your voice low.
Adv. She speaks low and distinctly.

More . . *Adj.* Ye are of more value than many sparrows.
Adj. Pronoun. They that would have more and more can never have enough.
Adv. Honesty is more valuable than brilliancy.

Near . . *Adj.* The scenes of my childhood are near and dear to me.
Adv. Do not come near.
Prep. The ship passed near the bar.
Verb. The ships near the shore.

Needs . . *Adv.* He must needs (necessarily) go through Samaria.
Noun. A boy must watch his employer's needs.
Verb. Man daily needs rest.

Only . . *Adj.* Only men of industry succeed.
Adv. One can only try.

So . . . *Adj.* Is that so?
Adv. He was so noble that all admired him.
Conj. He was noble; so they admired him.
Noun. Give me a dollar or so. (An idiom; perhaps it is more nearly an adverb: — "a dollar or about so much money.")

That . . *Adj.* That boy will succeed who is industrious.
Adj. Pronoun. That is the book I prefer.
Conj. They died that we might be free.
Expletive. We know that we are free.
Rel. Pronoun. The boy that is industrious will succeed.

The . . *Article* or *Adj.* The boy that thinks first of others is unselfish.
Adv. The more the better. (An idiom.)

While . *Conj. Adv.* Make hay while the sun shines.
Noun. That is worth while (adverbial objective).
Verb. Music whiled away the evening pleasantly.

Worth . *Adj.* Nobility is worth more than money.
Noun. Worth makes the man.
Verb. Woe worth (be to) the day.

131. GENERAL REVIEW.

TEST QUESTIONS. 1. How do you determine whether a group of words is a phrase, a clause, or a sentence? 2. What punctuation should not be used to close sentences? 3. When should a declarative sentence not be marked at its close by a period or an exclamation point? 4. How are words classified as parts of speech? 5. What part of speech does the predicate always contain? 6. What part of speech is used chiefly to connect? 7. What kind of verbs are used as connective words? 8. What parts of speech are used as modifiers? 9. In the expression *A new dress* does the word *new* increase or diminish the number of objects to which the word *dress* may be applied? Why? 10. When are two or more adjectives, used with one noun, not separated by commas?

11. What is the literal meaning of the word *infinitive?* 12. Wherein do infinitives and participles agree? 13. How do they differ in form? 14. Which form of the participle is never used as a noun? 15. Of what importance is the classification of nouns as concrete and abstract? As common and proper? 16. What eight uses of the noun require a capital letter? Illustrate. 17. How is the case of nouns determined? 18. In the sentence *All the* **air** *a solemn* **stillness** *holds* why is the case of the nouns *air* and *stillness* not clearly made known? 19. How many different forms of pronouns may be used to complete the sentence *He saw* ————? 20. Name the tenses of the indicative mode, and tell how each is formed. 21. What is the difference in meaning between *I waited* and *I was waiting?* Between *I waited an hour* and *I have waited an hour?* Between *I shall wait* and *I will wait?*

EXERCISE. *Classify the following sentence as to use and as to structure; tell the part of speech and give the syntax of each word; select four phrases, and tell how each is used; change the sentence to the declarative form, arrange the words in their natural order, and then diagram.*

> O what a glory doth this world put on
> For him who with a fervent heart, goes forth
> Under the bright and glorious sky, and looks
> On duties well performed, and days well spent!
> — *Longfellow.*

II. COMPOSITION.

PART I.

NARRATIVES AND LETTERS. ACTS THAT SHOW CHARACTER. PUNCTUATION.

(To be studied in connection with Part I of the Grammar on pages 7–48.)

1. "HOW TO WRITE."

In the making of a composition, or essay, success is possible only when the writer observes a few important principles. This lesson, which is merely to be read and talked over in class, is to call attention to these principles.

Whether composition writing is a task or a pleasure depends upon the pupil's knowledge of his subject. Therefore,

Choose a Familiar Subject.

Every young person has both seen and taken part in unnumbered incidents and experiences. If he writes of these he will have familiar subjects, for he knows all about them. He tells of these experiences freely and effectively when talking to his parents and companions. A little practice will enable him to write about them no less freely and effectively.

The subject being chosen, the next step is to decide what to say about it. The things that made an experience interesting to you will make it interesting to others. Study the experience; determine exactly the incidents, the acts, the motions, the colors, the odors, the sounds, the things said, that attracted and held your attention. You will often be surprised to find that little and seemingly unimportant things had much to do with the interest. These are the things you should tell of when you write. Doctor Edward Everett Hale[1] says:

Know What You Want to Say.

Having decided what you wish to say, your next duty is,

Say It.

This seems too simple to be stated. Yet every writer often finds himself tempted to tell of something not directly connected with his subject. To say all that one wishes to say, to say it clearly, and to say nothing more, is to carry out this principle. In saying it,

Use Your Own Language.

This means that you must not try to use "book language." If you make your composition sound like a book, it will not sound like you. It will not be natural. It is better to use almost the language you use when talking. Do not feel that pen and paper require long words or unusual sentences. The way you tell your mother of an experience is probably the best possible way for you to write of it. To write sentences wrong end first; to use "'tis" and "'twas" and "ne'er" and "e'er"; to say you "retired" when you really "went to bed" —

---

[1] This principle is taken from "How to Write," in Doctor Hale's volume "How to Do It," as are the principles that follow in the chapter. Teachers will do well to read and discuss Doctor Hale's chapter with their classes. The volume is published by Little, Brown, & Co., Boston.

all this weakens your work. You do not talk in this manner; why write so? The next principle grows out of this one:

Leave Out All Fine Passages.

Such passages are not a part of your conversation. When you find that you have used them, omit them.

Young people often feel, too, that the use of words with many syllables is a sign of power. This is not true. Therefore, remember that

A Short Word is Better Than a Long One.

The same principle that demands short words, also demands few words. To express a thought in twenty words is better than to express it in thirty, or in twenty-five, or in twenty-one, for the reason that it requires less exertion to read and understand twenty words. "Very" and other modifying words may often be omitted. They weaken rather than strengthen. The principle is:

The Fewer Words the Better.

The final direction is based on the fact that one's best work is never done at the first trial. Write; then go over your work and omit unnecessary words and expressions, change the location of sentences and paragraphs, substitute phrases for clauses and clauses for phrases, make clear the antecedents of pronouns, use words that are more exact and more suggestive, be sure that your punctuation marks really add to clearness. Keep your compositions, and after several months again examine each one and make the corrections that you failed to make earlier. Constant writing and continuous wise revision will result in an ability to write effectively. This principle Dr. Hale states thus:

Cut It to Pieces.

2. A KIND ACT.

As I was coming through the Allegheny parks one day I noticed a large Newfoundland dog standing near a pump, looking longingly at it. A little girl with some books under her arm stopped near the dog and pumped him a drink of cool water. When the dog had had enough he licked her hand, and looking up into her face he seemed to try his best to thank her. After patting his head for a moment, she went on her way. — *School Work.*

Exercises.

Ex. I. What is your feeling toward this little girl? What has caused that feeling? What in the second sentence helps to make clear for us a picture of the little girl? Why did she pat the dog's head before she started on? How many pictures are given of the dog? Which one seems most distinct?

Ex. II. You have seen or taken part in some act showing kindness or cruelty to a dog or to some other domestic animal. Tell of it, and afterward write an account of it. Or tell and write of any act of kindness you have seen.

3. THE WHISTLE.

When I was a child of seven years old, my friends, on a holiday, filled my pocket with coppers. I went directly to a shop where they sold toys for children, and being charmed with the sound of a whistle that I met by the way in the hands of another boy, I voluntarily offered and gave all my money for one. I then came home and went whistling all over the house, much pleased with my whistle but disturbing all the family.

My sisters and brothers, understanding the bargain I had made, told me I had given four times as much for it as it was worth, put me in mind what good things I might have bought with the rest of the money, and laughed at me so much for my folly that I cried with vexation; and the reflection gave me much more chagrin than the whistle gave me pleasure.

— *Autobiography of Benjamin Franklin.*

Exercise.[1]

Tell first, and later write in two or three paragraphs, of an experience of your own, — you paid too much for an article, bought the wrong article, forgot what you were to buy, lost, broke, or spilled what you had bought. Tell of the experience as a whole, — its beginning, the experience itself, and its results. Use short sentences and words as simple as Franklin's.

Write a paragraph about a pet or a toy that you very much enjoyed during your childhood. Tell how you got it, how you played with it by yourself or with your companions, and how you lost it, broke it, or got rid of it.

Write a paragraph about a childhood experience with a sled or with skates.

Write two or three paragraphs about any experience of your own before you were seven or eight years old.

What unnecessary word is there in the first clause of the selection?

4. THE FRIENDLY LETTER.

The most interesting letters are those full of the little details that make to-day different from yesterday and that suggest the whole life of the writer. To tell of many of these suggestive little acts and incidents is to write a letter that will be read with delight.

Read the following letter, adapted from one [2] written by a lad of eight or nine, a lad who became one of the most famous authors of our country. James Russell Lowell wrote "The Vision of Sir Launfal" and many other beautiful poems, as well as several volumes of delightful essays.

---

[1] When several subjects are mentioned under an exercise, as a rule it will be wise to let each boy and girl choose one and write of it only. Different subjects are suggested in order that every pupil may find one within his own experience.

[2] From Volume I. of "Letters of James Russell Lowell," by Charles Eliot Norton. Copyright, 1893, by Harper and Brothers.

Nov. 2, 1828.

My dear Brother:—I am going to tell you melancholy news. I have the ague together with a gumbile. I presume you know that September has a lame leg, but he grows better every day and now is very well but still limps a little. We have a new scholar from Round Hill. His name is Hooper. . . .

I am going to have a new suit of blue broadcloth clothes to wear every day and to play in. Mother tells me that I may have any sort of buttons I choose. I have not done anything to the hut, but if you wish I will. I am now very happy; but I should be more so if you were here. I hope you will answer my letter. If you do not I shall write you no more letters. . . . Mother has given me three volumes of " Tales of a Grandfather." Farewell.

Yours truly,

JAMES R. LOWELL.

Having read this letter you wish to know the place at which it was written, but there is nothing to tell you. In omitting this item the young writer made a mistake. Before the date of his letter he should have put the name of the place at which it was written. The "heading" then would have read thus:

Cambridge, Mass., Nov. 2, 1828.

We always wish to know in what place a letter was written, when it was written, and by whom it was written. In all the letters that you write be sure to make known each of these facts.

Exercise.

Are the sentences in this letter easily understood? Do you think they are long or short? When talking, do boys and girls as a rule use long or short sentences? How many words are in the longest sentence in the letter? Does the writer mention to his brother the same things he would mention if he were talking to him? Are they said in nearly the same language he would use if talking, or are they said in different language? What does he mean by *gumbile?* What word should he have used? Forms thus corrupted by carelessness or ignorance should be avoided.

LETTERS

What is the punctuation after *My dear Brother?* What is the punctuation after each of the words in the heading? What is the punctuation after *Yours truly?* In your own letters use exactly the same punctuation.

5. RULES FOR COMPOSITION.

When talking, both young people and old, as a rule, use short sentences. In writing, the same principle should be observed. So, too, in written composition practically the same language should be used as is used in spoken composition. This of course makes it necessary for boys and girls to form the habit of speaking accurately and clearly.

From the facts suggested above we may draw the following rules:

Write as you speak. This means, of course, to use short sentences and simple words; *not* to use slang, incorrect expressions, etc.

Seldom write a sentence containing more than thirty words or more than two statements joined by *and*.

Avoid corrupt forms of words, as well as inelegant and incorrect expressions.

Exercises.

Ex. I. Discuss in class a number of words and expressions that your teacher will tell you are often incorrectly used by you.

Ex. II. Write a letter to a relative or friend, telling of events that have happened at home and in your vicinity during the past week. Tell of real events, the ones that have been of especial interest to you. Use the language you would use in talking to the person to whom you are writing. Avoid long sentences. Punctuate properly.

Keep all letters and compositions that you write, and occasionally examine them for undetected errors.

6. WORDS TO WATCH.

Besides using incorrect forms of words, careless speakers and writers often use words in meanings not approved by the majority of educated people. From time to time such words will be introduced under the above title.

Like means *to enjoy, to be pleased with.*

Love means *to regard with affection*, as one's mother, one's country, or one's God. One does not *love* what one eats.

Exercise.

Insert the proper word in the blanks in the following sentences:

Oh, I do _____ olives so much! Don't you _____ to see a game of football? I _____ to skate. Do you not _____ that old gentleman? George Washington _____ his mother. I _____ to spend my leisure reading poetry. Every lad should _____ his country. Thou shalt _____ thy neighbor as thyself. Golf is a game that many people _____.

7. A SUDDEN SHOWER.

Barefooted boys scud up the street
   Or scurry under sheltering sheds;
And schoolgirl faces, pale and sweet,
   Gleam from the shawls about their heads.

Doors bang; and mother-voices call
   From alien homes; and rusty gates
Are slammed; and high above it all,
   The thunder grim reverberates.

And then, abrupt, — the rain! the rain! —
   The earth lies gasping; and the eyes
Behind the streaming window pane
   Smile at the trouble of the skies.

The highway smokes; sharp echoes ring;
    The cattle bawl and cow-bells clank;
And into town comes galloping
    The farmer's horse, with steaming flank.

The swallow dips beneath the eaves
    And flirts his plumes and folds his wings;
And under the Catawba leaves
    The caterpillar curls and clings.

The bumblebee is pelted down
    The wet stem of the hollyhock;
And sullenly, in spattered brown,
    The cricket leaps the garden walk.

Within, the baby claps his hands
    And crows with rapture strange and vague;
Without, beneath the rosebush stands
    A dripping rooster on one leg.
        — *James Whitcomb Riley.*[1]

Exercises.

Ex. I. What three pictures do you see, with closed eyes, as the first stanza is read? What idea is in *scud* that is not in *scurry*? What sounds are mentioned in the second stanza? What does the second statement in stanza two mean? Why do doors bang? Why are rusty gates slammed? What pictures are in the third stanza? What is meant by *The earth lies gasping*? Whose eyes are looking from the window? What pictures and what sounds in stanza four? Explain *smokes* and *steaming*. What pictures in five? Have you ever seen the swallow and the caterpillar thus? What does *Catawba* mean? What pictures in the sixth? What does the first half of six mean? What pictures in seven?

Because of the pictures and sounds given in the poem, what experience have we undergone in imagination? Are unusual or usual pictures and sounds given? Which of the pictures and sounds have you never seen or heard in reality?

---

[1] From "Rhymes of Childhood," by James Whitcomb Riley. Used by permission of the Bobbs-Merrill Company.

Ex. II. Using such simple pictures and sounds as will be suggestive of the whole experience, write four or five short paragraphs about the first day of school; about a snowstorm; about a thaw; about the coming of spring or autumn; about a bright summer day; about a very cold winter day; about a thunderstorm. The teacher and the pupils should discuss together one of these subjects.

8. THE FRIENDLY LETTER.

In preparing for college your older brother or sister may be reading some of the essays of Thomas Babington Macaulay, who was a noted English historian and essayist. You have perhaps read "Horatius at the Bridge" or other of the "Lays of Ancient Rome."

The following letter [1] was written by the boy Macaulay when thirteen years old, just after he had been sent from his home to Mr. Preston's school at Shelford, England:

Shelford, Feb. 22d, 1813.

My dear Papa: — As this is a whole holiday I can not find a better time for answering your letter. . . .

In my learning I do Xenophon every day, and twice a week the "Odyssey," in which I am classed with Wilberforce, whom all the boys allow to be very clever, very droll, and very impudent. We do Latin verses twice a week, and I have not yet been laughed at, as Wilberforce is the only one who hears them. . . . We are exercised also once a week in English composition, and once in Latin composition. . . . We get by heart Greek grammar or Virgil every evening. . . .

My room is a delightful, snug little chamber, which nobody can enter, as there is a trick about opening the door. I sit like a king, with my writing desk before me, . . . my books on one side, my box of papers on the other, with my arm chair and my candle; for every boy has a candlestick . . . of his own. . . .

Your affectionate son,

THOMAS B. MACAULAY.

[1] From Volume I. of Trevelyan's "Life and Letters of Lord Macaulay."

Exercise.

Does this letter sound as much like ordinary conversation as the former one? In length of sentences how does it compare? May this explain the answer to the first question? Notice that *Odyssey* is inclosed in quotation marks (" "). What in the letter on page 228 is thus inclosed? Are the two in any way alike? Notice that in different places four periods are found. The first of these is for punctuation, while the other three are to indicate that something of the original letter has been omitted.

9. RULES FOR COMPOSITION.

Inclose in quotation marks (" ") the names of books, of papers and magazines, and of vessels.[1]

Inclose in quotation marks the exact words of another when you include them within your own writing.

Exercises.

Ex. I. *Considering the following paragraph as your own composition, insert the necessary quotation marks:*

I see by the Pittsburg Times that the author of The Lean Years has gone abroad on the Philadelphia, accompanied by the editor of the New World. It is said that they contemplate the purchase of the London Collegian as well as the Old Century Magazine. When asked about this just before sailing, Mr. Blank stated that he could make public only the fact that they expect to return on the Majestic early in January; that while in London they hope to meet the author of The Jungle Book, and the editor of the London Times, and to see Henry Irving in King Lear.

Ex. II. Write a letter to a friend telling him of your companions, of your work at school, of your room at home, and of the bright saying or reply of a companion. Use his exact words. Do not forget quotation marks and other punctuation marks. Write short sentences. Make known when and where the letter is written.

[1] Italics, indicated in writing by underscoring once, are sometimes used instead of quotation marks.

10. THE FRIENDLY LETTER.

This time read a letter[1] written by Robert Louis Stevenson when he was a boy about fifteen. Later he became an English author, who is particularly noted for the beauty and perfection of his writing. He wrote essays that you will wish to read when you are older, as well as stories, poems, and many interesting books for both young and old.

Here is the letter, written from a famous watering place in southwestern England:

> 2 Sulyarde Terrace, Torquay,
> Thursday, April —, 1866.

Respected paternal Relative: — I write to make a request of the most moderate nature. Every year I have cost you an enormous, nay, elephantine, sum of money for drugs and physician's fees, and the most expensive time of the twelve months was March.

But this year the biting Oriental blasts, the howling tempests, and the general ailments of the human race have been successfully braved by yours truly.

Does not this deserve remuneration?

I appeal to your charity, I appeal to your generosity, I appeal to your justice, I appeal to your accounts, I appeal, in fine, to your purse.

My sense of generosity forbids the receipt of more, my sense of justice forbids the receipt of less, than half a crown.

Greeting, from, Sir, your most affectionate and needy son,

R. STEVENSON.

Exercise.

To whom is this letter written? Is the language such as the boy would use if he were asking his father orally for half a crown (63 cents)? Why does he use the long words and the high-sounding phrases? Would you call this a serious or a mock-serious

---

[1] From Volume I. of "Letters of Robert Louis Stevenson," by Sidney Colvin.

style? Why does he insert the plea that he has caused no expense in the way of physician's fees? Meaning of *Oriental*, of *remuneration*, and of *accounts?*

11. RULE FOR PUNCTUATION.

Notice the apostrophe and *s* ('s) added to the word *physician* in the above exercise. Why is it there? From this we draw the following rule:

Add an apostrophe and *s* ('s) when writing the possessive form of the noun, except when the noun is plural and ends in *s*. Then the apostrophe alone is added (Gr. 73, p. 122); as, *physician's;* but *three boys' hats*.

Exercises.

Ex. I. *Insert the necessary apostrophes:*

Johns father said that he might go to the mens shop and try to find the childrens books, after which he might go to the two boys home for an hour. He must then go to the grocers to ask about his mothers purchases, and to the confectioners to order the bon-bons for his sisters party. On his way home he must stop at Mr. Browns and then at Mr. Rosss, asking at each place for the owners permission to remove the leaves from his lawn.

Ex. II. Write a note to your mother asking for half a dollar, using the language you would use in talking to her. State the purpose.

Write a note to your father asking for a dollar to go to the county fair, adopting a mock-serious style and making use of some nonsensical plea.

Examine these notes and also the letters and compositions previously written, and see whether you have observed all the rules for composition and punctuation that have so far been given.

Ex. III. When you get up some morning you find that your father has already gone to work and that your mother is so ill you will have to stay at home to help care for the younger children. Write a note to your teacher, stating these facts. In the note use the same language you would use if you were standing at her desk telling her about it. Strive to be as free and natural.

Never be frightened by a sheet of paper and a pen or pencil. *Never try to write unless you have something definite in mind about which to write*, and then say it as easily and as freely as you would say it when talking. An effort is made in this book to give only such subjects as appeal directly to experiences you have had, and consequently subjects about which you have definite thoughts.

12. THE ARTIST.
After the Painting by Von Toussaint.

Ex. I. What is in the lower left corner of the picture? Why has the boy his cap on? Where did he get the crayon or charcoal with which he is making his picture? What does the expression of his face seem to tell about his feelings? Does he know that grandma is behind him? Whose portrait is he drawing? How do you know? Why has the smaller girl forgotten all about her dolly? What does her expression seem to suggest? Why is her thumb at her lips?

Assume the position and expression of the larger girl as nearly as possible, — body, face, hands, fingers. Does your position now seem to kindle any feeling within you? What feeling does the girl's face suggest? If she were wanting grandmother to come would her fingers be in the position they are in? In what position, then? Does grandma approve or disapprove of her new portrait? Why your answer? Does the position of her hands tell anything of her moods or feelings? Suppose she were in some other mood, how would she be holding her hands? Illustrate with your own hands. What has grandma been doing?

Are these people poor, rich, or in moderate circumstances? Is there anything to tell whether this is a scene in the United States? Do you think these children are as a rule good or naughty? Why?

Ex. II. Tell a story suggested by this picture. Tell, if you wish, of the events that have just preceded the moment pictured, and the events that follow soon after; or tell an entirely imaginary story in which these children are introduced. If you prefer, tell of some experience of your own in making pictures. Write the story.

THE ARTIST.

13. THREE BOYS AND A DOG.

One day while I was at the seashore I found my cousin Walter and his friend Dave playing on the beach. With them was Trixey, Walter's dog. He seemed quite tired out, as he had been swimming in the surf and going after sticks that Dave threw into the water.

Walter was afraid to let him go again, but Dave kept him going until the poor little animal was fairly trembling with cold and fatigue. As he came dragging his stick up the sand and laid it at Walter's feet the little master hugged him and said, "There, now; that's enough. You shan't go any more."

"Oh, bother! What a silly boy you are! It won't hurt him any. What are you afraid of?" scolded Dave.

"Don't send him again. It's cruel to urge him when he doesn't want to go," said Phil, another boy that now came running up.

"Oh, go on! Don't you be so wise!" sneered Dave. "There, Trixey, just once more! Good dog! Go on, now!" and he flung the stick far out into the surf. Quick as thought the little spaniel was plunging after it.

"Don't let him go! He's too tired, and I'm afraid the surf is too strong for him," pleaded Walter.

"Oh, Trixey, come back!" he called, and the faithful little creature, obedient to his master, turned and started for the shore.

"He shan't come back! I am going to make him get that stick. Go on, there!" shouted Dave, throwing a stone after the dog.

His aim was only too true. The stone hit the struggling creature on the head, and he disappeared under the water, and the strong current from the shore carried him out to sea. — *School Work*.

Exercises.

Ex. I. With which paragraph does the incident proper begin? What then is the purpose of the first paragraph? Is the introduction easy and natural? How are the different speeches separated from one another? Notice how the quotation marks are used in the third paragraph and in the fourth. How are they used in the fifth? In the other paragraphs? Notice the use of *oh* to show feeling. How is it spelled? What mark of punctuation follows it? What different feelings are here expressed by it? What different expressions are used to correspond with *said* in the second paragraph? Is the conclusion a part of the incident proper or a mere final thought added by the writer?

Why did Walter hug the dog? Tell your opinion of each of these boys.

Ex. II. Write in the form of a conversation an imaginary incident in which these three boys take part. Make each speech a separate paragraph. Watch the quotation marks. Use another word than *said* when mentioning the speaker.

Write of an incident you have seen in which several boys or girls take part. Use conversation. Change what they really said if by doing so you can make it sound better.

Tell the story of an experience of your own playing on the beach at the seaside, or along a small stream or river.

14. WORDS TO WATCH.

Oh, followed usually by a comma, occasionally by an exclamation point, should be used in all ordinary cases of emotion, both when the word precedes a name used in address, and when it is used merely as an exclamation.

O should be used only in a spirit of solemnity. Then it should be followed either by a noun in the case of address or by the expression of a wish. It should never be followed by a mark of punctuation.

As children are practically never under the solemn spell calling for *O*, they should use *oh*.

Write " O grave! where is thy victory!" " O mortal men! be wary how ye judge!" " O for that high nobility!"

But write " Oh, what a good time we did have!" " Oh, mother, may I go to the picnic?" " Oh, the roads were really awful!" " Oh, Mary, papa is going to take me with him to Chicago." " And when we reached there, oh, we were almost covered with mud!"

15 WHAT A BOY DID.

Ex. I. You have seen a boy do something that made you like him. In as simple and clear a manner as possible tell the teacher and the class about the act. Try to mention all the details, the little things, that were helpful in causing you to like him; omit all the details that were not helpful. If you repeat anything that the boy said, use his exact words. Remember that the plainest language is the best. Talk as freely and as frankly as though you were telling your father or mother.

Ex. II. Write an account of the act told of as directed in the exercise above, using as nearly as possible the same words. Do not write until you have told it orally either in class or at home. Be careful to use capital letters, periods, interrogation points, and quotation marks correctly.

After you have finished writing, read aloud what you have written, either to some one else or to yourself. If any sentences do not sound well, try to improve them.

16. SUGGESTION IN LITERATURE.

In 2 (p. 226) we learn of a little girl who pumped a drink for a dog. We like her because of this act. We feel that she often is kind, both to people and to animals. In fact, we feel that she always tries to be kind.

In other words, this single act *suggests* to us the kind of girl she is; that is, it suggests her *character*.

So the act of which you have told and written in 15, made you like the boy who did it by causing you to feel that if he performed one such act he would perform many others similar to it. That act suggested the kind of boy he is; it suggested his character.

In the same way a single mean, cowardly act has made

you dislike a boy. You feel that he will do other similar acts. His act suggests the kind of boy he is, suggests a character very different from that of the little girl told of in 2 and of the boy written of in the last lesson.

The things people like and the things they do *because they like to do them* make us know the kind of people they are; make us know their *characters*.

In life such suggestions, or hints, are almost daily making us *feel* that we like or dislike people. So in literature authors tell of the acts of their boys and girls, of their men and women, in order to *suggest* the kind of people they are and thus to make us like or dislike them.

Literature is full of suggestions, or hints, of this kind. Boys and girls, therefore, in order to read to the best advantage, must learn to understand easily and accurately the suggestions given by authors.

In the following selection the author makes several different persons do things that suggest character. Read the selection, notice whether you like or dislike the various persons, determine why, and see whether you *feel* what kind of people they are:

Oliver Horn.

Suddenly, while he was still resenting the familiarity of the constable, Oliver's ears were assailed by the cry of a dog in pain. Some street-boy had kicked him.

Oliver sprang forward as the dog crouched at his feet, caught him up in his arms, and started for the boys, who dodged behind the tree-trunks, calling "Spad, spad," as they ran. Then came the voice of the same constable.

"Hi, you can't bring that dog in here."

"He is not my dog. Somebody has hurt him," said Oliver in an indifferent tone, examining carefully the dog's legs to see whether any bones were broken.

"If that ain't your dog what are you doin' with him? See here:

I've been watchin' you. You've got to move on or I'll run you in. Do you hear?"

Oliver's eyes flashed. In all his life no man had ever doubted his word, nor had any one ever spoken to him in such terms.

"You can do as you please, but I will take care of this dog, no matter what happens. You ought to be ashamed of yourself to see him hurt, and not want to protect him. You're a pretty kind of an officer." — *Adapted from F. Hopkinson Smith's " The Fortunes of Oliver Horn"; used by permission of Charles Scribner's Sons.*

Exercises.

Ex. I. What do the street-boys do? What *character* do these acts suggest? What does Oliver do? What kind of boy is he? What do you learn about the character of the policeman?

In answering the above questions, make your answers the same as they would be if you had seen the acts yourself. Have you seen similar things done? Tell of them in class. Tell exactly what conclusions you reached about the character of the persons doing them.

How do you suppose Oliver treats his father and mother? His brothers and sisters? His own dog and his sister's kittens? His companions? How do you think he acts in school?

Ex. II. With what kind of letter does each sentence in the narrative begin? Why does *Spad* begin with a capital letter? With what mark of punctuation does each sentence end? Notice that each of the sentences ending with a period (.) makes a statement, while each ending with an interrogation point (?) asks a question. *Somebody has hurt him* is a statement. Why is it not followed by a period?

Examine all the quotation marks (" ") used. Tell why each pair is used. Why is there one at the end of the third paragraph? Why is there not one at the end of the fourth paragraph? Are the punctuation marks within or without the quotation marks?

Notice that in the conversation each separate speech forms a paragraph. Would it be more easily or less easily understood if all of the conversation were in one paragraph? How many words are in the longest sentence in the narrative?

Ex. III. Do you ever use the form *can't?* The form *ain't?* Of what words are these contractions? Which of the two is correct when used in conversation? What does the apostrophe (') stand for in the words *'re, doin', and watchin'?* Even in conversation would it not be better to say *are?* Do not omit the final *g* in words ending in *ing.* Never use the form "ain't" and *never fail to pronounce the final letter in words that end in "ing."*

17. RULES FOR CAPITALIZATION, PUNCTUATION, AND COMPOSITION.

Begin every proper noun with a capital letter.

Begin every independent sentence with a capital letter.

Begin every complete exact quotation with a capital letter.

Put a period (.) at the end of a complete declarative (statement-making) sentence.

Put an interrogation point (?) at the end of an interrogative (question-asking) sentence.

Use the apostrophe (') to indicate the omission of a letter or letters; as, he's for he is.

Use the hyphen (-) between the parts of a compound word; as, street-boy.

Use the hyphen (-) *after a syllable* at the end of a line, when part of the word must be written or printed at the beginning of the next line. Be sure that the hyphen comes at the end of a syllable. The hyphen is never used between the letters of a word of only one syllable. The letters of such a word must all be on one line.

Exercises.

Ex. I. Examine the letters and compositions you have written, and correct any violations of the rules so far given.

Ex. II. Tell of an incident seen by yourself somewhat similar to that told of in the selection under 16. Write the story.

To the Teacher. Have several of these compositions written on the blackboard, including some containing the "exact words" of the person with whom the composition deals. Have the class examine them for violations of the rules thus far given. Opposite a line containing an error place the number indicating the principle violated (see pages 343–345) and let each pupil discover and correct the mistake. Compositions should all be written with a wide margin at the right that this plan may be followed when indicating errors. The pupil should then make his corrections in red, and the paper should be examined a second time to learn whether the corrections have been properly made. Unless it is possible for the teacher to mark all papers the plan of blackboard correction should be used frequently.

18. THE FORM OF LETTERS.

A letter perfect in form contains the following parts:

The Heading. — This includes the complete post-office address of the writer and the date on which the letter is written.

The Address. — This includes the name and the complete post-office address of the person to whom the letter is written.

The Salutation. — This is the word or phrase of address used in beginning the body of the letter. In a friendly letter the salutation may be *My dear Cousin*, *My dear Virginia*, *Dear Uncle John*, etc.; in a business letter *to an individual* it should be *Dear Sir* or *My dear Sir;* in a business letter *to a firm or company* it should be *Gentlemen*. Notice when *dear* begins with a small letter.

The Body of the Letter. — This consists of the communication made to the person to whom the letter is written.

The Closing Phrase. — This is the word or phrase just preceding the name of the writer. In a friendly letter it may be *Your loving cousin*, *Your sincere friend*, *Yours affectionately*, etc.; in a business letter it should be *Yours respectfully*, *Yours most respectfully*, *Very respectfully yours*, or the like. Which word begins with a capital?

The Signature. — This is the name of the person writing. In business letters and in all other letters except those to members of one's own family the full name should be used. In family letters it is permissible to use only the given name or even a nickname. When writing *to a firm or to a stranger* a woman should sign her name thus:

(*Miss*) *Elizabeth Noman* (if unmarried).

Elizabeth Noman
(*Mrs. John Y. Noman*) } (write both, if married).

(*Mrs.*) *Elizabeth Noman* (if a widow).

Exercises.

Ex. I. *In the following business letter give the proper name to each of the different parts:*

Crafton, Allegheny Co., Pa.,
Oct. 27, 1902.

American Book Co.,
  100 Washington Square,
    New York, N.Y.

          Gentlemen: — Inclosed find money order for Fifty-six cents ($.56), for which please send me a copy of Rolfe's edition of Shakespeare's "Hamlet."

Yours respectfully,
JOHN Y. NOMAN.

Ex. II. Notice again the punctuation of each of the different parts. What punctuation marks follow *Co* and *Pa* and why? What punctuation mark follows the salutation? If the body of the letter begins on the line below the salutation, only the colon (:) is used, the dash (—) being omitted. Write the letter in this form.

19. RULES FOR PUNCTUATION.

Follow every abbreviation with a period.

Use a colon (:) after the salutation in a letter when the body of the letter begins on the following line. When it begins on the same line, follow the colon with a dash (:—).

Exercises.

Ex. I. *Write the abbreviations for each of the months, for each of the States of the Union, and for the following phrases, words, and titles:*

And so forth; County; Mister; Mistress (usually pronounced Missis); Honorable; Member of Congress; Master of Arts; Reverend; Doctor; Doctor of Philosophy; Doctor of Laws; Professor; Governor.

Ex. II. *Prepare perfect letter forms, using the following facts:*

F. H. Williams, living at 1800 Fifth Avenue, Pittsburg, Pennsylvania, writes on the 2nd of January, of the present year, to George F. Thuma, who lives in Kittanning, Armstrong County, Pennsylvania. Use the proper abbreviations, and punctuate and arrange correctly.

George F. Thuma writes to F. H. Williams thirty days later.

Sarah T. Arond writes to Perry Mason & Co., 201 Columbus Avenue, Boston, Massachusetts, from her home at 24 White Street, Station D, Pittsburg, Pennsylvania, on the 5th of December, 1901.

Perry Mason and Company write to Sarah T. Arond thirty days later.

F. J. Smith's wife, Martha, writes on August 23d, 1902, to J. K. Maintenon and Company, who do business at 17 Rue de l'Opéra, Paris, France.

A month later J. K. Maintenon and Company write to Mrs. Smith.

Ex. III. Cut slips of paper into the form of an envelope (6½ by 3½ inches) and address each of the above letters in the proper form, as shown below and on the next page. Near the upper right-hand corner outline a place for the stamp. Always put the stamp on this part of the envelope, as the government machines are made to cancel at this place.

American Book Company,
100 Washington Square,
New York,
N. Y.

> Messrs. E. F. Anderson & Co.,
> 305 Diamond St.,
> Chicago,
> Ill.

> Mr. John Y. Noman,
> Crafton,
> Allegheny Co.,
> Pa.

TO THE TEACHER. In correcting these letters and envelopes, keep in mind the additional rules for punctuation given in 19.

20. WORDS TO WATCH.

Don't is a contraction for *do not*.
Doesn't is a contraction for *does not*.

Exercise.

Insert the proper contraction:

He _____ know the way. We _____ wish to go. They _____ care for heat. You _____ know where they have gone. It _____ make any difference to us. She _____ seem to like to go to school. The men ———— stay after 4 o'clock. In the evening she ———— go out alone. To love one's neighbor ———— mean to hate one's self. The wheat ———— seem ready to cut.

WARNING. Say *he doesn't, she doesn't,* and *it doesn't,* rather than *he don't, she don't,* and *it don't.*

21. WORN OUT.

After the Painting by Faed.

Ex. I. Where in the house is this room? How many rooms are occupied by this family? What is the relation of the man to the child? What on the floor behind the man seems to suggest his trade? Has he probably been working the day before the time here shown? What time of day is it now? What shows that it was yet dark when he went to sleep? How long probably did he watch before he fell asleep? Why has the candle been placed where it is? How much longer will the candle burn?

What two things in the picture tell that it has been a cold night? Why has the father removed his coat? How do you feel toward him for this? Why is the mouse in the picture? How long has it been very quiet in the room? Why has the artist put the flowers on the window-sill and the violin on the wall? What is in the man's right hand? What is beside the bowl on the floor? What evidently was the man doing just before he dropped asleep? What is probably in the bowl? Was it for the child or the man? Why has it been left thus on the floor? What is in the pitcher behind the man?

Is there anything that indicates that the child's mother is dead? What has been left undone that a mother would probably have attended to? Why is the child's right hand where it is? What are the fingers doing? Why? What one detail in the child's expression seems especially to show that he is very ill? But what makes us feel that he will get well? How long has he been sleeping quietly?

Why has the artist made the bright light fall just where it does?

Ex. II. Tell and then write a story suggested by this picture.

Write an account of some illness of your own, or of one of your family or friends.

Worn Out.

22. THE FRIENDLY LETTER.

Friendly and social letters may contain all the parts of the perfect letter form, but very often the address is omitted. In case a friendly or social letter is of special importance, however, the address should be inserted.

The following is the proper form for informal friendly and social letters:

Lakeville, N.Y., July 17, 1903.

My dear Father:

[Body of Letter.]

Yours with love,
Junior.

Exercise.

Write a letter to your cousin or friend telling of something done by one of your companions which seems to you to suggest his character. Write from your own home. Punctuate all the parts as above.

Write a letter to your father or mother, who is visiting at 258 Thirty-second Street, Chicago, Illinois, telling that you have recently become acquainted with Oliver Horn, and explaining why you like him.

Write a letter to your cousin James, whose address is Rural Free Delivery 27, Mayville, Chautauqua County, New York, telling him how Oliver defended the dog and asking him how he treats the various animals about the farm. Use proper abbreviations. Cut envelope as in Comp. **19**, Ex. III., and address it.

Write a letter to Perry Mason and Company (see Comp. **19**), inclosing a dollar and seventy-five cents for " The Youth's Companion " for one year beginning with next January. Cut and address envelope.

23. A GENTLEMAN.

Read carefully the following selection. What suggestion of character do you find in it?

My grandfather came to see my mother once at about this time and visited the mills. When he had entered our room and looked around for a moment, he took off his hat and made a low bow to the girls, first to the right, and then towards the left. . . . We had never seen anybody bow to a room full of mill girls in that polite way, and some one of the family afterwards asked him why he did so.

He looked a little surprised at the question, but answered promptly and with dignity, " I always take off my hat to ladies."

— *Lucy Larcom in " A New England Girlhood."*

Exercises.

Ex. I. Tell the class or a friend of an act performed by an aged person suggestive of his character. It may show a thoughtful and lovable nature, or one of a very different kind. Perhaps you can tell of several incidents suggesting different kinds of character.

Ex. II. Write an account of one of these incidents, using much the same language as that used when you told of it.

Write a letter to some aged relative or friend, telling of an incident suggesting the lovable nature of an old lady or gentleman. If possible tell of an incident that you have seen.

Ex. III. What mark of punctuation just precedes the quoted words of the grandfather in the above? What mark of punctuation precedes or follows the quoted words in the following sentences?

1. *Nathan said to David, "Thou art the man."*
2. *" Our antagonist is our helper," says Burke.*
3. *" There are more men ennobled by study," says Cicero, " than by nature."*

How does the punctuation of the last sentence differ from the punctuation of the others? Notice the quotation marks.

From these illustrations we derive the following rule:

24. RULE FOR PUNCTUATION.

Set off a brief quotation from the rest of the sentence by a comma or by commas.

Exercise.

Make sentences using the following quotations. In each case put the words you add, first before and then after the quotation, and when possible put them within the quotation, as in the third illustrative sentence in Ex. III., p. 251.

1. They never fail who die in a great cause. — *Byron.*
2. Talkers are not good doers.
3. Some temptations come to the industrious, but all temptations attack the idle. — *Spurgeon.*
4. Thought takes man out of servitude into freedom. — *Emerson.*
5. Time wasted is existence, used is life. — *Young.*
6. Lack of desire is the greatest riches. — *Seneca.*
7. The only jewel that you can carry beyond the grave is wisdom. — *Langford.*
8. A man must either imitate the vicious or hate them.

— *Montaigne.*

TO THE TEACHER. Have several compositions read in class each day, asking pupils to tell what kind of person is suggested. In the manner already outlined (p. 243; see also p. 343), correct as many papers as possible. Often resort to blackboard corrections, requiring all pupils to write an improved form for each error pointed out.

25. BUSINESS LETTERS.

Read carefully the following business letter:

Maizeville, N.Y., March 1, 1902.

Robert Durham, Esq.,
    105 Fifth St.,
        New York, N.Y.

Dear Sir:

    I have a place that will suit you, I think. It can be bought at about the figure you name. Come and see it. I shan't crack it up, but want you to judge for yourself.

Respectfully yours,

John Jones.

Exercise.

What in this letter suggests the character of John Jones? What kind of man do you think he is? Why have you this idea? What sort of man will write the last sentence of the letter? Would you have liked him more or less if he had told of all the advantages and attractions of the farm he wishes to sell? If he had told of both its advantages and disadvantages? Does he suggest either? How?

Do you consider *crack it up* an expression that should be used by educated people? Give the reason for your answer. Note the use of the word *place*. Do not use it in this meaning. Say *farm* or *home*.

26. RULES FOR COMPOSITION.

From the above exercise we may draw the following rules:

Avoid the use of slang, both in conversation and in written work.
Use a word only in the meaning in which it is used by the majority of educated writers and speakers.

Exercise.

Write a letter to William Finland, who lives in Sharon, Mercer County, Pa., telling him of a dog you have for sale. Try to impress him so favorably that he will wish to buy the dog. Will you suggest or declare its good points? Be careful to make the letter complete in form and perfect in punctuation, capitalization, and spelling.

Write a letter to Margaret Manning, who lives in Brockwayville, Jefferson County, Pennsylvania, telling of canary birds you have for sale.

Write a letter to some person you know, telling of something you really have for sale.

27. WORDS TO WATCH.

Affect means *to act upon, to influence*.
Effect means *to bring about, to accomplish*.

Exercise.

Insert the proper word:

The change was _____ after a long struggle. **Did the failure** _____ your business? Will you be able to _____ your purpose? How little did his death _____ his family! He undertook to _____ a consolidation of all the glass manufactories.

28. THE STORY OF A TRIP.

Every boy and girl, after a trip to the woods, to a friend's, to grandmother's, or after any other pleasant outing, wishes, when again at home, to tell of the pleasures of the day. To give an outline of the trip is not enough. There is no interest in an account that simply amounts to "We started, we reached there, we stayed till dusk, and we came home." The details — the little events that excited your delight, your fear, your merriment, that made the day pleasant or unpleasant — are the points that give interest. The things you did, the sights you saw, the sounds you heard, — tell of these and you put life into your story, you make it real. Contrasts, too, help to give interest: the gloom of the forest contrasted with the sunshine of the meadow; the despair of the person you met contrasted with your own feeling of delight; the hovel and the great farmhouse; the hot sunshine and the cool shade; your own warmth and the cool spring; the dusty road and the rippling stream. In telling such a story the various events should be given in their proper order.

Exercise.

First orally, and then in writing, tell the story of a day's outing, trying to observe the suggestions given above.

29. THE FOREIGN GENTLEMAN.[1]

Read the following selection, watching carefully for every character suggestion :

"As I went down stairs soon after, I saw something I liked. The flights are very long in this tall house, and as I stood waiting at the head of the third for a little servant-girl to climb slowly up, I saw a gentleman come along behind her, take the heavy hod of coal out of her hand, carry it all the way up, put it down at the door near by, and walk away, saying, with a kind nod and a foreign accent,

"'It goes better so. The little back is too young for such a weight.'

"Wasn't it good of him? I like such things, for, as father says, trifles show character.

—*Adapted from Louisa M. Alcott in " Little Women."*

Exercises.

Ex. I. What kind of person employs the little servant-girl, judging from the work the child must do? What of the character of the foreign gentleman? What feeling have you toward Jo, the young girl who tells of the incident and who is so pleased with it?

Ex. II. Notice that each of the paragraphs begins with quotation marks. The selection is from a letter written by Jo and quoted by Miss Alcott in her book. She, quoting it, puts it in quotation marks. As the letter consists of a number of paragraphs, she puts the quotation marks at the beginning of each paragraph, but at the end of only the last. Why, then, are there no quotation marks after the last paragraph quoted here?

Notice further that the second paragraph is within single quotation marks (' '). When Jo wrote the letter what marks did she put around this paragraph? The rule is that a quotation within a quotation should be inclosed in single quotation marks.

---

[1] This and later selections from Miss Alcott's "Little Women" are used by permission of Little, Brown and Company, Boston.

Why would it be less easy to get the meaning if the comma following *after* were omitted? The clause *As I went down stairs soon after* is really restrictive, or necessary in order to get the writer's full meaning, and as such it should not be separated from the rest of the sentence by a comma. But to add clearness, to avoid a possibility of at first giving a wrong idea, the comma is used.

30. RULES FOR PUNCTUATION.

When a passage consisting of several paragraphs is quoted, place quotation marks at the beginning of each paragraph, but at the end of none except the last.

A quotation within a quotation should be inclosed within single quotation marks (' ').

Use a comma whenever, by appealing to the eye, it will make the meaning of a sentence clearer.

Exercise.

Tell in class and then write a paragraph about some act of kindness you have seen a man or a woman do for a boy or girl.

Tell in class and then write a paragraph about some act you have seen showing a kind of character opposite to that suggested in the last selection.

In the next letter you write to a friend tell of something showing character.

31. TELEGRAMS.

When a telegram is to be sent there is no time to stop to learn how to send it. Therefore boys and girls should become familiar with the details connected with the sending of telegrams, and should have some practice in condensing messages to the rate-limit of ten words. The meaning, however, must be clear, no matter how many words may be required.

The telegraph form, which is found lying on the counter

in the telegraph office, has blanks for the date of the message, for the name and address of the person to whom it is sent, for the message proper, and for the name of the sender. The lines for the message are generally divided into five equal parts, the intention being that a single word shall be written within each division, thus enabling the operator to count the words with speed and accuracy. The following is an illustration of a message ready to hand to the operator:

December 24, 1902.

J. H. Johnson,
    133 Ellicott Square,
        Buffalo, N.Y.

| Unexpected | vacation. | Will | be | home |
| at | eleven. | Friend | with | me. |

                                    FRED F. JOHNSON.

Exercise.

For each of the following telegrams make a blank like the one shown. Try to put each message into ten words or fewer. The address and signature are not counted in the number of words.

Write a telegram to your father stating that your brother is in the Bellevue Hospital in New York, having been thrown under a car and having had his foot crushed. Ask your father to come at once.

Write a telegram to American Book Company, 100 Washington Square, New York, asking them to send you at once by Adams Express thirty copies of this book and thirty copies of Baldwin's "Fifty Famous Stories Retold."

Your best friend has won a prize of $25 in the annual prize essay contest of the Carnegie Museum, Pittsburg, Pa. Send him a telegram of congratulation, and state that you will pass through Pittsburg this evening on the seven o'clock train from Chicago to New York.

Send a telegram to your uncle, C. M. Miles, Atlanta, Ga., telling him of the death of F. H. Doyle, and stating that the funeral will be Thursday afternoon at 2 o'clock.

Telegraph to your grandmother at 9 Sixby Street, Harrisburg, Pa., that your house burned last night, that you all escaped safe, that everything was destroyed, and that you will all leave on the ten-thirty train to-morrow morning to stay with her till other arrangements can be made.

32. HOW TO PLAY A GAME.

EXERCISE. Tell in a paragraph how to play some game with which you are familiar. Choose a simple one. Connect your account of the game with a picnic or a party. Tell it so that you will have to use quotation marks.

Write a letter to a friend, asking for full directions for playing the game you took part in last Thursday night at her home. Explain that you are going to a party at your aunt's in the country, and that you wish to be able to suggest this game, as you enjoyed it very much.

Write an answer to this letter.

33. A BOY'S SONG.

Where the pools are bright and deep,
Where the gray trout lies asleep,
Up the river and o'er the lea,
That's the way for Billy and me.

Where the blackbird sings the latest,
Where the hawthorn blooms the sweetest,
Where the nestlings chirp and flee,
That's the way for Billy and me.

Where the mowers mow the cleanest,
Where the hay lies thick and greenest;
There to trace the homeward bee,
That's the way for Billy and me.

Where the hazel-bank is steepest,
Where the shadow falls the deepest,
Where the clustering nuts fall free,
That's the way for Billy and me.

. . . .

But this I know: I love to play,
Through the meadow, among the hay;
Up the water and o'er the lea,
That's the way for Billy and me. —*James Hogg*.

Exercises.

Ex. I. Give the meaning of the following words as used in this poem: *lea, latest, hawthorn, nestlings, trace, homeward, deepest*. What are the four pictures in the first stanza? What pictures are found in the other stanzas? What sounds are introduced? With closed eyes try to see the various pictures. Try to hear the various sounds. Of the various pictures suggested, which do you like best?

Ex. II. Tell the class of a place that especially pleases you. It may be in the country, in the city, or in the suburbs; it may be along the highway or in the deep woods. Try to present simple, everyday pictures and sounds, as is done in the poem given. Write a description of the place in three or four short paragraphs.

34. RECEPTION OF COLUMBUS AT BARCELONA.
After the Painting by R. Balaca.

Ex. I. Where did the event pictured on the next page take place? Before whom? Who is the man seated on the platform? The woman? But at which man are most of the people in the picture looking? Who is this central figure? Why are they looking at him?

Judging from the position of his body and of his hands, what is Columbus doing? From what place has he recently returned? What in the picture assures you of this? What else shown in the picture has he brought back with him? What is on the floor that has been taken from the chest? At the left is a man on one knee; what is he doing?

Find all the people in the picture that are not looking at Columbus.

RECEPTION OF COLUMBUS AT BARCELONA.

At whom are most of them looking? Why? **What are the women at the left of the picture interested in?** At what are the Indians looking? Why? Which one of them is showing the greatest feeling? How?

How do you sit when you become deeply interested in what some one is saying? How is the king sitting? The queen? Which seems the more interested in the story Columbus is telling? Why your answer? Why, perhaps, has the artist represented the woman as leaning forward? What does the position of the king's head indicate? Where are the officers at the right and left of the dais looking? Are they supposed to look straight forward or to look about in every direction? In what is the boy at the queen's right interested? What would you be interested in if you were sitting in his chair?

Of what is the floor of this room made? What kind of windows let light into this room? What is hanging behind the king and queen? What is on the steps of the platform? What is under the chest and curiosities?

Who is the most commanding figure in this picture? Why has the artist made him taller and more noble-looking than any of the other men? How is he dressed? How are the other principal characters in the picture dressed?

Take a position similar to that in which Columbus is represented,—body, head, feet, hands. Similar to that of the queen; to that of the king; to that of the nearest Indian. Does the change in position result in any change in feeling? If so, try to state the different feelings.

Look at this picture in every part; then close your book and with eyes shut try to see it as clearly as you saw it with the book open. Do this again and again until you can see the picture clearly with closed eyes.

Ex. II. Tell an imaginary story about the little boy at the right of the queen; about one of the Indians.

Tell briefly a story you have read or heard about Columbus. Write the story.

Write an account of a visit you have made to a magnificent public building.

Give orally or in writing a description of this picture, first from memory and then with open book. Tell of the king and queen, of Columbus, of the Indians, of the curiosities, of the spectators, and finally of the room.

35. WORDS TO WATCH.

Get means *to obtain, to come into possession of.*
Have means *to own, to possess.*

The word *got*, a form of *get*, is often incorrectly used with *have* to indicate ownership or possession; as, *I have got a new suit* instead of *I have a new suit.* This usage should be avoided.

Get is also often used in such expressions as *I must get my lessons, I got sick, I have got to do it,* etc. This is using a general word where a special word will be much more precise. Say *I must learn my lessons, I became sick, I must do it,* etc. Keep the word *get* in all its forms for its precise meaning, *to obtain, to come into possession of.*

Exercises.

Ex. I. State the difference in meaning between *I have a new suit* and *I have got a new suit.*

Use correctly *get* (or *got*) in at least ten sentences.

Ex. II. *Use a more precise word than* **get** *or* **got** *in each of the following sentences:*

I got a new cap. I got a dollar for the dog. I have got cold. Get me a pair of shoes. They are going to get married. When did you get home? I have got the book you wished. May I get warm? Why don't you get him a doctor?

36. CHRISTMAS MORNING.

Christmas morning is a time of keenest interest to all boys and girls. Here is a little picture of a Christmas morning scene. Four girls, although without money to

ACTS THAT SHOW CHARACTER

give one another presents, determine each to remember their mother, their father being away with the army.

"There's mother. Hide the basket, quick!" cried Jo, as the door slammed and steps sounded in the hall.

Amy came in hastily, and looked rather abashed when she saw her sisters all waiting for her.

"Where have you been, and what are you hiding behind you?" asked Meg, surprised to see, by her hood and cloak, that lazy Amy had been out so early.

"Don't laugh at me, Jo! I didn't mean that any one should know until the time came. I meant only to change the little bottle [of perfumery] for a big one. I gave *all* my money to get it, and I'm truly trying not to be selfish any more."

As she spoke, Amy showed the handsome flask that replaced the cheap one, and looked so earnest and humble in her little effort to forget herself that Meg hugged her on the spot, and Jo pronounced her "a trump," while Beth ran to the window and picked her finest rose to ornament the stately bottle.

—*Adapted from Louisa M. Alcott in "Little Women."*

Exercises.

Ex. I. What do you conclude Amy had done first? Why? But what has she done this morning? How do you feel toward her for doing it? What do you think of Beth's act told of in the last line?

Notice the passage inclosed within brackets [ ]. When a person is quoting from another and wishes to insert in the quoted passage an explanation, the explanation is placed within brackets. Who has inserted this passage?

Ex. II. Tell and then write of an unselfish act at Christmas.
Tell of any Christmas event that comes clearly to your mind.
Write of an act performed on Christmas that seems to you selfish.

37. WHICH WAY SHALL I GO?

Boys and girls are often stopped on the street and asked to give directions to reach a certain place. Sometimes, even when they know just where the place is and just the streets to follow in order to reach it, they find it far from easy to give the desired directions.

A few exercises in writing directions will perhaps make you more ready and clear when you next have an opportunity thus to be of service to a stranger.

One principle must be observed in giving directions, and it may be expressed in two words: *Be clear!* A second principle is, *Be brief!* But never be brief at the expense of clearness.

When giving directions, begin at the point from which one is to start. Tell the number of blocks to go, the way to turn, and mention any landmarks that will be helpful, such as "sky-scrapers," fountains, statues, hotels, public buildings, etc., in the city, and groves, hills, farmhouses and barns, railroad crossings, mills, fields of corn or wheat, etc., in the country.

Exercise.

Tell me how to reach your home from the schoolhouse; how to reach the railway station from your home; how to reach the park from the best hotel in your city; how to find the home of a friend of yours, starting from your house; how to start from the city hall and reach a point that will require me to ride on two car lines.

Write directions for one or more of the journeys called for above.

Write directions for me to reach the home of a friend whom you occasionally visit in the country. Tell me how to find the station, where to leave the train, and how to go from that point to her home.

Write directions for me to go to the postoffice nearest your farm.

Write directions for me to reach the farm of friends living five miles from your farm.

PART II.

ACTS THAT SHOW FEELING. PUNCTUATION.

(To be studied in connection with Part II of the Grammar on pages 49–93.)

38. ACTS DUE TO FEELING.

The following selection contains some suggestions of a kind different from any yet considered. See whether you can discover them:

Heavy Hearts.

"That reminds me," said Meg, "that I've something to tell. It isn't funny, like Jo's story, but I thought about it a good deal as I came home. At the Kings' to-day I found everybody in a flurry, and one of the children said that her oldest brother had done something dreadful and her papa had sent him away. I heard Mrs. King crying and Mr. King talking very loud, and Grace and Ellen turned away their faces when they passed me, so I shouldn't see how red their eyes were. I didn't ask any questions, of course; but I felt very sorry for them, and was glad I hadn't any wild brothers to do wicked things and disgrace the family."

— *Louisa M. Alcott in "Little Women."*

Exercises.

Ex. I. Why was everybody in a flurry? Why was Mrs. King crying? Why was Mr. King talking loud? Why did Grace and Ellen turn their faces? Why were their eyes red? Why is there an apostrophe (') after the *s* in *Kings'*? Why the other apostrophes?

Ex. II. Tell in class exactly what you saw a boy do when his mother refused to let him go where he wished to go.

Tell in class what you saw a boy do when his father handed him a pair of new skates.

Tell in class what you saw a girl do when she was told she might take an unexpected pleasure trip.

Tell in class what you saw a woman do when she was told that the telegraph boy was at the door.

Tell in class what you saw a man do when he hit his finger with a hammer.

Tell in class what you saw a cat do when it found itself facing a strange dog.

Tell in class what you saw a pair of birds do when a boy began to climb the tree in which their nest was built.

Tell in class what you saw a girl do when she thought a dog was about to bite a child whom she had no possible means of helping.

39. MERTON'S PROMISE.

Read the following selection, watching for every suggestion:

"All right, Merton," I said; "you shall have the book and a breech-loading shotgun also. . . . "

The boy was almost overwhelmed. He came to me and took my hand in both his own.

"Oh, papa!" he faltered, and his eyes were moist, "did you say a gun?"

"Yes, a breech-loading gun on one condition, — that you'll not smoke till after you are twenty-one. A growing boy can't smoke with safety."

He gave my hand a quick, strong pressure, and was immediately at the farther end of the store, blowing his nose suspiciously. I chuckled to myself: "I want no better promise. A gun will cure him of cigarettes better than a tract would." — *Selected*.

Exercise.

Why was Merton almost overwhelmed? Why did he take his father's hand in both his own? Why did he falter when he began to speak? Why were his eyes moist? Why did he give his father's hand a quick, strong pressure? Why did he at once go to the farther end of the store? Why was he blowing his nose?

40. ACTS DUE TO FEELING.

The acts you told of in the second exercise of 38 were due to feeling. So, too, in 39 Merton's acts are all due to his feelings. He is surprised, for the promise comes unexpectedly; he is delighted, for a gun, long and eagerly wished for, has seemed an impossibility; he is thankful; he is appreciative. These feelings of surprise, delight, thankfulness, and appreciation are made known to us by what he does. The strength of these various feelings is shown by the fact that he rushes to the farther end of the store. He will not let his father see that he has lost his self-control, and that tears are on his cheeks.

Feelings, then, may be suggested by what one does. In fact, we are continually telling those about us what our feelings are, by the expression of the face, by the tones of the voice, by the motions of the head, of the hands, and of the body, and by the things we do. The last selection shows how such acts are used by authors.

We have seen that these acts make us know Merton's feelings. But we must not forget that acts as a rule make known character, or what a person always is. So from these acts, besides learning Merton's feelings, we also learn that he is a manly, sensitive boy, and we feel that as a rule he acts honorably and nobly. That is, the same acts that make us know his feelings also make us know his character.

We shall find, then, that acts often show both feelings and character.

Exercises.

Ex. I. From the selection in 39 what have you learned about Merton's father? What kind of man is he?

Notice how the quotation marks are used. Note that all explanations inserted by the writer are excluded from the quotation marks. Notice further that such explanations are set off from the quotation by means of commas or of other punctuation marks. Note again that each speech forms a paragraph by itself. What do the four periods at the end of the first paragraph mean? Notice that *Merton* and *papa* are set off by commas. They are words used in addressing a person, and such words are always set off by commas.

Ex. II. Write a conversation that you have heard between a son or daughter and mother or father, during which one of the speakers has acted in a way to suggest his feelings. For example, a boy has been refused permission to go somewhere or to do something; what did he say and how did he act? A father has brought his daughter a present; a father has told his son of a new bicycle, or of a trip to grandfather's, or of a hunting trip; a mother has told her daughter of friends who are coming, or of a Hallowe'en party, or of a new dress. *Be sure to write from experience.*

Correct this paper after it has been marked according to the plan on page 343.

41. SUGGESTION OF FEELINGS.

Ex. I. Turn to the selection on pages 241, 242, and examine it for suggestions of feelings, answering the following questions:

Why did Oliver spring forward? Why did the dog crouch at his feet? Why did Oliver catch the dog in his arms? Why did he start for the boys? Why did they dodge behind the tree-trunks? Why Oliver's indifferent tone? Why did his eyes flash? Why does he speak as he does to the officer?

Ex. II. Write a friendly letter to your cousin, making known character and feelings by means of things done. Tell of acts that you have seen. Make your letter a brief character sketch of a boy or girl you know. Try to select acts that show his character as you know it.

Be sure that in form and punctuation your letter is in harmony with the form given in **22,** p. 250.

Cut a slip of paper into the shape of an envelope and address this letter in proper form.

42. THE RESCUE.

Read the following selection, watching especially for acts suggestive of feelings:

Running as I never ran before, I followed, reached the bank where there was an eddy in the stream, sprang in up to my waist, and dragged them [Bobsey, the child who had fallen into the creek, and Junior, the lad who had jumped in and brought him to a shallow place] to solid ground. Merton and Winnie meanwhile stood near with white faces.

Bobsey was conscious, . . . and I was soon able to restore him so that he could stand on his feet and cry, "I — I — w — won't d — do so any — any more."

Junior, meanwhile, had . . . seated himself upon a rock, emptied the water out of his shoes, and was tying them on again, at the same time striving with all his might to maintain a stolid composure under Winnie's embraces and Merton's interrupted handshakings. But when, having become assured of Bobsey's safety, I rushed forward and embraced Junior, his lips began to quiver, and two great tears mingled with the water that was dripping from his hair. Suddenly he broke away, took to his heels, and ran towards his home, as if he had been caught in some mischief and the constable were after him.

I carried Bobsey home.

Mrs. Jones [Junior's mother] came over, and we made her rubicund face beam and grow more round, if possible, as we all praised her boy. I returned with her, for I felt that I wished to thank Junior again. But he saw me coming, and slipped out at the back door.

— *Adapted.*

Exercises.

Ex. I. Why did the father, who is telling the story, run so rapidly? Why did he spring in up to his waist? Was it necessary? Why the white faces? What is indicated by the dashes in Bobsey's sentence? Why did the father clasp him to his heart so tightly?

Is Junior's seating himself on the rock, etc., due to his feelings, to his character, or to both? Why does he try to maintain a stolid composure? Why the embraces and handshakings? Why the rush forward, etc.? Why the quiver of the lip and the tears? Why does Junior run home? Why did Mrs. Jones's face beam and grow rounder? Why did Junior slip out at the back door?

What do you conclude about the character of the father? Of Junior? Upon what do you base your opinion?

Ex. II. Tell the class or a friend of a more or less thrilling rescue you have made or seen.

Write an account of the same incident, using only short sentences. Try to be suggestive, to tell of acts that hint at feelings or character in all you write.

Tell or write of a boy or girl who exercised self-control when under some especially strong feeling, — when hurt, when embarrassed, when nervous, when delighted, when frightened. Be sure to include all the suggestive details which made you know his feeling and which showed how he was trying to conceal it.

43. MOZART AND HIS SISTER BEFORE MARIA THERESA.
After the Painting by Borckmann.

Ex. I. How many persons are shown in this picture? How many are women? How many are children? At which persons are all the others looking? Why? Who are the children at the piano? How old do you judge they are? Why your answer? What are the books on the floor? For what are they there?

Maria Theresa was empress of Germany. Which figure here represents her? Which of the women seems most richly dressed? Why are several of the company leaning forward? Why is the hand of the woman near the center lifted, and her fingers outspread?

What do the various things used in furnishing and decorating this room make known about its owners? What is suggested by the dress of the various persons? Why have most of them white hair? How are the children dressed? Which one has white hair?

Why is this a supreme moment in the lives of these children? What will be the result if this company approve of their music?

How great a musician did this boy become? How long ago did he live?

Ex. II. Write an imaginary story about a day in the lives of these children.

Write a story of an experience of your own in connection with music lessons or with a musical performance.

MOZART AND HIS SISTER BEFORE MARIA THERESA.

Write an account of an experience of your own watching a parade or the passing of a band; or give such an account orally.

Write an account of some important event or day in your own life.

Write or give orally a description of this picture.

44. POSTAL CARDS.

EXERCISE. Cut a slip of heavy paper or cardboard $3\frac{1}{4}$ by $5\frac{1}{2}$ inches. This represents a United States postal card. On one side indicate the place for the stamp near the upper right corner. On this side address your card to Joseph Howe Company, Penn Avenue and Fifth Street, Columbus, O. Use proper abbreviations, and punctuate and capitalize correctly. On the other side, writing the long way of the card, ask this firm to send you a copy of their latest catalogue. Will it be necessary on a postal card to include that part of the perfect letter form called the Address? Why your answer? Will it be correct to omit any other parts of the perfect letter form?

Write another postal card, this time asking the postmaster at Clarion, Clarion County, Pennsylvania, to forward to you at your home address any letters for you that may be sent to his office. In addressing the card, in place of the man's name use the words "Post Master."

45. WORDS TO WATCH.

Lend is always a verb, and *should never be used as a noun.*
Loan is usually a noun, and *should rarely be used as a verb.*

Exercises.

Ex. I. *Insert the proper word:*

Will you ———— me your knife? He received the watch as a ————, not as a gift. ———— me a dollar.

Ex. II. In sentences, use each of these words correctly three times.

Ex. III. Turn to Composition **28,** page 254, and note again the suggestions made there for giving a narrative life and reality. Then write an account of some recent trip you have taken.

46. THE HEROISM OF JOHN BINNS.

Thirteen years have passed since, but it is all to me as if it had happened yesterday — the clanging of the fire bells, the hoarse shouts of the firemen, the wild rush and terror of the streets; then the great hush that fell upon the crowd; the sea of upturned faces with the fire glow upon it; and up there, against the background of black smoke that poured from roof and attic, the boy clinging to the narrow ledge, so far up that it seemed humanly impossible that help could ever come.

But even then it was coming.

Up from the street, while the crew of the truck company were laboring with the heavy extension ladder that at its longest stretch was many feet too short, crept four men upon long, slender poles with cross-bars, iron-hooked at the end. Standing in one window they reached up and thrust the hook through the next one above, then mounted a story higher. Again the crash of glass, and again the dizzy ascent. Straight up the wall they crept, looking like human flies on the ceiling, and clinging as close, never resting, reaching one recess only to set out for the next; nearer and nearer in the race for life, until but a single span separated the foremost from the boy. And now the iron hook fell at his feet, and the fireman stood upon the step with the rescued lad in his arms, just as the pent-up flame burst lurid from the attic window, reaching with impotent fury for its prey. The next moment they were safe upon the great ladder waiting to receive them below.

Then such a shout went up! Men fell on each other's necks and cried and laughed at once. Strangers slapped one another on the back with glistening faces, shook hands, and behaved generally like men gone suddenly mad. Women wept in the street. The driver of a car stalled in the crowd, who had stood through it all speechless, clutching the reins, whipped his horses into a gallop and drove away, yelling like a Comanche, to relieve his feelings. The boy and his rescuer were carried across the street without any one knowing how.

Policemen forgot their dignity and shouted with the rest. Fire, peril, terror, and loss were alike forgotten in the one touch of nature that makes the whole world kin.

Fireman John Binns was made captain of his crew, and the Bennett medal was pinned on his coat on the next parade day.—*Jacob A. Riis in "Heroes who Fight Fire" in "The Century" for February, 1898. Used by permission of The Century Company.*

Exercises.

Ex. I. Keeping in mind that a composition should consist of an introduction, a middle, and a conclusion, tell what the first paragraph is intended to do. What general picture does it present? What details, or items, are mentioned to suggest that picture? With eyes closed try to see the picture clearly. How many paragraphs make up the middle of the composition? What does the short one do? What does the third paragraph picture? The first time you read this paragraph what effect did it have on you? How did it make you feel? What details are given to produce this effect? What is pictured in the fourth paragraph? What different things are mentioned as being done by the men and women? Why are these things done? What feeling do you have as you read what the different persons did? What is done by the last paragraph? Does each paragraph deal with one main thought or with several?

After you have studied this selection, talk with your teacher in class about the power of details to suggest pictures and to stir feelings.

Ex. II. Give a brief account of an experience you have had with a fire—when your home was on fire or was likely to be, when a neighbor's house burned, when a great fire occurred in the city, when you saw the engines and trucks going to a fire, when the fire-drill took place at your school. Write the same story.

Be as simple and as clear as possible. Think before you write, and pick out the details that will be most effective in suggesting the pictures and the experiences. Do not forget the value of details of sound and of smell.

Or tell and write of an experience in a flood. If you can think of nothing in your own experience, ask your mother or grandmother to tell you of an experience she has had or knows of, and write a simple account of it.

47. THE COMMA.

Punctuation marks are used in order that the reader may get the writer's meaning with the least possible effort. A punctuation mark should never be used unless it adds to clearness.

The fact that the comma is frequently used, even by educated persons, when it is neither necessary nor helpful, suggests the following rule for punctuation:

Never use a comma unless its presence will make the meaning clearer.

It has been shown in 40, Ex. I., p. 268, that words and expressions used in addressing a person are set off by a comma or by commas. The rule is this:

Set off with a comma or with commas every word or expression naming a person addressed (Gr. 6, p. 15); as, *John, hand me the book. Hand me the book, my little lad. Will you, dear boy, hand me the book?*

Exercise.

Insert the necessary commas:

Why Willie did you do that? Be careful my beloved hearers not to think lightly of what he says. Yes sir I will go. No ma'am your pleading will do no good. Listen father I beseech you. Boast not my dear friends of the morrow. Ladies and gentlemen I wish to introduce Mr. Noman. Why sir I did it. Yes sir I will pay for it. He said, "Father I wish to ask you a question." Will you tell me ma'am where Mr. James lives? Well sir that is the end of it. How long will you be gone mother?

48. THE COMMA (*Continued*).

I like Irving's life of Goldsmith a great deal better than the more authoritative life by Forster, and I think there is a deeper and sweeter sense of Goldsmith in it. — *W. D. Howells.*

In the above sentence put a period in place of the comma after

Forster. What effect does it have upon the part of the sentence preceding the comma? Omit the *and* following the comma. What effect does the change to a period have on all that follows?

Of how many independent statements, then, is the sentence quoted made up? What connecting word binds them together? What punctuation mark precedes this connecting word? If the statements are written separately what punctuation mark should be used? Why?

Examine the following sentences, see of how many statements each is composed, note the punctuation of each, and determine what change in punctuation should take place if the statements were written separately:

Justice is the end of the law, and love is the work of the ruler.

Mr. Howells's people are like those I have known, while Mr. James's are mostly of a sort I have never known.

It is easy to struggle, but the hardest thing in the world is to surrender.

No evil agency can harm the dead, but the living are in constant danger.

Clowns are best in their own company, but gentlemen are best everywhere.

To think a score of times of helping your neighbor is good, but to help him only once is far better.

Determine how the following sentences differ from the ones just quoted:

Since the time of Addison English prose has steadily broadened in range and increased in literary importance.

Defoe at sixty turned from journalism and pamphleteering and produced "Robinson Crusoe."

With one hundred and forty dollars Bayard Taylor crossed the ocean and spent two years in Europe.

What do these sentences lack that the earlier ones have? Are the separate statements complete in each of the sentences? If not, what is lacking? Compare the length of the final statements in these sentences with the length of the final statements in the earlier ones.

From these various sentences may be drawn the following rule:

PUNCTUATION

When one complete statement is joined to another complete statement by such connectives as *and, but,* etc., use a comma at the end of the first statement. When the statements are brief or have the same grammatical subject, the comma is usually omitted.

Exercises.

Ex. I. Examine the selections in 2, 23, and 46 (pp. 226, 250, 251, 273, 274), and determine which commas are governed by this principle. Also determine all points at which the comma is omitted because the statements are closely connected in meaning and are brief.

Examine in a similar manner several pages in your reader.

Examine in a similar manner several compositions that you have written, inserting commas wherever they are required by this principle.

Ex. II. *Combine each of the following pairs of statements by means of a suitable connective, and insert the required commas:*

1. We must conquer our passions. Our passions will conquer us.

2. A wise man seeks to shine in himself. A fool seeks to outshine others.

3. A young and unknown poet asked for five minutes. Mr. Longfellow listened to his poems for two hours.

4. Once the boy Longfellow shot a robin. He came home with his eyes full of tears.

5. Hawthorne had little taste for music. He used to say he could never distinguish between "Yankee Doodle" and "Hail, Columbia."

6. Holmes as a boy was especially fond of flowers and trees. When a man he did not lose his childish love for them.

7. Lowell the boy made friends with the robins and thrushes, the orioles and sparrows. He kept this friendship after he had become a famous man.

8. Taylor asked the young poet Stoddard to visit him. He was glad to accept the invitation.

9. Mr. Stedman has never lived for himself. He has always practiced Emerson's gospel, "Help somebody."

10. Thackeray began his career as a painter. He soon abandoned that pursuit for literature.

49. POSTAL CARDS AND LETTERS.

EXERCISE. Write a postal card (see page 272) to Perry Mason & Co., 201 Columbus Avenue, Boston, Massachusetts, asking them to change the address of your "Youth's Companion" from Indiana, Indiana County, Pennsylvania, to your present address. Use the proper abbreviations. Which part of the perfect letter form may be omitted from a postal card? Be sure to address the card correctly. When making such a request *always give the former address as well as the new address.*

Write a letter to The Century Company, Union Square, New York City, inclosing a postal money order for seven dollars to pay for a year's subscription to " The Century Magazine " and for a year's subscription to "St. Nicholas," the former to be sent to your aunt, Mrs. Sarah K. Mendon, 117 Hawthorne Avenue, Northwest, Washington, D.C., and the latter to yourself at your home address. Before writing this letter read again the directions and the model letter in **18**, pp. 244, 245.

In writing this letter be careful to use proper abbreviations and to punctuate correctly. Address the envelope in harmony with the model given on p. 246.

50. HOW I MADE AN ANCHOR.

Read the following selection, noticing that the various events are recorded in the exact order of their occurrence. Such a piece of writing, being practically without suggestion, can not be notable as literature. Its interest is due to the simple, clear explanation of the things done.

Last summer, during July and a part of August, while spending my vacation at Chautauqua, I kept my sailboat fastened to a keg buoy about sixty yards from the shore. The buoy was held in place by a heavy rope tied around two large flat stones, which I had wired together and dropped into the lake opposite the gymnasium. One morning, however, my boat was gone. Inquiry brought out the fact that a stray sailboat had been seen about five miles down the lake. It proved to be mine, still attached to the buoy. The buoy was clinging to the anchoring stones, which had been dragged all that distance by the force of the night's storm.

This summer I determined not to be caught again. The first thing I did, therefore, was to buy an empty gasoline barrel, which I took to the beach near the gymnasium. There I drove off the two hoops near one end, and drove a third hoop part way off. I then had no trouble in taking out one head of the barrel without breaking any of its edges. I now encircled the barrel with part of a thirty-foot chain, making it fast with well-clinched staples. Next I gave the barrel, inside and out, three coats of deck paint. Now I was ready for the completion of my work.

I fastened the sterns of two rowboats close together. From one to the other I laid heavy planks, leaving the bows eight or ten feet apart. On the planks I set the barrel, and filled it closely with large and small stones. I then carefully replaced the head, and drove the hoops down as far as possible. To the end of the chain I fastened a new keg buoy, to which I had given several coats of paint.

The day was still and the lake was perfectly smooth. When no steamer was in sight, for I did not want any waves rolling in while I was at the rest of my work, with the help of a friend I slowly paddled the boats out into the lake to the place chosen as the anchoring ground. Having reached it, I dropped the buoy over, and then gently pushed the barrel from the planks. It fell forward between the boats, and we gave a shout of applause. I now had an anchor that would not drag.

But I made one mistake. I had not expected the barrel to sink into the mud so far as it did, and when the lake is high the chain is sometimes too short and my buoy is under water. The next time I shall be sure to have plenty of chain. — *Adapted*.

What idea of the writer's character do you get from the selection? How is each new paragraph indicated? How do you indicate paragraphs in your own composition? What is the purpose of the last paragraph?

Notice that each paragraph deals with a single prominent division of the explanation. The first deals with the facts that led to the making of the anchor. This is a beginning paragraph, or a paragraph of introduction. The second deals with the preparation of the barrel up to the time it was ready to be placed on the planks; the third with filling it and making it ready to drop into the water; and the fourth with putting it into the lake. The fifth is a concluding paragraph, containing an implied warning to any one who may make a similar anchor, and bringing the composition to an easy close.

Every composition should have a beginning, a middle, and a conclusion. The first and last may be only a sentence, but must be enough to open and close harmoniously. In the brief compositions written thus far a single sentence is sufficient; in longer compositions a brief paragraph is usually given to each.

A very necessary condition of a composition is that it shall be a unit, that is, that it shall deal with one subject and with nothing else. In the above selection, for example, a paragraph telling how much the writer enjoyed his vacation, or one dealing with the scenery about Chautauqua Lake, would be out of place.

In the same manner a paragraph must deal with one definite part of the general subject of the composition; it, too, must be a unit, but a smaller one. For example, a sentence stating that a severe storm had occurred the night the sailboat dragged its anchor, would be entirely out of place in the second, third, fourth, or fifth paragraph of the selection, but might have been properly introduced in the first.

So, too, a sentence must be a unit. It must deal with a single idea definitely related to the paragraph subject. For example, the first two sentences of the second paragraph of the selection, if made into a single sentence, would not be a unit, as they deal with different thoughts, although both are definitely related to the paragraph subject. The second and third sentences are more closely related in thought, but even they would not form a harmonious unit.

In all writing, then, endeavor to have a composition deal with one subject, a paragraph deal with one definite part of that subject, and a sentence deal with one thought about the part of the subject which is considered in the paragraph.

Exercise.

Tell of an experience of your own somewhat like the one told of above. For example, tell how you made a raft, how you took a photograph, how you trapped some animal, how you caught a butterfly, how you caught a fish, how a game was won, how you made the garden, how you made a window garden, etc. Be careful to tell of the events in the order of their occurrence, and to make your explanation simple and clear. Have at least a beginning paragraph, two middle paragraphs, and a concluding paragraph.

Have you any general suggestions to make to others trying to do something of the same kind, as the author has suggested something in the last paragraph quoted?

51. WORDS TO WATCH.

Ain't is a form often used for *am not*, *is not*, or *are not*. This form is incorrect. The contraction *I'm not* may be used. *You're not*, *He isn't*, and *They're not* are also allowable, as are *We're not* and *We*, *You*, or *They aren't*. BUT NEVER USE "AIN'T."

Exercise.

Insert the proper contraction:

He _____ at home to-day. They _____ willing to stay till 6 o'clock. The boy _____ studying to suit his father. You _____ doing all you should for him. I _____ going to the city. We _____ invited to the picnic.

52. DRIVING HOME THE COWS.

Out of the clover and blue-eyed grass
    He turned them into the river lane;
One after another he let them pass,
    Then fastened the meadow bars again.

Under the willows and over the hills
    He patiently followed their sober pace;
The merry whistle for once was still,
    And something shadowed the sunny face.

Only a boy! And his father had said
    He never could let his youngest go;
Two already were lying dead
    Under the feet of the trampling foe.

But after the evening's work was done,
    And the frogs were loud in the meadow-swamp,
Over his shoulder he slung his gun,
    And stealthily followed the foot-path damp;

Across the river and through the wheat,
    With resolute heart and purpose grim;
Though the dew was on his hurrying feet
    And the blind bat's flitting startled him.

Thrice since then had the lanes been white,
    And the orchard sweet with apple-bloom;
And now, when the cows came back at night,
    The feeble father drove them home.

For news had come to the lonely farm
    That three were lying where two had lain;
And the old man's tremulous, palsied arm
    Could never lean on a son's again.

The summer day grew cool and late;
    He went for the cows when the work was done;
But down the lane as he opened the gate
    He saw them coming, one by one:

Brindle, Ebony, Speckle, and Bess,
  Shaking their horns in the evening wind;
Cropping the buttercups out of the grass;
  But who was it following close behind?

Loosely swung in the idle air
  An empty sleeve of army blue;
And worn and pale from the crisping hair,
  Looked out a face that the father knew.

The great tears sprang to their meeting eyes,
  For the heart must speak when the lips are dumb;
And under the silent evening skies
  Together they followed the cattle home.
        — *Kate Putnam Osgood, in "Harper's Magazine."*

Exercises.

Ex. I. Why is the whistle still? Why the sunny face shadowed? Who has said "Only a boy"? Does the son agree? Do we now sympathize with the father or with the son? Why does he go stealthily? Where is he going? Why is this sturdy young man startled by the bat? What makes us know the length of time that intervenes before the second part of the poem? Would it be better to say that the son had lost an arm than thus to make it known indirectly? Why the tears? Why are the lips dumb?

With closed eyes try to see clearly the pictures suggested by each line of the poem. Try to smell the clover and to hear the rustle of the willows, as well as really to enjoy the sweetness of the orchard. In each line determine upon the one or two words that especially appeal to the feelings.

Ex. II. Write a paragraph about a boy or a girl in the woods. Try to suggest a half dozen pictures, remembering that almost every line in this poem suggests a picture.

Have one of your grandparents or an aged friend tell you about an incident connected with the war; then write an account of it.

Write an imaginary story of the life of this young man during the three years he was away. Tell of his reaching the army, of his being wounded, of his hospital experience, and of his trip home.

53. THE COMMA (Continued).

Last summer, during July and a part of August, while spending my vacation at Chautauqua, I kept my sailboat fastened to a keg buoy about sixty yards from the shore.

The leading thought in the sentence just quoted is, "Last summer I kept my sailboat fastened to a keg buoy about sixty yards from the shore." In the original sentence, then, there are two parts that in meaning are of secondary value: *during July and a part of August,* and *while spending my vacation at Chautauqua.* Each of these is set off by commas from the part of the sentence containing the important idea; for they convey ideas of less than prime importance. Such expressions are said to be **parenthetical**.

Parenthetical expressions should be set off from the rest of the sentence by a comma or by commas.

Notice the following sentences, each of which contains an **Appositive,** that is, a substantive expression meaning the same as the noun or pronoun that it follows:

APPOSITIVE PARENTHETICAL.

1. Mr. Brown, *the well-known carpenter*, has recently visited Cuba.
2. My dog, *a fine collie*, must be kept tied.
3. Have you met my sister, *the girl with the black hair?*
4. John Stuart Mill, *the philosopher*, was born in Scotland.

APPOSITIVE RESTRICTIVE.

5. My sister *Elizabeth* is to go abroad soon.
6. The artist *Millet* was a French peasant.
7. My dog *Noble* must be kept tied.
8. The philosopher *John Stuart Mill* learned the Greek alphabet when he was three years old.

Most appositives (probably all of over two words except an occasional proper name) are parenthetical, or non-restrictive (see 1 to 4, p. 284). They are not absolutely necessary to the expression of the author's primary thought, but are inserted for emphasis or for explanation.

A few appositives, however, including the great majority of those consisting of a single word, of a noun and its article, or of a proper name, are restrictive in their nature (see 5 to 8, p. 284). They are needed in order to express the author's primary meaning, and *are never set off by commas.*

A parenthetical or **Non-restrictive Expression,** as has been explained, is one that can be omitted without changing the author's primary meaning. It is one that adds a new idea or an emphasizing idea of secondary importance. (See left column below.)

But a **Restrictive Expression** is one that is absolutely necessary in order to express the author's primary meaning. To omit a restrictive expression is to lose or change the meaning of the sentence. (See right column below.) This explains why a non-restrictive expression is set off by commas and why a restrictive expression must be written without commas.

As the correct use of the comma depends largely upon a power to determine quickly and accurately whether an expression is restrictive, the following illustrative examples are inserted to show how clauses, the various kinds of phrases, and even single words may be either restrictive or non-restrictive:

Non-Restrictive — Set Off.	Restrictive — Not Set Off.
1. His only son, John, was present.	1. His son John was present. (He has other sons.)
2. A Greek philosopher, Diogenes, lived in a tub.	2. The Greek philosopher Diogenes lived in a tub.

NON-RESTRICTIVE — SET OFF.	RESTRICTIVE — NOT SET OFF.
3. Mr. Roosevelt, the president, effected the settlement of the strike.	3. Peter the Hermit was the preacher of the first crusade.
4. The man, rowing rapidly, soon came to the island.	4. The man rowing rapidly is my father.
5. The general, careless of all advice, was defeated.	5. A general careless of all advice deserves defeat.
6. To speak candidly, I don't understand it.	6. He doesn't know how to speak candidly.
7. It is mind, after all, that does the work.	7. He came after all the work was done.
8. The diamond, which is pure carbon, is very expensive.	8. The diamond that I lost was very expensive.
9. I then moved to Cincinnati, where I lived in comfort many years.	9. I then moved to a town where I had lived many years of my youth.
10. Words, which are the signs of ideas, are divided into classes.	10. Words that stand for nouns are called pronouns.

Considering together parenthetical and appositive expressions, we may formulate the following rule:

All parenthetical and all non-restrictive appositive expressions should be set off from the rest of the sentence by a comma or by commas.

Exercises.

Ex. I. *Determine which of the following sentences contain non-restrictive expressions, and insert the necessary commas:*

1. Webster the statesman lived in Massachusetts.
2. Daniel Webster who was a statesman lived in Massachusetts.
3. The balloon rising swiftly was soon lost to sight.
4. The noise coming from the kitchen must be stopped.
5. A balloon made of silk is very durable.
6. The boy from whom I bought the paper could not be found.
7. No accident occurring we shall soon be there.
8. He lost all his money the bank having failed.
9. James cowardly by nature was not fitted to be a soldier.

10. England's debt to put it in round numbers is $4,000,000,000.
11. These are the flowers that sister gave us.
12. The lion which is the king of beasts is found in Africa.
13. The lion that we saw at the circus came from Africa.
14. It will break if you touch it.
15. Paper was invented in China if the Chinese tell the truth.

Ex. II. Which of the expressions in the left column on pp. 285, 286, are parenthetical and which are appositive?

In the discussion under 53 find all the parenthetical expressions; all the restrictive expressions.

54. THE COMMA (*Continued*).

Occasionally an expression that is restrictive in nature is set off by a comma, following this rule:

Insert a comma whenever, by appealing to the eye, it will make the meaning clearer.

RESTRICTIVE — SET OFF FOR CLEARNESS.	RESTRICTIVE — NOT SET OFF.
1. By these, various opinions are held.	1. By these we acquired our liberties.
2. To each, honor is given.	2. To each much honor is given.
3. When it is red-hot, glass bends easily.	3. When it is red-hot all glass bends easily.
4. To the intelligent and virtuous, old age presents a scene of tranquil enjoyment.	4. To the intelligent and virtuous our old age presents a scene of tranquil enjoyment.

Note that the word following the comma might seem in meaning to belong with the word just before the comma. It is this fact that renders the comma necessary.

5. Whatever is, is right.   5. Whatever is good is beautiful.
6. The machine that was successful in doing the work of harvesting at less than the cost of labor by hand, made possible the boundless wheat fields of the Northwest.

The sentences numbered 5 show that a subject ending in a verb, even though very short, is usually separated from its predicate by a comma; while 6 shows that a long subject, even though not ending in a verb, is similarly separated. These commas, by appealing to the eye, add much to clearness.

Exercise.

Two of the following sentences need a comma to set off a restrictive expression. Determine which they are:

When we arrived the minister had already begun his sermon. In the morning I will stop and see it. Even if this does seem to apply to some it should not be applied. If I am able I will go with you. When we entered the room was already comfortably warm.

55. HARVESTERS' RETURN.

After the Painting by Alfred Seifert.

Ex. I. What shows that this picture does not represent an American scene? Where do you suppose it is located? Who are the main figures in the picture? What has the girl on the left had in her basket? In the jug that is now in the basket? Which girl is carrying something in the skirt of her dress? What do you suppose she is carrying? Why have some of the other girls turned up their skirts? What shows that this is a picture of the return of the harvesters rather than of their departure? What shows that this is a group of harvesters? How many sickles are in the picture? Are the men or the women carrying them? How many scythes? Who is furnishing the group music? Who is the man in the long coat walking near the load of grain? Or is it a load of hay? Why your answer? Notice the little girl behind the boy at the left. What has she on her arm? Why?

Into what two groups has the artist divided the six prominent figures? Which girl of the group of four is being watched by the other three? Why are they watching her? What does she seem to be doing? Which of the groups is the more happy? What is causing

HARVESTERS' RETURN.

the happy expression of their faces? Why perhaps do the others show less sunshine in their faces? But what shows that the two groups are friendly? Where is the left hand of the girl at your left in the picture? Of the girl next to her?

What in the background shows the hour of the day?

Ex. II. Write a story about the boy, the girl, and the dog shown in the picture.

Write an account of an experience of your own during some harvest time.

Write any story suggested by the picture.

56. THE COMMA (*Continued*).

Notice the use of commas in the following sentences:

1. The United States now owns Porto Rico, the Canal Zone, the Hawaiian Islands, Guam, and the Philippines.

2. No form of vice — not worldliness, not greed of gold, not drunkenness itself — does more to un-Christianize society than evil temper.

3. A busy lawyer, editor, minister, physician, or teacher has need of greater physical endurance than a farmer, trader, manufacturer, or mechanic.

4. The city can use bright, thinking, progressive boys, strong in health, vigorous in mind, clear in thought, energetic in action, honest in purpose.

5. The old horse neighed, snorted, kicked, rolled, and finally darted across the prairie.

6. It is necessary to have rapid plates, bright sunshine, and short exposure.

7. He said that he had to go to the city, stop at the bank, buy his tickets, and be back by three o'clock.

Exercise.

Which of these sentences contain several nouns used in the same way, that is, in a series? Several adjectives used in a series? How are these words separated from one another? Which contain several modified nouns used in a series? Several verbs? Several infinitive phrases? How are the individual members of these various series separated from one another?

The rule governing the use of commas in a series may be thus stated:

Place a comma after each except the last of a series of words or expressions in the same construction.

NOTE. When a series of adjectives precedes a noun they are not separated by commas unless they are in the same construction; that is, unless each adjective modifies the noun alone. In the following sentences each adjective modifies the substantive idea that follows; that is, the idea made up by combining the following adjective or adjectives and the noun; and so no commas are necessary.

She carried a new white willow basket.
He lives in the old red brick house.
All children love Andersen's delightful fairy tales.

See Gr. 120, I., p. 198; p. 32, footnote.

Exercises.

Ex. I. *Insert the necessary commas:*

1. The earth the air and the water teem with life.
2. John James and Henry were present.
3. His characteristics were greatness strength and sagacity.
4. Mary honors obeys loves and serves her Creator.
5. He was a brave generous and patriotic prince.
6. Wise cautious and eloquent was Ulysses.
7. The lecture was clearly forcibly and eloquently delivered.
8. Meekly truthfully and disinterestedly he trod the path of life.
9. We sailed down the river along the coast and into a little bay.
10. Seldom is a person at the same time wise in his own eyes wise in the eyes of the world and wise in the sight of the Creator.

Ex. II. Examine closely the selection "How I Made an Anchor" (pp. 278, 279), and give the rule governing each comma used.

Ex. III. Examine several of your compositions and insert commas wherever they are needed in order to conform to the rules given. Omit all commas that are not clearly governed by one of the rules.[1]

Ex. IV. Tell the story of a trip to the woods, of a hunting or fishing trip, of a day on a farm, of a day in the city, of a day on the ocean, of a day at the zoo, or of a trip to the museum. Before writing, read again the suggestions in 28 (p. 254).

57. SUGGESTION OF FEELINGS.

Read the two opening stanzas of Gray's "Elegy Written in a Country Churchyard," watching for the details used to make the reader experience the coming on of evening:

> The curfew tolls the knell of parting day,
>   The lowing herd winds slowly o'er the lea,
> The plowman homeward plods his weary way,
>   And leaves the world to darkness and to me.
>
> Now fades the glimmering landscape on the sight,
>   And all the air a solemn stillness holds,
> Save where the beetle wheels his droning flight,
>   And drowsy tinklings lull the distant folds.

Exercises.

Ex. I. In each of the eight lines is one detail typical of the coming of evening in the country. Four of them appeal to the hearing. Which four? To what do the others appeal?

Why does the plowman *plod?* What does *knell* mean? *Parting? Wind? Lea? Save? Wheels? Lull?* Why does the landscape *glimmer?* Why does the author say the way is *weary* and the tinklings are *drowsy?*

In each line pick out the words that seem especially to appeal to

[1] For the rules given together see pp. 343-345.

the feelings. Do these words make you think of anything more than their dictionary meaning? For example, does *toll* make you think of anything except the slow ringing of a bell? Try to determine definitely what each word *suggests* in addition to its dictionary meaning.

Ex. II. Write a paragraph or two about early morning in the country, using eight or ten details typical of that time of day.

The same of early morning in the city. The same of the city between 8.30 and 9 o'clock on a morning when school is in session. The same of a very hot afternoon in the city or country.

Pick out details that are seen only at the time you are trying to describe. Use if possible words with a wider suggestiveness than the mere meaning given in the dictionary.

58. A LADY'S MISTAKE.

After reading the following selection carefully, study it with the questions given below:

Towards evening once, John was coming. . . home with some stalks of the sweet-flag in his hand. . . . As he was walking along he met a carriage, which stopped opposite him; he also stopped and bowed, as country boys used to bow in John's day. A lady leaned from the carriage and said,

"What have you, little boy?" . . .

"It's sweet-flag stalk; would you like some?"

"Indeed, I should like to taste it," said the lady, with a most winning smile. "I used to be very fond of it when I was a little girl."

John was delighted. . . . He handed up a large bunch of it. The lady took two or three stalks, and was about to return the rest, when John said,

"Please keep it all, ma'am. I can get lots more. I know where it is ever so thick."

"Thank you, thank you," said the lady; and as the carriage started she reached out her hand to John. He did not understand the motion until he saw a cent drop in the road at his feet. Instantly all his . . . pleasure vanished. Something like tears were in his eyes as he shouted,

"I don't want your cent. I don't sell flag!"

John was intensely mortified. " I suppose," he said, " she thought I was a sort of beggar-boy. To think of selling flag ! "

At any rate he walked away and left the cent in the road.
— *Charles Dudley Warner in* " *Being a Boy.*"

Exercises.

Ex. I. Why does the author intimate that country boys of John's day were more thoughtful and polite than boys of to-day ? Was the lady thinking of herself or of the little boy when she stopped and spoke to him ? What suggestion of John's character in his answer to her first question ? Why the most winning smile ? Why did John hand up a large bunch ? What is suggested by John's asking her to keep it all ? What was the woman's feeling in dropping the penny for John ? Why did his pleasure vanish ? Do the tears primarily suggest feeling or character ? Was he polite in what he shouted after her ? Why did he do it ? Do you admire him more or less because he left the cent in the road ? Why did he leave it ? Is there more of feeling or of character suggested by this selection ?

Ex. II. What do the three periods in the first line show ? Why are there four at the end of the first sentence ? Why are there but three after the lady's first question ? Tell why each comma, apostrophe, and quotation mark is used, referring to the rule governing it. If the comma after *lady* (paragraph four) is omitted what change will be made in the meaning ?

Ex. III. Tell of an experience of your own in which your feelings were much hurt by the intended kindness of another. Write an account of the same in about the language in which you told it.

Suppose you had been at the roadside and had seen the incident told of in the selection quoted. Write a letter to a friend, telling of it and expressing your opinion of the lady and of the boy.

Write a letter to a friend telling of an experience of your own in which your feelings were hurt.

Which part of the perfect letter form may be omitted from a friendly letter ? Which parts must be included ? (Comp. **18**, p. 244.)

Address an envelope for your letter.

59. THE SEMICOLON.

In the last selection are found the following sentences:

As he was walking along he met a carriage, which stopped opposite him; he also stopped and bowed, as country boys used to bow in John's day.

"It's sweet-flag stalk; would you like some?"

"Thank you, thank you," said the lady; and as the carriage started she reached out her hand to John.

In each of these sentences will be found a semicolon (;). In the first two it will be noticed that no connective follows the semicolon, while in the third the semicolon is followed by *and*.

The first two sentences might have been written thus:

As he was walking along he met a carriage, which stopped opposite him. He also stopped and bowed, as country boys used to bow in John's day.

"It's sweet-flag stalk. Would you like some?"

When writing these sentences, however, the author *felt* that the meaning of the two parts was a little too closely related to permit the use of the period, and consequently he used the semicolon. Many writers would prefer the period to the semicolon. Boys and girls, under similar circumstances, should use the period.

The third illustrative sentence reads:

"Thank you, thank you," said the lady; and as the carriage started she reached out her hand to John.

The first statement of this sentence contains two commas, and is followed by a semicolon. A sentence *meaning the same* would be punctuated thus:

The lady thanked John, and as the carriage started she reached out her hand to him.

The first statement in this sentence contains no commas,

and consequently it may without confusion be followed by a comma instead of a semicolon. When one or both of two connected statements contain a comma or commas, a semicolon is sometimes used between the statements in order to prevent possible misunderstanding.

Boys and girls, however, should as a rule use a period when they are tempted to use a semicolon.

From the above discussion we deduce the following rules:

Use the semicolon between two statements united by a connective, if a comma is found in either or both of the statements and if a comma at the point of connection might endanger clearness.

Use a semicolon between two statements not united by a connective when they seem too closely allied in meaning to permit the use of the period.

NOTE. The semicolon is sometimes used to separate phrases or clauses depending upon a common declaration. For illustration see Composition 60, Ex. II. It is also occasionally used when the statements are long, and when the second statement gives a result of the first, an explanation of it, or a reason for it; as, *It was dark and the path was stony; so we took a lantern with us.*

It is also regularly used before *as* introducing an example, as is shown just above.

Exercise.

Determine the rule governing each semicolon used in **38, 39, 46,** and **50** (pp. 265, 266, 273, 274, 278, 279). How many do you find? Do authors make frequent use of the semicolon?

Examine several of your compositions and determine whether periods could not be substituted for any semicolons you have used.

60. THE MOUNTAIN AND THE SQUIRREL.

The Mountain and the Squirrel
Had a quarrel;
And the former called the latter "Little Prig."

Bun replied:
"You are doubtless very big;
But all sorts of things and weather
Must be taken in together
    To make up a year
    And a sphere;
And I think it no disgrace
To occupy my place.
If I'm not so large as you,
    You are not so small as I,
    And not half so spry.
I'll not deny you make
A very pretty squirrel-track;
Talents differ; all is well and wisely put;
If I can not carry forests on my back,
Neither can you crack a nut." — *Ralph Waldo Emerson.*

Exercises.

Ex. I. Does Emerson wish us to think about the squirrel and the mountain, or about something else? What? Which statement of two words seems to sum up the principal thought of the poem?

Ex. II. Write an imaginary conversation between a robin and an oak tree, in which each tells what its worth is to the world; between a boy and a locomotive; between a dog and a horse; between a pin or a needle and a crowbar. Use quotation marks correctly, and make each speech a separate paragraph.

61. WORDS TO WATCH.

Either means *one of the two.*
Both means *the one and the other.*

Exercises.

Ex. I. *Insert the proper word:*

I will land you on _____ side of the river. Trees covered _____ banks of the stream.

Ex. II. *Determine the meaning of each of the following sentences:*

I will give it to both of you. Either of you may have it. He left his boat for both of them. He said that either of them might use the boat.

Ex. III. Write five sentences using each of these words correctly.

62. A PLEASANT ROOM.

Read carefully the following selection, watching for hints, or suggestions, of character and for all other suggestions:

It was a comfortable old room, although the carpet was faded and the furniture was plain; for a good picture or two hung on the wall, books filled the recesses, chrysanthemums and Christmas roses bloomed in the windows, and a pleasant atmosphere of home-peace pervaded it. — *Louisa M. Alcott in " Little Women."*

Exercises.

Ex. I. What does this description of the room tell about the character of the inmates? Just what things suggest character? Shut your eyes and try to see the room. Are you able to see it? Notice that you are enabled to see it because of the few suggestive details that are given. Just what details are mentioned? What things were in the room that are not mentioned? When describing a room will you mention a large number of things that it contains? If a few details will do, what must the few be, — those that are common to every room, or those that give the character, so to speak, of the special room? Give a rule governing each punctuation mark in this selection.

Ex. II. Write a description of a room that you have seen. Make use of the four or five details that individualize the room, and if possible suggest by these details the character of the inmates. Remember that a person tries to have in his room the things he cares for.

63. DESCRIPTION.

The last lesson illustrates the whole theory of successful literary description, as does Composition 57. In his descriptions an author aims to be suggestive, and in order to be suggestive he depends primarily on picturing details, or hints, just as he depends upon character details, or hints, in making us know his people. When he wishes to make us know his hero he selects two or three typical acts out of the hundreds the hero performs and lets us see him do these. Such typical acts are suggestive details out of the hero's life. So when he wishes to make us see a room, a person, a landscape, or a city street, he chooses a few suggestive details and presents them to us in a manner as vivid as possible.

The details, or hints, of character being given, the imagination tells much of the character of the man; the few suggestive details of the picture being given, the imagination puts in for us the other details, and we see the room, the person, the landscape, the city street, — whatever it may be that the author wishes us to see.

Read a further illustration :

Laurie led the way from room to room, letting Jo stop to examine whatever struck her fancy; and so at last they came to the library, where she clapped her hands. . . . It was lined with books, and there were pictures, and statues, and . . . little cabinets full of coins and curiosities, and sleepy-hollow chairs, and queer tables, and bronzes; and, best of all, a great open fireplace with quaint tiles all around it. —*Louisa M. Alcott in " Little Women."*

Exercises.

Ex. I. Shut your eyes and see the room. How does it differ from the room you saw in 62? What are the suggestive details, or hints, that are given? How many are given? Which ones are most effective in making you see? An old gentleman lives in this room; what idea do you form of his character? What gives it to you? Are these, then, character-revealing details, as well as picturing details?

Ex. II. By means of picturing details that are also character-revealing details, describe the room of one of your companions.

Use your imagination, if necessary, to describe the room of a girl that is untidy and unrefined, although she is rich.

Describe the room of a girl that is ladylike, cultured, and neat, although very poor.

Describe the room of a boy that loves hunting, photography, and all manner of games.

In all this work draw as much as possible from rooms that you have actually seen.

64. BREAKING THE HOME TIES.

After the Painting by Thomas Hovenden.

Ex. I. Which figures are most prominent in this picture? Who is the woman? Who is the boy? What does the title of the picture mean?

Why has the woman her hands on the boy's shoulders? Where is she looking? Why? Why so intently? What are her feelings, judging from the lines of her mouth? Is she speaking? What do you think is going on in her mind?

What is the boy looking at? Why not at his mother? If he looks at her, what do you think may happen? What are his feelings, judging from the way he is holding his head and from the expression on his face? Is he holding his hat loosely or firmly? Why? Do you think he wishes to go away? Where do you suppose he is going?

Who is the young woman seated near the dog? What is she looking at? Why not at the boy? Where is her hand? Why? What do you think is in the package on her knee? What is leaning against her knee? What is there that makes us know how she feels?

At whom is the dog looking? To whom does he belong? What kind of dog is he? What does he seem to be thinking?

Who is the man walking toward the door? What is he carrying?

BREAKING THE HOME TIES.

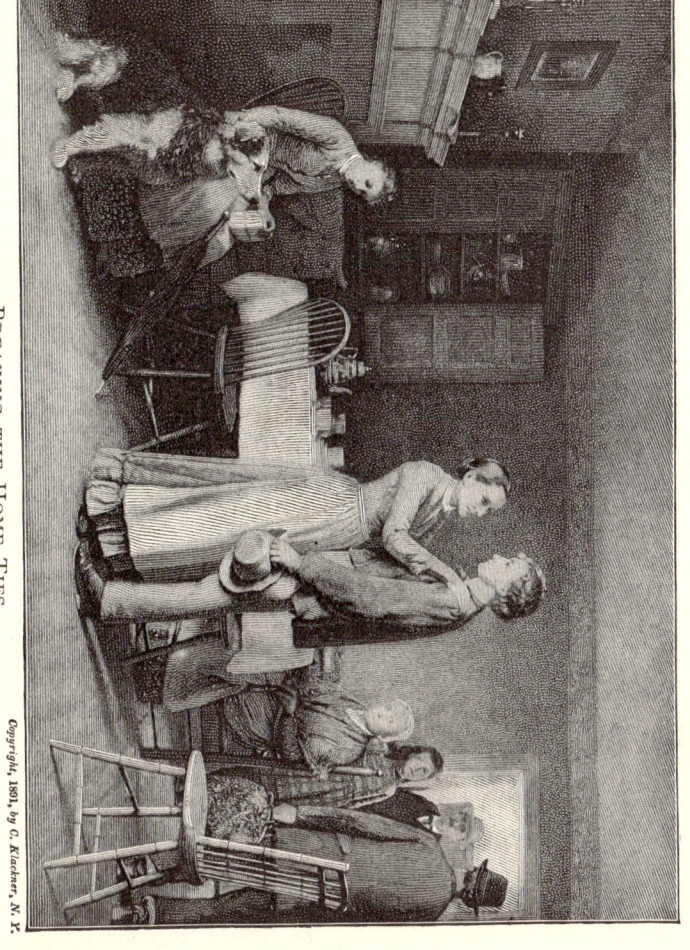

Copyright, 1891, by C. Klackner, N. Y.

Why has he picked it up and turned his back toward the woman and boy? Who is the elderly lady sitting near the table? At whom is she looking? What does her expression seem to tell about her thoughts? Who is the little girl back of her? At whom is she looking? Why? From the way she holds her head, what can you tell about her thoughts? Who is the man looking in at the door?

What time of year is it? What time of day? Why is the table set? Has the boy a long or a short trip before him? Who will go with him to the station? Does this family live in the city or in the country? What feeling do you have as you look at this picture?

Ex. II. With book closed describe this picture orally. Then write a description of it.

Write an account of a trip you have taken. Tell of leaving home, of your feelings when leaving, and of your feelings when away.

Write an account of this boy's trip, of an incident in his life in the city, or of his feelings the first night he is in a boarding house.

65. WORDS TO WATCH.

Beside means *by the side of*.
Besides means *in addition to*.

Exercise.

Insert the proper word:

I was in the house and there were three others _____ me. He is sitting _____ the house. He asked you to walk _____ him. What will you take _____ your trunk? In the yard was a tall maple _____ various fruit trees.

66. THE COLON.

The exercise in Composition **65** begins thus:
Insert the proper word:

In like manner many of the lessons containing selections

begin with a sentence that closes with a colon (:), just as the present lesson itself begins. These various sentences show the real nature of the colon. *It is a sign of expectation.*

It says to the reader, "Something else is coming; expect it." Look at the sentence beginning 39, 41, 42, 57, etc., and you will see that such is the nature of this mark of punctuation.

We have learned before that the colon is used after the salutation in letters. Here, as in the instances already cited, it says to the reader, "Something else is coming; expect it." An orator begins his address by saying "Ladies and Gentlemen:" and we know from his tones that we are to expect something, and the reporter indicates that expectation by putting a colon after the word *Gentlemen*. We may then formulate this rule of punctuation :

Use the colon to indicate expectation, — especially before a long quotation, before a formal enumeration, and after the salutation at the beginning of letters.

67. WORDS TO WATCH.

In indicates place *where*.
Into indicates place *to which*, and usually follows verbs of motion.

Exercise.

Insert the proper preposition:

Put the ashes _____ the can ; they are now _____ the ash-pit. We sat down _____ the library, but soon went _____ the parlor. Throw the paper _____ the basket. He asked him to go _____ the house. I wish that, when you are _____ the city, you would go _____ Davis's and get me a deed-box _____ which to keep my manuscripts.

68. GRANT'S BARGAIN.

A Mr. Ralston living within a few miles of the village owned a colt which I very much wanted. My father had offered twenty dollars for it, but Ralston wanted twenty-five. I was so anxious to have the colt that after the owner left I begged to be allowed to take him the price demanded. My father yielded, but said twenty dollars was all the horse was worth, and told me to offer that price; if it was not accepted I was to offer twenty-two and a half, and if that would not get him, to give the twenty-five. I at once mounted a horse and went after the colt. When I got to Mr. Ralston's house I said to him: "Papa says I may offer you twenty dollars for the colt, but if you will not take that I am to offer twenty-two and a half, and if you won't take that to give you twenty-five." . . . I could not have been over eight years old at the time. — *Personal Memoirs of U. S. Grant.*

Exercise.

Determine the reason for this foolish act of the boy Grant.

Tell and then write of some foolish act of your own when you were about eight or ten years old, or of some such act performed by another child. Remember to use short sentences, and to use about the same words in the written form that you used in the oral form.

69. THE NOTE OF INVITATION.

Read the following formal invitation and reply:

Mrs. Alan T. Gardiner requests the pleasure of Miss Ross's company at dinner on Thursday, May twenty-first, at six o'clock.
  11 Josephine Street,
    May Sixteenth.

Miss Ross regrets that illness prevents her acceptance of Mrs. Gardiner's kind invitation for Thursday evening.
26 Pointvue Avenue,
    May Seventeenth.

An affirmative reply would state that "Miss Ross accepts with pleasure Mrs. Gardiner's invitation," etc.

Exercise.

Notice that the invitation is written in the third person. Write a note to yourself in which Mrs. James Huntley Harper asks you to be present at a birthday party that she is to give for her daughter, Miss Harper, on Thursday evening, March 18th, at 180 High Street, Cleveland, Ohio. In a third person note write dates in words, not in figures.

Write an answer to this note, declining. Use the third person form.

Write an answer, accepting.

70. THE EXCLAMATION POINT.

Examine the following expressions:

"Jane! Jane! where are you?
"Such fun! Only see! A note of invitation from Mrs. Gardiner for to-morrow night!"

In these expressions the exclamation point (!) is used five times. The name *Jane* used in the first expression is a word of address. You have already learned that such words and expressions are usually set off from the rest of the sentence by commas. But here the exclamation point is used. This shows that the exclamation point is occasionally used as the equivalent in some respects of the comma.

In the next three uses it could not be replaced by any other mark of punctuation, for the sentence clearly shows strong emotion.

We may then formulate this rule of punctuation:

Use the exclamation point after words, phrases, sentences, or other expressions that show strong emotion.

Boys and girls, however, should seldom use the exclamation point.

Exercise.

Find other exclamation points in the selections given in this book or in several selections in your reader, and determine whether each follows an expression of strong emotion.

71. THE OTHER FELLOW.

Read the following brief selection and determine what is meant by "The Other Fellow."

Dr. Oliver Wendell Holmes says that in every one of us there are two persons. First, there is yourself, and there is the Other Fellow! Now one of these is all the time doing things, and the other sits inside and tells what he thinks about the performance. Thus, I do so and so, act so and so, seem to the world so and so; but the Other Fellow sits in judgment on me all the time.

I may tell a lie, and do it so cleverly that the people may think I have done or said a great or good thing; and they may shout my praises far and wide. But the Other Fellow sits inside and says, "You lie! you lie! you're a sneak, and you know it!!" . . .

Or, again, I may do a really noble deed, but perhaps be misunderstood by the public, who may persecute me and say all manner of evil against me falsely; but the Other Fellow will sit inside and say, "Never mind, old boy! It's all right! Stand by!"

— *William Hawley Smith in " The Evolution of ' Dodd.' "* [1]

[1] Used by permission of Rand, McNally & Company.

Exercise.

Write an account of something you have done for which you were blamed, but at which the Other Fellow said, "It's all right!"

Write an account of something you have done for which you were praised, but at which the Other Fellow said, "You're a sneak!"

You will not be asked to read these themes in class.

Write a paragraph describing an act that made you know a boy or girl was angry or was delighted.

Write a postal card to J. A. Grim, 1324 Park Building, Cleveland, O., asking him to call at your office and repair your typewriter. Do not fail to tell him where your office is.

In a letter to a friend describe two acts of a boy or girl that made you impatient.

In a letter describe a picture that you have seen so that a friend can buy you a copy of it. You do not know its name.

In an informal note invite a friend to go boating, driving, or walking with you.

In a letter tell a friend of a new game you have learned to play. Explain so fully that he will be able to play it.

PART III.

DETAILS THAT PICTURE. MISCELLANY.

(*To be studied in connection with Part III of the Grammar on pages 94-222.*)

72. PRACTICAL DESCRIPTIONS.

The following selection is a piece of description that is practical rather than literary. In what order does the author tell of the various acts of the boys?

The Eel Trap.

The Moodna creek had now become very low, and not more than half its stony bed was covered with water. . . . A holiday was given to the boys, and they went to work to construct an eel weir and trap. With trousers well rolled up, they selected a point on one side of the creek where the water was deepest, and here they left an open passage-way for the current. On each side of this they began to roll large stones, and on these placed smaller ones, raising two long obstructions to the natural flow. These continuous obstructions ran obliquely up stream, directing the main current to the open passage, which was only about two feet wide, narrowing it still more. In this they placed the trap, a long box made of lath, sufficiently open to let the water run through it, and having a peculiar opening at the upper end where the current began to rush down the narrow passage-way. The box rested closely on the gravelly bottom, and was fastened to posts. Short, close-fitting slats from the bottom and top of the box, at its upper end, sloped inward, till they made a narrow opening. All its other parts were eel-tight. The eels coming down with the current, which had been directed towards the entrance of the box, as has been explained, passed into it, and there they would remain. They never had the wit to find the narrow aperture by which they had entered. — *Selected.*

Exercise.

Describe the building of a "shanty"; the making and setting of a trap of some kind; the digging of a cave; the building of a dam and the placing of a miniature water-wheel; the planning, grading, and finishing of a tennis court; the making of a piece of fancy work; the making of bread, of cake, of candy. Be sure that you describe something that is within your own experience, something that you have made yourself, or done yourself, or in the making or doing of which you have had part.

73. LEAVING THE OLD HOME.

The description in this lesson has more of a literary flavor, its purpose being, by the mention of a few details, to make us feel as though we were really seeing the garret and the garden.

It was hardest for me to leave the garret. . . . The rough rafters, the music of the rain on the roof, the worn sea-chests with their miscellaneous treasures, the blue-roofed cradle, . . . the tape-looms and reels and spinning-wheels, the herby smells, and the delightful dream-corners, these could not be taken with us to the new home. Wonderful people had looked out upon us from under those garret-eaves. Sindbad the Sailor and Baron Munchausen had sometimes strayed in and told us their unbelievable stories; and we had there made acquaintance with the great Caliph Haroun al Raschid.

To go away from the little garden was almost as bad. Its lilacs and peonies were beautiful to me, and in the corner of it was one tiny square of earth that I called my own, where I was at liberty to pull up my pinks and lady's delights every day, to see whether they had taken root, and where I could give my lazy morning-glory seeds a poke, morning after morning, to help them get up and begin their climb. Oh, I should miss the garden very much indeed!

— *Lucy Larcom in " A New England Girlhood."*

Exercises.

Ex. I. Shut your eyes and try to see this garret. In the same way try to see the garden. The picture you see is made up of the details mentioned, and of various other details added by your imagination. The details added by your imagination have been drawn from your experience, that is, from the garrets and gardens you have seen and played in, and the ones of which you have read and heard and talked and day-dreamed.

What details are mentioned to make us see the garret? Does the music of the rain make you see it, or help you to feel as though you were really there? What other details are given that do not appeal to the sight? What ones appeal to your experience in a garden?

Ex. II. Describe a grove in which you have played. Use details appealing to the sight, to the hearing, and to the smell. What different sounds belong particularly to such a place? What odors? What words may be used to describe the sound made by the brook? By the birds? By the wind in the tree-tops? By the leaves? In the woods are all places on the ground reached by an equal amount of light? Is any sunshine to be seen?

Describe a play-room you have seen, using details that will suggest it vividly to the reader. What sounds are heard?

Describe a yard fitted up especially as a play-place for a number of children, taking for the moment of your description a time when the little ones are plainly happy. Use details of all possible kinds.

Correct all papers as explained on page 343.

74. THE RETURN OF THE "MAYFLOWER."

After the Painting by G. H. Boughton.

Ex. I. Does the word *return* in the name of the picture mean that the ship is going to England or is coming to the Massachusetts coast?

Which are the important figures in the picture? So far as beauty and attractiveness are concerned, what is the general nature of the shore where they are standing? What would have been the effect if the artist had introduced about them a very beautiful landscape? Granting that the real shore is beautiful, why would it not be wise to paint it so in this picture?

Why are the less important figures introduced? Why has the woman her handkerchief in her hand? What would have been the effect if the artist had omitted the ship at the extreme right?

THE RETURN OF THE MAYFLOWER.

What is the feeling of the man and of the woman? Where is the right hand of the woman? Why? Why is the woman put in a position that requires her to turn her head in order to look after the disappearing ship?

Why is the man holding his hat in his hand? Why is he heedless of the fact that his cloak has fallen from one shoulder? Do the faces have similar or decidedly different expressions? On which face is the expression more marked?

Is the sun shining bright? Why has the artist made it such a day? As you look at the picture do you feel that the day is warm or chilly? Why has the artist made you feel thus?

Assume the position of each of these figures in every detail. What effect does the position have on your feelings?

Tell the history lying back of this picture.

Ex. II. Tell a story suggested by this picture, — perhaps of a boy or girl left here by the return of the "Mayflower," describing his various adventures. Make it entirely imaginary. Or tell any story you please — imaginary, or founded on history. Write one story.

75. BILLS AND RECEIPTS.

You (George Williams) have been left in charge of your father's store. During the time he is away a gentleman comes in and lays down ten dollars and a statement, which you find reads thus:

    Joseph A. Williams,
        Grocer.

                         Dubois, Pa., Nov. 1, 1910.
  Sold to
    H. G. Kane, Dubois, Pa.

Oct.	2.	14 lb. Ham at 15¢	$2.10
"	7.	20 lb. Sugar at 6¢	1.20
"	10.	10 cans Tomatoes at 13¢	1.30
"	24.	1 Box Soap	4.50
			$9.10

BILLS AND RECEIPTS

After receiving the change Mr. Kane will wish something to show in case he should be asked again to pay the bill. Taking the bill, you write at the bottom of it

> Received payment,
> JOSEPH A. WILLIAMS,
>   by GEORGE WILLIAMS.

The word *by* is written before your own name in order to show that your father's or your employer's name has been written by you.

If Mr. Kane pays only part of the bill, you write a receipt like this, on a separate sheet of paper:

$2.25   Dubois, Pa., Nov. 7, 1910.
Received of H. G. Kane Two and 25/100 Dollars on account.
> JOSEPH A. WILLIAMS,
>   by GEORGE WILLIAMS.

Exercises.

Ex. I. On January 11, 1911, J. F. Goodwin, dealer in hardware, Titusville, Pa., sells to F. K. Linwood one sled for $2.00 and a pair of skates for $1.75; on January 20 he sells him 20 pounds of nails at 5 cents a pound; on the 24th he sells him a stove for $22.50; on the 28th he sells him a saw for $1.50 and an ax for $1.75.

Make out a bill on February 1st. Receipt the bill. Write a separate receipt for the amount of the bill. Write a receipt for money paid on account.

Ex. II. Make out a bill that a general merchant might send to a customer; one that a shoe dealer might send; one that a jeweler might send; one that a physician might send, saying "For Professional Services from Oct. 1st to date."

A real estate agent receives a check for $30.00 in payment of rent for house number 11 Josephine Street, Greensburg, Pa., the check being sent by John H. Roberts. Write a receipt for the same, showing date received, from whom, amount, rent for what month, and for what house.

76. WORDS TO WATCH.

Expect means to look for (mentally) *in future time*. It is often incorrectly used with reference to past or to present time, in the sense of *think* or *suppose*. It is not possible to *expect* a person was ill yesterday.

Exercise.

Insert **expect, think,** *or* **suppose:**

I _____ you were there last night. We _____ to start tomorrow. Do you _____ to go to New York soon? I _____ it was a close game. Where do you _____ to go next summer?

May is used to ask for permission or to grant it; to make known that permission has been granted; and sometimes to make known that something may possibly be done; as, *May I go? You may go. I may go if I care to. I may (possibly) go if the weather is pleasant.*

Can is used to state that one has power to do a given thing; as, *I can lift fifty pounds, and I can swim twenty yards. I can multiply but I can not divide in algebra.*

Exercises.

Ex. I. *How do these sentences differ in meaning?*

I can swim to the island if I may. I may swim to the island if I can.

Ex. II. *Insert* **may** *or* **can:**

_____ I go to the woods with the boys? You _____ if you _____ wear your shoe. Mother says I _____ go if you _____ go with me. He _____ cross the ocean next month. I think I _____ work that problem. _____ I sharpen my pencil?

77. JOYOUS DAYS.

Dandy and I took another walk this afternoon. We went over the hill, up the valley, and along the brook, where we found the pussy willows creeping out on almost every bough. Coming home across the fields we saw the robin redbreasts hopping in the furrow behind the plow, with eye intent for luckless worms. Of course Dandy raced after them, barking, but the dear fellow would not harm them, even if they would let him.

Some violets peeped at us from the awakening grass, and the dandelion show, an array of gold, again and again stopped us. A thistle finch, who had changed his dull coat for one of yellow, flew past, assuring us by his mere presence that the warm sun will soon make all nature happy.

Ten days ago, on a bright southern hillside, we found the fragrant arbutus nestling under its covers of brown leaves, and now unnumbered flocks of young anemones are dancing among the budding trees, all as joyous as a crowd of laughing girls let out of dull, dry school for a woodland holiday.

The days of joy have surely come again! — *Adapted.*

Exercises.

Ex. I. What time of the year is the author describing? What eight items or details does he use to suggest the beauty of this season? What is the pussy willow? The thistle finch? The anemone?

What does the expression *pussy willow* make you think of besides the willow with its silky catkins? That is, what associations, entirely apart from its dictionary meaning, are suggested by it? Does it recall the place where it grows and its beauty, the delight with which we see it each spring, etc.? What other pleasant associations has it? What does the word *brook* make you think of besides a small stream of water? What does *behind the plow* suggest? *Dandelion? Young anemones? Budding trees?*

What does the author mean when he says the pussy willows are *creeping* out on every bough? Do they really creep? Use *appearing now* instead of *creeping out;* which is the better expression and why? Do the thistle birds really change their *coats?* Use a literally true expression instead of this one. Which is the better expression? Why? Is it correct to speak of a great number of dandelions as a *show?* Use a literal expression. What is meant by saying that the dandelion show has begun in an array of *gold?* What is the literal word to use instead of *gold?* Which is better?

What two words in the third line of the third paragraph are not literally true? Substitute literal words. Is the literal word or the *figurative* word better?

The words *creeping, coats, flame, show, flocks, dancing, awakening, nestling,* and *covers* are said to be used *figuratively*. Such uses of words are called *figures of speech*. While it is not literally true to say that *flocks* of young anemones are *dancing* around the trees, yet there is a way in which the expression is true. Try to explain its truth.

Ex. II. In a paragraph or two, using six to ten details, describe one of the seasons. Seek words that will suggest more than their dictionary meaning, and also try to use two or three figures of speech.

Bring into class a list of five figures of speech used in conversation.

Ex. III. Describe a picnic dinner at which you have been present, using suggestive details.

Describe the unpacking of the picnic baskets. In doing so use many suggestive details drawn from color,— the color of the buns, of the jellies and cakes, of the eggs and of the various fruits, etc. Use adjectives or descriptive words that will make us see the tablecloth, the picnic plates, and spoons, knives, forks, etc.

Describe your ideal picnic place. Take a real place as the foundation of your description, adding such other details as will make it ideal. Use suggestive details to make us see the trees, the brook or the lake, the flowers, the old log, the vines, the rocks, etc. Remember that details suggestive to the hearing are helpful.

Ex. IV. Tell the story of a picnic you have recently attended. Make use of details to picture the various scenes you mention; use other details to make known your different moods; use other details to bring out contrasts (see 28, p. 254); use other details to suggest rather than to tell what you did. Be as vivid, as interesting, and as real as it is possible for you to be with a free use of suggestive details of various kinds.

78. THE PRONOUN: SOME DANGERS.

Notice the following sentence:

She announced that the coffee was ready, and every one settled themselves to a hearty meal.

In the above sentence the error is in the use of the pronoun *themselves*, a word meaning more than one, to refer to the word *one*. The sentence of course should read, "every one settled *himself* to a hearty meal." From this we may deduce the following rules for composition :

Be sure that a pronoun is in harmony with the word for which it stands.

When a pronoun refers to persons of both sexes, use the form of the pronoun that as a rule refers only to men and boys; as, *himself* above refers to *every one*, which includes both boys and girls. (See p. 99.)

(Review pp. 134–136, 140–141.)

79. THE DEN.

The following description not only makes us see the room, but does much towards making us know the character of the foreign gentleman (see Comp. 29) that occupies it:

"'Did you ever see such a den, my dear? Just come and help me put these books to rights, for I've turned everything upside down trying to discover what he did with the six new handkerchiefs I gave him [the foreign gentleman] not long ago.'

"I went in, and while we worked I looked about me, for it was 'a den' to be sure. Books and papers everywhere; a broken meerschaum, and an old flute over the mantelpiece as if done with; a ragged bird without any tail chirped on one window seat, and a box of white mice adorned the other; half-finished boats and bits of string lay among the manuscript; dirty little boots stood drying before the fire; and traces of the dearly loved boys, for whom he makes a slave of himself, were to be seen all over the room. After a grand rummage three of the missing articles were found, — one over the bird cage, one covered with ink, and a third burnt brown, having been used as a holder. — *Louisa M. Alcott in "Little Women."*

Exercises.

Ex. I. What do the books and papers suggest about his character? The flute? The birds and mice? The boats and bits of string?

The manuscript? The boots by the fire? The location and condition of the various handkerchiefs that were found? Note that these various articles are also suggestive details to make us see the room.

Ex. II. Describe a yard that you know, — one that makes known the character of its owner. First tell of it, then write about it.

Describe a room of the same nature, trying both to make us see the room and to make us know the character.

Describe a grocery store that you know, one showing a careless, negligent owner. Describe one showing a neat and careful owner.

80. SNARING FISH.

Read the following account of a sport familiar to boys:

The boy is armed with a pole and a stout line, and on the end of it a brass wire bent into a hoop, which is a slip noose and slides together when anything is caught in it. The boy approaches the bank and looks over. There the fish lies, calm as a whale. The boy devours him with his eyes. He is almost too much excited to drop the snare into the water without making a noise. A puff of wind comes and ruffles the surface so that he can not see the fish. It is calm again, and there he still is, moving his fins in peaceful security. The boy lowers his snare behind the fish and slips it along. He intends to get it around him just back of the gills, and then to elevate him with a sudden jerk. It is a delicate operation, for the snare will turn a little, and if it hits the fish he is off. However, it goes well, the wire is almost in place, when suddenly the fish . . . moves his tail just a little, and glides out of the loop, and . . . lounges over to the other side of the pool; and there he reposes just as if he were not spoiling the boy's holiday.

This slight change of base on the part of the fish requires the boy to . . . get a new position on the bank, a new line of approach, and patiently wait for the wind and the sun before he can lower his line. This time cunning and patience are rewarded. The hoop encircles the unsuspecting fish. The boy's eyes nearly start from his head as he gives a tremendous jerk and feels by the dead weight that he has him fast. Out he comes, up he goes in the air, and the boy runs to look at him. — *Charles Dudley Warner in " Being a Boy."*

Exercises.

Ex. I. What is done by the first sentence? Why should a new paragraph be begun just after the fish moves away? Which details are mentioned that are absolutely necessary in order to understand the facts? Which other details are inserted simply for the purpose of making the incident seem real, of making us feel as though we were there and were ourselves holding the pole and snaring the fish? Which details are most necessary to make this story interesting?

Ex. II. Tell and then write of some fishing experience of your own. Mention only the really suggestive details. Tell of the events in their exact order.

Tell and then write of a hunting experience; of a berrying experience; of an experience in catching a butterfly; in capturing a pet bird or animal that has escaped. Whatever subject you write on, let it be a recent and vivid experience.

81. THE LETTER OF INTRODUCTION.

The letter of introduction is a kind of letter that boys and girls, as well as men and women, occasionally find useful. Suppose you (Sarah Ganning) are going to Canton, Ohio, to live. A friend of yours, Martha Jordan, knows you are going and tells you that she has a very dear friend there, Margaret Wilson, to whom she will give you a letter of introduction. A day or two later she stops at your home and leaves it for you. You find the envelope addressed thus:

     Miss Margaret Wilson,
      134 Seelye Ave.,
Introducing Miss Sarah Ganning. Canton, Ohio.

Examining it, you discover that it is not sealed; for it is not customary to seal such a letter. Opening it, you find it reads as follows:

121 Park Ave., Meadville, Pa.,
December 2, 1902.

Miss Margaret Wilson,
   134 Seelye Ave.,
      Canton, Ohio.

My dear Margaret: — I learned only yesterday that a schoolmate and special friend of mine is to move to your city next week. She is Sarah Ganning, and I have asked her to hand you this letter, as I wish you and her, both so dear to me, to become equally dear to each other. I am sure that I do not need to ask you to do whatever is within your power to make Canton a real home for her.

With much love and many hopes that you and Sarah will speedily become the best of friends, I am,

Ever yours affectionately,
MARTHA JORDAN.

You at once realize that such a letter will make your life in Canton more full of sunshine, and of course you are grateful for it.

Such letters are often given by men to other men, both for business and for social reasons. The body of such a letter might read as follows:

My dear Sir: — The bearer of this letter, Mr. Joseph H. Moore, will be in your city for some weeks, engaged in the completion of a large commercial project. Any favors that you may show him in either a business or a social way will be fully appreciated by him and will be remembered by me as though granted to myself.

Exercise.

Insert the omitted portions of the above letter.

John Winters is going to Syracuse, N.Y., to live. Give him a letter of introduction to Frank H. Stacy, a close friend of yours living at 765 North Park Avenue. Address an envelope for the letter.

J. H. Jones, stationer and bookseller, is going to New York, to try to complete the purchase of a store on Fifth Avenue. Write for him a letter of introduction to William F. Adams, who lives at 348 West 31st Street.

Jane Merigan is to spend the winter studying music at Mt. Union College, Alliance, Ohio. Give her a letter of introduction to Mr. and Mrs. C. F. McAdams, 395 Aiken Avenue.

Mr. J. W. Stein wishes to ask a favor of L. K. Fitzon, who is a councilman in Youngstown, Ohio. Give him a letter of introduction.

Jeanette S. Dixon wishes to consult Dr. F. M. Heck, a noted oculist of Cleveland, Ohio, who is an intimate friend of yours. Give her a letter of introduction.

82. A NIGHT AFIELD.

The selection that follows, attempts by means of description to make the reader feel as though he himself were spending the night on the prairie, several miles from home:

Once the boys secured permission to camp all night [in the meadow] beside the wagon, and after the men drove away homeward they busied themselves eating supper and making up their beds on piles of hay, with the delicious feeling that they were real campers on the plains. This feeling of exaltation died out as the light paled in the western sky. The wind suddenly grew cold, and the sky threatened a storm. The world became each moment more menacing. Out of the darkness came obscure noises. Now it seemed like the slow, sinister movement of a rattlesnake — now it was the hopping, intermittent movement of a polecat.

Lincoln was secretly appalled by these sinister changes, but the feeling that he was shielding weakness made him strong, and he kept a cheerful voice. He lay awake long after Owen fell asleep, with eyes strained toward every moving shadow, his ears intent for every movement in the grass. He had the primitive man's sense of warfare against nature, recalled his bed in the garret with fervent longing, and resolved never again to tempt the dangers of the night. He fell asleep only when the moon rose and morning seemed near.

The coming of the sun rendered the landscape good and cheerful and friendly again, and he was ashamed to acknowledge how nervous he had been. When his father returned, and asked with a smile, "Well, boys, how did you enjoy it?" Lincoln replied, "Oh, . . . it was lots of fun."— *Hamlin Garland in " Boy Life on the Prairie."*[1]

[1] Used by permission of the Macmillan Company, owners of the copyright.

Exercises.

Ex. I. Notice that the boys are happy as long as they are busy. What is the first fact that brings a change to their feelings? What similar experience have you had? What senses detect the next details that bring terror? The appeal in the last sentence of the first paragraph is to what sense? How does the thought of the rattlesnake affect you?

What suggestion in the first sentence of the second paragraph? Why the strained eyes and the intent ears? What is suggested by the fervent longing and the resolve? Why the change in feelings brought by the return of the sun?

Ex. II. Tell and then write of an experience of your own in spending the night out of doors; or of an experience in passing by yourself along a lonely walk, path, or road, in the darkness; of an experience in remaining alone in the house all night or till very late; of an experience upon awakening in the night with the feeling that some intruder is in your room or in the house, is on the porch roof, or is trying to unlock the front door.

83. DAVID.

After the Painting by Elizabeth Gardiner.

And David said unto Saul, Thy servant kept his father's sheep, and there came a lion . . . and took a lamb out of the flock. And I went out after him, and smote him, and delivered it out of his mouth.
— *I. Samuel, xvii : 34-35.*

Ex. I. Where is this scene located? What is there that perhaps may suggest the time of day or the condition of the weather? Who is the chief figure in the picture? What has he just done? What is he now doing?

What is the position of his head? Of his eyes? Which arm is raised? Why? Why is he kneeling? Why has he knelt thus on the lion? What thoughts are probably in his mind?

In which arm is David holding the lamb? Is there any reason why he should hold it in this arm? What seems to be the feeling of the lamb? Why your answer?

DAVID.

Has David probably slain this lion with his hands alone? What did a shepherd lad usually carry? Why did he carry it? In a land infested with wild beasts would it be light or heavy? Why has the artist not shown it in the picture?

What will David do now?

Ex. II. Write an imaginary account of the contest between David and the lion.

Giving the lamb power to talk, write such an account of its experience with the lion as it might give to David.

From memory write an account of David's contest with Goliath. Then compare what you have written with the story given in I. Samuel, xvii: 38–54, and revise or rewrite.

Write a description of this picture.

84. ANSWERING ADVERTISEMENTS.

WANTED. — Boy to answer telephone and door-bell at physician's office, and to send out bills. Address in own writing, giving age and naming references. X 29, Press Office.

WANTED. — Girl to fold and address circulars. Address in own handwriting, giving age and time spent in school. References required. 34, Telegraph Office.

WANTED. — Boys and girls to address envelopes at home. For particulars write F. T. Smith, Dep't 23, 118 Strand, London, England.

FOR SALE. — Beautiful summer home on Lake George. 8 rooms; wide porches; plenty of shade; 100 feet from lake. For particulars address Owner, 116 South Oregon Ave., Boston, Mass.

FOR RENT. — Farm of 160 acres, 7 miles from city. Address Z. A. Young, R. F. D. 33, Crafton, Pa.

FOR RENT. — Brick house, 9 rooms, both gases, all conveniences. $45.00. Particulars from Owner, Room 1728, Frick Building.

Exercise.

Write letters of inquiry or application in reply to four of the above advertisements. Use the full business form of letter (p. 252). Be sure to give all particulars required and to ask for each separate item of information that you wish. Address envelopes for the letters.

85. WORDS TO WATCH.

Mad means *affected in mind, insane*.

Angry means *irritated, annoyed, provoked, enraged, wrathful* (followed by *with* before the name of a person and *at* before the name of a thing).

Exercise.

Insert the proper word:

I'm _____ _____ you, and I'll not play with you any more! That man was _____ because I went into his yard! An asylum for the insane is sometimes called a _____ house. John became _____ and so I came home. The officer said that the dog was _____.

He is angry _____ me for taking his sled. He is angry _____ what I did. He said that he was not angry _____ John but was angry _____ his actions.

WARNING. Be careful not to say that a boy "got mad."

86. WINTER.

When icicles hang by the wall
    And Dick, the shepherd, blows his nail,
And Tom bears logs into the hall,
    And milk comes frozen home in pail;
When blood is nipt, and ways be foul,
Then nightly sings the staring owl
        Tuwhoo!
Tuwhit! tuwhoo! A merry note!
While greasy Joan doth keel[1] the pot.

When all aloud the wind doth blow,
    And coughing drowns the parson's saw,[2]
And birds sit brooding in the snow,
    And Marian's nose looks red and raw;
When roasted crabs[3] hiss in the bowl —

---

[1] *Skim.* Or the meaning may be *cool*.
[2] Wise saying.
[3] Crab-apples.

> Then nightly sings the staring owl
> Tuwhoo!
> Tuwhit! tuwhoo! A merry note!
> While greasy Joan doth keel the pot.
>
> — *William Shakespeare.*

Exercises.

Ex. I. What things do these stanzas tell that men do in winter as a result of the cold? What other things mentioned are caused directly by the cold? What is meant by *hall?* By *nipt?* By *ways be foul?* Why, at this time in the evening, when it is so cold without, does Joan "keel the pot"? Why does Shakespeare speak of Dick and Tom and Marian and Joan rather than merely speak of the shepherd, the servant, the maid, etc.? What sounds are mentioned in order to make the winter seem more real? What word is used in order to make us see the owl?

Ex. II. By mentioning various things done by men, by the cold, etc., describe winter. Use the details here used, if you wish, but add others. In similar manner describe one of the other seasons.

Ex. III. Write a paragraph about any vivid winter experience you have had: how you were caught in a storm, how you went sliding or skating or sleighing, what you saw in the woods in winter, etc.

87.[1] SUGGESTIVE WORDS. — A NEW ENGLAND SCENE.

(Before studying this lesson review Comp. 57 and 77.)

Brookfield village lay in a great wide meadow through which strayed one of the mountain's lost brooks, — a brook tired out with leaping from bowlder to bowlder, and taking headers into deep pools, and plunging down between narrow walls of rock. For here in the

---

[1] Lessons 87 to 91 inclusive are intended for study and discussion in class. Many of the questions call for composite answers, made up of the various replies received, rather than for complete answers from one pupil. In these lessons the teacher should work with the pupils and should not expect too much from them.

meadow it caught its breath and rested, idling along, stopping to bathe a clump of willows; whispering in the shallows; laughing gently with another brook that had locked arms with it, the two gossiping together under their breath as they floated on through the long grasses fringing the banks, or circled about the lily pads growing in the eddies. In the middle of the meadow, just where two white ribbons of roads crossed, was a clump of trees pierced by a church spire. Just outside of this bower of green — a darker green than the velvet meadow-grass about it — glistened the roofs and windows of the village houses.

— *F. Hopkinson Smith in "The Fortunes of Oliver Horn."*

Exercises.

Ex. I. Mention all the mental pictures that the word *meadow* calls up; also the sounds it causes you to hear, the odors it recalls, the kind of day or weather it suggests, and any other associations that the word has, in addition to its dictionary meaning of a tract of level land regularly mown for hay.

In like manner discuss in class the pictures, sounds, odors, and other associations suggested by each of the following words: *mountain, brook, willows, shallows, banks, eddies, church spire.*

Ex. II. What does the author mean when he says the village *lay* in a meadow? When he says the brook *strayed?* When he says that the mountain had *lost* a number of brooks? When he says that the brook was *tired out* with *leaping* and *taking headers* and *plunging?* When he says the brook *caught its breath, rested, idled, stopped to bathe the willows?* When he says that it *whispered?* When he says that another brook *locked arms* with it and they *laughed* and *gossiped* together as they *floated* where the grasses *fringed* the banks? When he says that the roads were *white ribbons* and the clump of trees was *pierced* by a spire? That the grass was *velvet?*

Discuss in class each of these words, and put in its place if possible a word or expression that says exactly the truth the author had in mind. If necessary, use a sentence to state the truth.

Write a paragraph about one of the italicized words in the last line of Exercise I., mentioning everything that it brings to your mind, both things you have seen, heard, smelled, tasted, or touched, and things of which you have read and heard.

88. SUGGESTIVE WORDS.

Can a brook do the various things ascribed to it in 87? Who or what can do these things? These words, then, are regularly words used in talking of men, and not words used in talking of a brook. Here, however, they are taken from the *man* class and used in the *brook* class.

Three words belonging to the brook class are *run, flow*, and *ripple*. Which of these seems rather to belong to the man class? Use each of these in speaking of men, transferring them from the brook class. Use *laughter* as the subject of one of them, and *life* as the subject of another.

Does any one of these words, when used outside of its own class, tell the literal truth? When words telling the literal truth are substituted for these words, which are the more pleasing? Which the more suggestive? Why do you prefer "The brook caught its breath and rested" (man words used in talking of a brook) to "The brook flowed slowly" (brook words)?

Exercises.

Ex. I. What does each of the following combinations of words (*literary phrases;* note that they differ from *grammatical phrases;* p. 69, footnote) suggest in the way of pictures, sounds, odors, and other associations: *from bowlder to bowlder; deep pools; narrow walls of rock; a clump of willows; the long grasses; lily pads growing in the eddies; a clump of trees pierced by a church spire; velvet meadow-grass.*

Are the same associations aroused if these words are taken separately? Which one of the phrases is made up of words that, taken alone, are almost entirely without suggestion? Which contains a word not used literally? Which contain words that have much suggestion when used alone?

Ex. II. Determine the various details used to bring before the reader this New England scene. Which ones are stated in words suggestive in themselves? Which ones in words used figuratively (out of their usual class)? Which ones in literary phrases? Which ones in words having little suggestive power? (Note that these divisions somewhat overlap.)

89. SUGGESTIVE WORDS (*Continued*).

Literature is largely made up of the various kinds of detail. The more important of these are *things done*, or acts suggesting character and feelings (see pp. 226 (2), 238, 240 (15), 241, 265, etc.); and *things seen, heard, smelled*, etc., which suggest pictures and experiences (see pp. 230 (7), 298, 299, etc.).

These details may be made known in plain prose words, as, *Women wept in the street* (p. 273); in words suggestive in themselves, as, *The hawthorn blooms on the hedges* (p. 330); in figurative words (words suggestive because used out of their usual class), as, *The night drags by* (p. 330); and in literary phrases (combinations of related words that become more suggestive because used together), as, *velvet meadow-grass* (p. 327).

Details that make known character and feeling are usually stated in plain prose words; details to recall experiences and to paint pictures should be stated in words full of suggestion.

Boys and girls, then, both that they may learn to read appreciatively and that they may learn to express their own thoughts and feelings, should gain all possible skill in determining the suggestions hidden within the details and within the words used in literature.

Exercise.

Write a description, containing perhaps a hundred words, of a valley, of a lake, of a mountain, of a seashore, of a meadow, of a grove or other bit of woods. Try to use all three kinds of suggestive words as well as suggestive details. After writing this and making it as perfect as possible in its suggestion, lay it aside for several days. Then take it up again and try to use yet more suggestive words. Do not be satisfied until each word is exactly the right word. It is known that one of the two or three most prominent living writers occasionally spends a whole day seeking for a single word. He is noted for using words that say exactly what he wishes to say, and it is only by such unceasing labor that he finds them.

From the recent lessons we deduce the following principle of composition:

Often a suggestive word may be substituted to advantage for a prose word.

90. STUDY OF A POEM.

Much of the enjoyment of poetry depends upon a power to appreciate fully and quickly the suggestions found in the words used by the poet, as well as upon a power to understand the details he uses. The following stanzas, by Mr. Thomas Bailey Aldrich, well illustrate the wondrous suggestiveness in well-chosen words:

Seadrift.

The night drags by: and the breakers die
  Along the ragged ledges;
The robin stirs in his drenched nest;
  The hawthorn blooms on the hedges.

In shimmering lines, through the dripping pines
  The stealthy morn advances;
And the heavy sea-fog straggles back
  Before those bristling lances.

> Still she stands on the wet sea-sands:
> The morning breaks above her,
> And the corpse of a sailor gleams on the rocks —
> What if it were her lover?

Exercises.

Ex. I. Copy these stanzas and underscore each suggestive word, that is, each word that has more than a mere fact or dictionary meaning. What details are made use of? What tells the time of year? What kind of night has it been? How do you know? What are the *bristling lances?*

How long has she stood on the shore? Is *wet sea-sands* better than *shore?* Why? Is the last stanza in harmony with or in contrast with the first two? For whom is it that the night drags? Substitute for *drags* a literal word. Why is the figure of speech better? Substitute for each of the figurative words a literal word and note the loss of power. Substitute prose words for the words that are suggestive in themselves. What difference does it make? With closed eyes try to see distinctly each of the eight or ten pictures in the poem.

What associations cluster about *drags, die, ragged, stealthy, straggles, bristling,* and *breaks?* About each of the words suggestive in themselves?

Ex. II. In the poem quoted are 74 words. In about as many words describe the earth and the air after an April shower, an autumn pour, or a winter storm. Use as many suggestive details as possible, and as many suggestive words, both literal and figurative. Work at this description for several days, trying to make each word the very best possible.

91. THE POET'S SONG.

The following stanzas by Lord Tennyson give a poet's feeling about the power of poetry. Read them at least twice carefully, trying to understand the meaning, before you refer to the exercise:

The rain had fallen, the Poet arose,
  He passed by the town, and out of the street,
A light wind blew from the gates of the sun,
  And waves of shadow went over the wheat,
And he sat him down in a lonely place,
  And chanted a melody loud and sweet,
That made the wild swan pause in her cloud,
  And the lark drop down at his feet.

The swallow stopt as he hunted the bee,
  The snake slipt under a spray,
The wild hawk stood with the down on his beak,
  And stared, with his foot on the prey,
And the nightingale thought, "I have sung many songs,
  But never a one so gay,
For he sings of what the world will be
  When the years have died away."

Exercise.

Why did the poet leave the town and street? What tells the direction from which the wind is blowing? What makes us see the effect of the wind? What is the most suggestive word in the fifth line? How many different results of the poet's song are definitely mentioned? How does the swallow hunt the bee? Have you ever seen it? What two suggestions make us see the hawk? What is *the down*? What is your idea of the meaning of the nightingale's thought?

What words in the poem are suggestive as figures of speech? What other words are suggestive? What suggestive details are in the poem?

Are the facts told in these stanzas the literal truth? If not, why did Lord Tennyson make the statements?

92. PERSUASIVE WRITING.

You wish your father or another person to give you something or to permit you to go somewhere or to do a certain thing.

You determine to put into writing your reasons for feeling that your wish should be granted. You first make a list of these reasons. Then you remember that your father will have reasons why your wish should not be granted. You think out all the reasons he will advance, make a list of them, and determine an answer for each.

Now you are ready to write. You first make a brief opening paragraph. Then you give a paragraph to each of the main reasons why your wish should be granted, and a paragraph to each of your answers to possible objections. This constitutes the body of your paper. In a brief concluding paragraph you sum up your reasons, and close with a request that your desire be granted.

This kind of composition, whether oral or written, is called persuasion or argumentation.

Exercise.

You wish your cousin or friend to spend the holidays at your home. Make a list of three or four reasons why he should come and one or two answers to possible objections. After making this brief outline write a letter to him. Use a brief opening paragraph, then a separate paragraph for each reason and answer, add the short concluding paragraph, and sign as usual. Be easy and natural, and write as you would talk if your cousin were present.

In the same way write a letter to your father to persuade him to let you spend the summer on your uncle's farm, at your aunt's city home, at Chautauqua Lake, or at the ocean.

Write a similar letter to a friend who is talking of leaving school, endeavoring to persuade him that it will be better for him to remain in school for at least another year.

Write a letter to a friend urging him to go to the woods with you on Saturday instead of taking a bicycle ride.

Write a letter to your grandmother urging her to come to visit you.

Write a letter to your father in order to persuade him to buy you a bicycle or anything else that you especially wish.

Write a letter to your father, endeavoring to persuade him to let you go through high school after you have completed the grammar school course.

Write a reply to any of the above letters, refusing the thing asked and giving reasons for the refusal.

93. THE GLADIATOR CONDEMNED.
After the Painting by Gérome.

Ex. I. In what city may we imagine this scene is taking place? In what building? How long has the present series of contests been in progress? Why your answer? How many bodies are on the sand of the arena? Which ones are bodies of dead men?

With whom has the standing gladiator just been fighting? With what have they been fighting? Where are the conqueror's feet? Why is he looking up? (When his opponent was defeated it was customary for a gladiator to look to the spectators — usually to the group of spotless vestal virgins — to learn whether he should kill his fallen foe or grant him life.) To which special group is this conqueror looking? Is it a group of men or women? How are they dressed? Do the spectators wish him to spare his foe or kill him?

What is the position of their bodies? Why are they leaning forward? Why are their arms extended? What is the position of their thumbs? What does this mean? (Reversed thumbs demanded the death of the conquered.) Will the gladiator be compelled to kill his foe?

What is the position of the head of the conquered? Why is his mouth open? Where is the conqueror's foot? What is the position of the conquered's right arm? Toward whom is it extended? Why? Where is his left hand? Why? What is the position of his feet? Why is his right foot and leg raised?

Toward what point are all the spectators looking? How important a moment in the sport is this? How much pity do you find in the faces or attitudes of the spectators? How is the conquered dressed? Was he better prepared for the contest than his foe? What is on his left arm? On his right arm? On his head? Legs? Had the conquered a shield? How did he use the net and the trident on the sand at his right? Did the short sword at the left of the picture probably belong to him or to the man near whom it lies?

THE GLADIATOR CONDEMNED.

Does the conqueror seem to wish to kill or to spare? Why your answer?

What signs do we see here of luxury and splendor? How many people are here? How many did the Colosseum at Rome seat? (See encyclopedia.) What other sports took place in the arena? What are the eagles at the tops of the columns? How far are the gladiators from the nearest spectators? That they could thus demand death and look upon it, indicates what kind of people? In what century did gladiatorial sports most flourish?

Do you believe that the world is better now than it was at the time here pictured? Why your answer?

Ex. II. Write a description of this picture.

Suppose that these two men are brothers: write their story.

Write any story, or an account of any incident, suggested by this picture.

94. WHAT THE LONG NIGHT SAID.

The last day we saw the sun, only the upper half was above the horizon at noon, and just as the rim was ready to sink I fancied I heard the " Long Night" say to me:

"For one night of six months I rule at the North Pole. Then I am most powerful. In the course of countless ages I have frozen the sea and I have built a wall of ice so thick and so broad and so hard that no vessel will ever be strong enough to break through, and no man will ever reach the pole. I guard the approach to the pole and watch carefully the wall of ice I have built around it. When the sun drives me away and rules in his turn one day of six months at the pole (for the whole year is equally divided between us), he tries with his steady heat to destroy the wall I have built. On my return I repair the damage the sun has done and make the wall as strong as it was before. I send terrific gales and mighty snowstorms over oceans and lands and even far to the south of my dominion, for my power is so great that it is felt beyond my realm."

There was a pause; then I thought I heard the sardonic laugh of the " Long Night." It seemed like a laugh of defiance.

— *From " The Land of the Long Night" by Paul du Chaillu.*

Exercise.

Write in about as many words as this selection contains, an address that the sun might make, telling of what he has done and is doing for the people of this earth. Write a brief introduction and an appropriate closing paragraph similar to those found above.

Write an answer made by some brave explorer to the boast that no man will ever climb Mt. Everest.

Write a speech of the telephone, in which it tells what it has done for men. The same of electricity; of the locomotive; of natural gas.

Write a speech that spring might make, telling of what she brings to the earth; a speech that winter might make; summer; autumn.

95. ORGANIZATION AND CONDUCT OF A SOCIETY OR MEETING.

The pupils of the seventh and eighth years of your school wish to hold a picnic. They meet to make arrangements for it. When all are in the room, George rises and says, "The meeting will please come to order. I move that Sarah act as chairman of the meeting." Frank rises and says, "I second the motion." George then says, "It has been moved and seconded that Sarah act as chairman of this meeting; those in favor of the motion will say *aye*." After the vote has been taken he says, "Those opposed will say *no*." If the motion is carried he continues, "The motion is carried. Sarah will please take the chair." If the motion is lost he asks for further nominations, and proceeds in the same manner until a chairman is elected.

As soon as Sarah takes the chair she says, "The next business in order is the election of a secretary," at which some one rises and makes a nomination. Several nominations may be made, if desirable. Usually these names are voted on by ballot if more than one nomination is made. The one receiving the majority of the votes cast is declared elected.

Then the various matters of business are taken up in order; first a motion is made and seconded that a picnic shall be held; if this is carried a place is suggested and voted on, or a motion is passed to leave the selection of a place to a committee; etc., etc.

Suppose the purpose is to organize a society. The first meeting is conducted precisely as above.

A committee is elected to prepare and submit a constitution and also by-laws. At the next meeting the report of this committee is heard. It may be adopted as a whole, it may be adopted as amended, or some parts may be adopted and the rest referred back to the committee for further consideration. As soon as enough of the constitution is adopted, an election is held to fill the offices provided for. The temporary chairman then gives the chair to whoever has been elected permanent president, the new secretary takes his place, and the regular order of business is followed.

A constitution should be as brief as possible, and should include only the few important items that must not be changed without careful and prolonged consideration. It usually contains the following items:

1. Name and object of the society.
2. Qualification of members.
3. Officers, their election and duties.
4. Meetings (put details in by-laws).
5. How to amend the constitution.

The by-laws give the various details of more or less importance: the time of regular meetings, the manner of calling special meetings, dues, initiation fees, fines, order of business, book of parliamentary law that is to be authoritative, etc.

Officers for a permanent society should as a rule be a president, a vice president, a secretary, a treasurer, and an executive committee.

The president presides at all meetings, if present; otherwise the vice president takes the chair.

The secretary keeps a record of the meetings. This is called the minutes. The form of minutes is shown by the following suggestion:

The regular meeting of the ——— Society was held on Friday afternoon, Nov. 21, 1902. President John Way was in the chair. The minutes of the previous meeting were read and approved.

The following program was then carried out:

[Insert Program.]

After criticisms and suggestions by the critics, Mr. Jay and Miss Kay, the following report was received from the committee on badges and was adopted upon motion of Mr. Smith:

[Insert Report.]

Mr. Jack moved that the second meeting in December be devoted especially to the presentation of the annual drama. Carried.

On motion of Mr. Say, it was determined that each member be given two tickets to the drama for presentation to friends.

Mr. Dee moved that the meetings in January be devoted especially to debates. Miss Goe moved to amend that it read "that the first three meetings in January be devoted to debates." Amendment passed. Motion as amended was then passed.

After hearing the report of the executive committee on program for the next two meetings, the society adjourned on motion of Miss Loy.

WILLIAM BEST, Secretary.

The minutes may make no mention of motions that are lost; it is better, however, to record all motions.

The treasurer has charge of the money of the society,

pays bills upon orders signed by the president and the secretary, collects dues, fines, etc. At the end of his term he makes a complete report of money on hand when he came into the office, of money received, of money expended, and of balance on hand.

The executive committee consists usually of five members. Its duty is to consider matters of business referred to it by the society, and also to prepare programs, etc.

The following is the usual order of business in a society :

1. Reading of minutes, followed by corrections and approval.
2. Program.
3. Reports of standing committees.
4. Reports of special committees.
5. Unfinished business (matters considered but not disposed of at former meetings).
6. New business.
7. Adjournment.

The president announces the order of business.

Exercise.

Write the minutes of an imaginary session of a society. Insert a program, a report, and a record of at least four motions.

96. LETTERS AND ADVERTISEMENTS TO WRITE.

Ex. I. Write a letter asking a friend to spend Thanksgiving and three or four succeeding days with you. Make your letter informal and very friendly.

Write a note thanking a friend in the country for sending you a box of beautiful arbutus, the first of the spring; or a note thanking a city friend for a bunch of chrysanthemums; or your country cousin for a fine hunting dog he has sent you by express; or your city cousin for a new rifle such as you have been wanting for a year. Show your appreciation and hearty thanks.

Write a note to the principal of a preparatory school or the president of a college asking for a catalogue.

Ex. II. Write a letter ordering at least ten different articles from a grocery store. Be sure that you mention real prices and order real articles. Ask that the articles be sent to your home C. O. D. (that is, "collect on delivery," meaning that you will pay for the articles when they come). Use a line for each article you order.

From a real catalogue order at least ten articles from a great department store. (Your teacher will have several catalogues at her desk.) Inclose money order for the amount of your purchase. Ask that the articles be sent by the express company that has an office near your home. Do not urge the house to give the order their immediate attention; that is customary. Use a line for each item.

One article received among goods ordered as above was very much soiled. In a letter state the exact trouble and ask what action you shall take, assuming that of course they will make the matter right.

Ex. III. Write an advertisement to rent the house you live in; an advertisement to sell your bicycle, used for one year; to sell a horse and carriage; to buy a second-hand typewriter; a second-hand upright piano; a lot at least 50 by 150 feet in the residence district; a farm of at least 100 acres within three miles of town.

97. THE BOY TO THE SCHOOLMASTER.

" You've quizzed me often and puzzled me long,
    You've asked me to cipher and spell,
You've called me a dunce if I answered wrong,
    Or a dolt if I failed to tell
Just when to say *lie* and when to say *lay*,
    Or what nine-sevenths may make,
Or the longitude of Kamchatka Bay,
    Or the I-forget-what's-its-name lake.
So I think it's about *my* turn, I do,
    To ask a question or so of you."

The schoolmaster grim he opened his eyes,
  But said not a word for sheer surprise.

"Can you tell where the nest of the oriole swings,
  Or the color its egg may be?
Do you know the time when the squirrel brings
  Its young from the nest in the tree?
Can you tell when the chestnuts are ready to drop,
  Or where the best hazelnuts grow?
Can you climb a high tree to the very tiptop,
  Then gaze without trembling below?
Can you swim and dive, can you jump and run,
  Or do anything else we boys call fun?"

The master's voice trembled as he replied,
  "You are right, my lad; I'm the dunce," he sighed.[1]
                  — *Edward J. Wheeler.*

Exercises.

Ex. I. Why did the schoolmaster open his eyes? Why was he silent? Why did his voice tremble? Why did he sigh? Where has the boy lived who asks these questions?

Ex. II. Write a paragraph telling whether you like or dislike these stanzas, and giving your reasons.

Write two or three paragraphs telling of the things you know which you have not learned at school. Think carefully about this, determine upon as many as possible, and tell of the value they are to you.

Ex. III. Write two or three paragraphs telling of the things you have learned at school, and of the value they have been to you. Be as definite as possible.

Write two or three paragraphs of the things you have learned from this book during the time you have been studying it, and tell of some occasions when the information has been of use to you. Make no general statements. Be particular.

[1] Used by permission of the author.

98. PRINCIPLES OF COMPOSITION.

To the Teacher. The following summary, which includes only principles that should be emphasized in grammar-school work, is intended to be used for the marking of compositions. On the margin opposite an error is placed the number of the principle violated. After reading the principle and with the aid of the index looking up the Composition and Grammar references, the pupil must discover the error he has made at the point indicated, and must correct it, preferably with a pencil or ink of a color different from that with which the composition is written.

Much of this work should be done with compositions copied on the blackboard, each pupil in the class being required to correct every error indicated. As often as time permits, all compositions written for a given exercise should be marked by the teacher, returned to the pupils for correction, and examined a second time to see that the corrections are properly made. The teacher should regularly mark and return at least four or five papers taken from each set written, as pupils are more careful when they know that their papers may be examined.

A few numbers are added in blank, that teachers may include any other principles that they wish to emphasize.

The following paragraph shows concretely the method suggested:

	1
A kind act.	*2b*
As I was coming through the allegheny parks one	*5d*
day i noticed a large, " Newfoundland " dog standing	*5g–8–3a*
near a pump looking longingly at it. a little girl with	*9h–5a*
some Books under hir arm stopped beside the dog and	*3b–4*
pumped him a cool drink of water When the dog had	*20a–6a*
had enough he licked her hand and looking up into her	*9f*
face he seemed to try his best thank her after patting	*9f–25–6a–5a*
his head for a moment she went in her way.	*15*

As an introductory exercise, children may be asked to correct the errors indicated in the above paragraph. Most of these principles may be used from the beginning, even before they have been formally studied in either the Grammar or the Composition.

Rules of Composition.

1. Write your name at the top of the first page of each written lesson, preferably to the right.

2. (a) About two inches from the top of the first page write a title. (b) Begin its important words with capitals. (c) Under-

score it with three lines. (d) Leave an even margin of half an inch or more at each side of written work. (e) Begin the first line of each paragraph about half an inch from the margin.

3. Avoid unnecessary (a) punctuation marks, including quotation marks and the apostrophe, (b) capital letters, and (c) italics.

4. Spell correctly.

5. Begin with a capital letter (a) every sentence; (b) every formal quotation; (c)[1] every name of the Deity, but not pronouns referring to these names; (d)[1] every proper name and proper adjective; (e) the principal words in titles of office or respect, in titles of books and poems, in headings of chapters, in names of firms, etc.; (f) the first word of each line of poetry; (g) *I* and *O*, but not *oh*.

6. Use a period (.) (a) at the end of a declarative or imperative sentence; (b) after an abbreviation; (c) after *yes* and *no* when used alone; (d) after initials.

7. (a) Use an interrogation point (?) after direct questions. (b) Use an exclamation point (!) after exclamatory sentences and expressions.

8. Never use a comma unless its presence will add to clearness.

9. Use a comma (,) (a) to set off words of address; (b) to set off a quotation and to set off words that divide a quotation; (c) after *oh,* and usually after *yes* and *no* when not used alone; (d) after each word or expression in a series except the last; (e) to separate two complete statements united by *and, but,* and similar connectives; (f) to set off parenthetical expressions and non-restrictive appositives; (g) to set off non-restrictive expressions beginning with *who* and *which;* (h) to set off independent participial elements; (i) wherever its presence, by appealing to the eye, will add to clearness.

10. Inclose in quotation marks (" ") (a) the exact words of another included within your own writing; (b) the names of books, of poems, of papers and magazines, and of vessels. (c) Inclose in single quotation marks (' ') a quotation within a quotation.

11. Use the apostrophe (') (a) with *s* ('s) when writing the possessive form of the noun, except when the noun is plural and ends in *s;* (b) at the end of nouns in the plural ending in *s* when writing the possessive form; (c) to show the omission of a letter or of letters belonging to a word. (d) Do not use the apostrophe with *ours, yours, hers, its,* and *theirs.*

---

[1] When a name of the Deity or a proper name consists of several words, begin each important word with a capital; as, *Son of Man, Gulf of Mexico, Abraham Lincoln.*

SUMMARY OF RULES

12. Use a hyphen (-) (a) at the end of a line, *after a syllable*, when part of the word must be written on the next line ; (b) between the parts of compound words when the parts have not become united into a single word.

13. Use short sentences. Make two or three sentences out of a single long one.

14. Use simple words.

15. Use words in their proper meaning. See p. 239 for *oh;* p. 147 for *lie, lay, rise, raise, sit,* and *set;* p. 184 for *shall* and *will;* p. 138 for *who, which,* and *that.*

16. Avoid slang.

17. Avoid abbreviations, contractions, and corrupt forms of words (p. 229).

18. Be sure that a verb agrees with its subject.

19. (a) Do not use the past participle instead of the past tense, or vice versa. (b) Use verbs in the proper tense. (c) Use the subjunctive form of the verb to express conditions contrary to fact.

20. (a) Place adjectives where they must modify the word desired. (b) Use *a* and *an* correctly. (c) Use *than* after an adjective in the comparative degree. (d) Use *other* to exclude the thing being compared.

21. Place adverbs near the words they modify.

22. Do not use adjectives for adverbs or adverbs for adjectives.

23. Use pronouns according to the rules of grammar.

24. (a) Punctuate and capitalize as shown in the perfect letter form, p. 245. (b) Use only a colon (:) after the salutation when the body of the letter begins on the following line; when it begins on the same line use the colon and the dash (:—). (c) Do not omit any parts of the letter form.

25. Do not omit necessary words.

26. Omit unnecessary words.

27. (a) A paragraph should deal with one definite part of a subject. (b) A sentence should include only closely related thoughts. See pp. 87 and 279–281.

28. Make your sentences express exactly your meaning.

29. Make every sentence complete.

30. Show the beginning and the end of each sentence.

31. *And* should connect only similar elements.

32. Find and correct an error in the line marked.

ADDITIONAL EXERCISES.

PAGE 8. *Determine which of the following are sentences:* 1. History of New England. 2. A turkey strutted before the barn. 3. Near the farmhouse was a large orchard. 4. Sometimes tearing up the earth with his feet. 5. The man's mouth watered. 6. An apple in his mouth. 7. The rich fields of wheat, of rye, of buckwheat, and Indian corn. 8. Mounted on the top of a wagon loaded with beets. 9. The boy went home. 10. Loving my country. 11. About the effect of this speech on the people. 12. By spring the feeling of the people had changed very greatly. 13. To describe the school as divided into classes. 14. André, under a false name, with papers betraying military secrets. 15. The constitution was not new.

PAGE 8. *Determine the sentences that tell, that command or request, and that ask a question:* 1. By the dawn's light you can see the flag. 2. He came from the deserts of Nevada. 3. The first said, "I did!" 4. I will tell a tale in praise of the right. 5. Will you rebuke wrong throughout your life? 6. So live that thy days are full of helpfulness. 7. To have a good friend is one of the highest delights of life. 8. Do you forgive as you would be forgiven? 9. Think before you speak. 10. If friendship is not given to you, earn it. 11. See what is making that noise. 12. What did you find it to be? 13. It was the escaping steam. 14. What time is it? 15. Tell me the time. 16. Is that the truth? 17. Did you finish it yesterday? 18. Tell me when you finished it. 19. That will do.

PAGE 9. *Tell which of the following sentences are declarative, which interrogative, and which imperative, and give reasons. Mention those that are also exclamatory:* 1. I breathed a song into the air. 2. Where did I find the song? 3. I found it in the heart of a friend. 4. Let me come in. 5. I will be of service to you. 6. Does your pupil do well? 7. Pardon the praise! 8. Ah, here is the home of my childhood! 9. There is always a song somewhere. 10. What is money in comparison with being useful! 11. Never mind about money! 12. What a beautiful night it is! 13. Stop that noise! 14. I will not do it! 15. Who were on the program last night? 16. I think you are right. 17. Go into the spelling contest!

ADDITIONAL EXERCISES

PAGE 12. *Analyze the following declarative sentences, and diagram (as on p. 11):* 1. The early sunlight entered the room. 2. I love thy rocks and rills. 3. He answered every roll call. 4. Each guest started at the word. 5. A boy's mother is his best friend. 6. Candles are lighted. 7. Our fathers brought forth a new nation. 8. The woods, the blossoms, and the mosses please men in their simple way. 9. The bell's deep tones are swelling. 10. The birds sing gayly in the trees. 11. Time goes by, by little minutes. 12. "Goodby" is a sad word. 13. The leaves are turning to a beautiful gold. 14. The school bell rings at nine o'clock. 15. A machine of that kind can be bought for one hundred dollars. 16. I finished the work at noon. 17. Roosevelt spoke at the fair. 18. A hook-nosed rag-peddler knocked at my door at six o'clock. 19. He walked rapidly across the street.

PAGE 13. *Change the following interrogative sentences, as nearly as possible, to the declarative form; tell the subject and predicate of each; and diagram:* 1. What do you mean? 2. What is the meaning of this noise? 3. Did you bring any message? 4. How was this done? 5. Why did you insist? 6. Is he confined to bed? 7. What does he say? 8. Where are the books you mentioned? 9. How is your master? 10. Was the stick nailed to the limb? 11. Will you tell me his name? 12. Were you at the picnic? 13. Who are you? 14. Who is the man with the black eyes? 15. Are many new pupils here? 16. Which boy is the best runner? 17. Does the baseball team promise well? 18. Why did you come to this school? 19. Where is your home?

PAGES 13-14. *In the following sentences supply the omitted subjects, and diagram:* 1. Tell me the whole story. 2. Try to be helpful. 3. Hand me that book. 4. Always be industrious. 5. Cast the log out of your own eye. 6. Please open the door. 7. Don't you do it. 8. Do not neglect the little things. 9. Keep thy tongue from evil and thy lips from guile. 10. Never forget your mother. 11. Be a brother to the unfortunate.

PAGE 16. *Which of the following expressions are sentences, and why? Diagram each sentence as in the examples given:* 1. Oh, why not? 2. Excellent idea. 3. Turn the lamps out. 4. Go, then! 5. Look! I am even now a dead man. 6. Gently, sir. 7. Very little, truly. 8. That is true. 9. "Nonsense!" was what he said. 10. Has any one called? 11. Sir, consider. 12. Rot! 13. Hurry! 14. Oh, for a team that could play ball! 15. Pell-mell, rush, slam, bang, into the bleachers! 16. They carried him off on their shoulders. 17. What a sight it was! 18. Good-by!

PAGE 18. *Determine the subject and the predicate of each of the following sentences, arrange them in their natural order, and diagram:* 1. Slowly his pale arms reached forward. 2. On the grass the rain is gently falling. 3. On earth are no fairies. 4. The bells I hear. 5. For you are bouquets and wreaths. 6. Holy is thy name. 7. Suddenly out came a rabbit. 8. Such a wreck I never before saw. 9. Wonderful is the ability of man. 10. A man of unusual strength was he.

PAGE 19. *Analyze the following sentences to determine the subject and predicate, and then diagram them:* 1. There is no death! 2. To him there was no meaning in the bullet's hiss. 3. There the snowflakes drifted. 4. There is reason for urging the boys to play. 5. There is a blessedness in happy hearts. 6. There I left my people. 7. There on the orchard path I met him. 8. There hangs a saber. 9. There are dreams that mean nothing. 10. There I found a violet.

PAGE 21. *Diagram the following sentences and observe how they are punctuated:* 1. I myself heard it. 2. It is wisdom to dislike folly. 3. It is good to be the best of men. 4. The word "beautiful" is an adjective. 5. It is really I, your old friend and neighbor. 6. Here it is, the dear remembered spot! 7. It is easy to do things wrong. 8. It became necessary to revolt from England. 9. It is foolish to waste time. 10. I gave it to him myself.

PAGE 27. *Make a list of the nouns on this page, and tell whether they are concrete or abstract.*

PAGE 31. *Point out the verbs:* 1. We gave him no reply. 2. He looked about for his own image. 3. He broke down all at once. 4. "And so did I!" exclaimed Henry. 5. When the clock struck eleven this domestic ball broke up. 6. My time is short. 7. Is it so that he deserves this praise? 8. They went in. 9. Clear away! 10. Trifles show character. 11. Maud Muller on a summer's day raked the meadow sweet with hay. 12. It falleth like the gentle rain from heaven. 13. Sweet land of liberty, of thee I sing. 14. Wake Duncan with thy knocking! 15. I went to the door and opened it quickly. 16. The wind rushed in and blew out my lamp. 17. I read the book while you rested.

ADDITIONAL EXERCISES

PAGE 32. *Select the subject and the predicate in each of the following sentences, and diagram (p. 32):* 1. There dwelt a mighty emperor. 2. Then the gentle lady spoke courteously. 3. The brave knight came soon. 4. Thou speakest foolishly. 5. The noble king went quickly. 6. A quarrel soon broke out. 7. Her violent sorrow gradually lessened. 8 Gently the feathery flakes floated down. 9. The forward pass succeeded admirably. 10. The sure-footed mule descended carefully. 11. The wounded bandit ate ravenously. 12. The weird sounds increased. 13. Steadily the cold rain fell. 14. The phantom slowly, silently approached.

PAGE 33. *Select the verbs and determine those made up of two or more words:* 1. I seek a friend. 2. I have laid my hand to the plow. 3. Be ruled by me, and go back. 4. Come then, good neighbor. 5. Then they went, both together. 6. Crowns of glory will be given to us. 7. What company shall we have here? 8. As I was going there, I fell in here. 9. But why did you not look for the steps? 10. Fear followed me so hard that I fled and fell in. 11. I may go to the game. 12. I might have been elected if I had asked that my friends vote for me. 13. What would you have done? 14. He had been cut with broken glass. 15. He has gone home. 16. We shall certainly ask them all. 17. What has he done for the school?

PAGES 34-35. *Fill the blanks with appropriate adjectives, and tell what each modifies:* 1. Give me my _____ cottage again. 2. Farewell, _____ home. 3. From _____ trip the _____ ship comes in. 4. Reach out to me a _____ hand. 5. A _____ welcome awaits us from our _____ mother. 6. The _____ moonlight lights up the _____ clouds. 7. Life is an _____ struggle. 8. He made a _____ blunder. 9. He walks the _____ streets. 10. This is our _____ land. 11. I see the _____ _____ house. 12. This is a _____ grove. 13. We went on a _____ train. 14. He rides a _____ _____ horse. 15. My father has the _____ garden in town.

PAGES 35-36. *Fill the blanks with appropriate adverbs, and tell what each modifies:* 1. He came in _____. 2. I know them _____. 3. Walk _____ to the station. 4. We heard _____ that you were here. 5. I saw it _____. 6. The snow is falling _____. 7. Tender words are _____ welcome. 8. Some boys find work _____. 9. Some boys sleep _____. 10. Lincoln _____ loved the common people. 11. Pleasures of the senses pass _____.

12. Pleasures of the mind _____ pass. 13. Do your kind deed _____. 14. I love my country _____ _____. 15. He did his duty _____. 16. They lived _____ for _____ many years. 17. It is vanity to desire to live _____ and not to care to live _____. 18. The wind blew _____ and the rain fell _____. 19. And hark! how _____ the thrush sings!

PAGE 37. *Tell which of the indicated words are adjectives and which are adverbs, and tell what each modifies:* 1. A **little, lowly** cottage it was. 2. A **soft** answer turneth away wrath. 3. The wind bites **sharply**; it is a **very cold** wind. 4. I come to pluck your berries **harsh** and **crude**. 5. After life's **fitful** fever, he sleeps **well**. 6. The sublime and the ridiculous are **often nearly** related. 7. He prayeth **best,** who loveth **best** all things, both **great** and **small.** 8. This is my **best** work. 9. She has a **soft, gentle,** and **low** voice, — an **excellent** thing in woman. 10. **Undoubtedly** he was a hero.

PAGES 38–39. *Analyze and diagram the following:* 1. She dropped on her knees. 2. He fell into imbecility. 3. The man went on this errand. 4. I served through the war. 5. They rode from the palace to the town. 6. The sentinels at the door fled. 7. The church bells of the city rang in the night. 8. The candle in her hands went out. 9. His duty to his friend interfered. 10. A man at bay seldom hesitates. 11. The little playful streams hurry down the hillside. 12. Beneath the palms he wanders again. 13. The clown was standing on his head.

PAGE 42. *Diagram:* 1. He asks for work and shelter. 2. He went with swinging gait and erect shoulders for milk and eggs. 3. The happy man works with his brain and with his hands. 4. I sing in merry time and tune of home and friends and love. 5. He came with prayer and praise. 6. That book was printed in Berlin or in Vienna. 7. He never looked for admirers and friends. 8. In rain and wind he came. 9. He speaks in the blush of morning and in the evening glow.

PAGE 44. *Which of the indicated words are prepositions? Why? Which are conjunctions? Why?* 1. It is strange, **yet** stranger things have happened. 2. **No** great artist ever sees things **as** they really are. 3. What did he know **about** slavery? 4. There must be work done **by** hands **or** none **of** us could live. 5. Little minds are subdued **by** misfortune, **but** great minds rise **above** it. 6. Drink **to** me only **with** thine eyes, **and** I will pledge **with** mine. 7. **I can study books** # ADDITIONAL EXERCISES 351

at any time, **for** they are always **at** hand. 8. Sink **or** swim, live **or** die, survive **or** perish, I give my hand **and** my heart **to** this vote. 9. If you survive yellow journalism, you need not be afraid **of** yellow fever. 10. I could not enjoy anybody's lectures **unless** I entirely disagreed **with** some parts. 11. They all went **but** me. 12. I went **for** apples, **for** we wished to make cider. 13. I did it **against** his advice. 14. He ran **against** a tree. 15. In 1830 the population **of** the United States was **under** thirteen millions. 16. He has been here **since** noon. 17. It has been years **since** he graduated. 18. He came **and** he conquered. 19. He came **for** the purpose **of** conquering.

PAGE 47. *Tell part of speech of indicated word, and give a reason:* 1. The streams run **down** the hillside. 2. The **down** of the dandelion tells our fortune. 3. He went **down** and I went up. 4. They **dance** very well. 5. The **dance** will be in the barn. 6. I saw the fish **swallow** the hook. 7. A **swallow** flew from the chimney. 8. A **swallow** of water may save a life. 9. That **study** occupies all their time. 10. They **study** all the time. 11. He sits in his **study** chair. 12. The **man** is without money. 13. A **man** child had been born. 14. They **man** the boat and push from shore. 15. He admires her **fancy** gown. 16. Her **fancy** makes wonderful stories. 17. I **fancy** she will be disappointed. 18. He raised his **left** hand. 19. I **left** the house at 9 o'clock. 20. I went from the gate and turned to the **left**. 21. He picked up the **paper** and trimmed it with a **paper** knife which the men who came to **paper** had left in a **paper** box. 22. I **shot** from the fort at the sound of the **shot** and found that the **shot** tower was in flames as the result of hot **shot** fired by the besiegers. 23. Of all the saws I ever saw saw, I never saw a saw saw as this saw saws. 24. **Like** natures **like** the same things. 25. The **fence** is too high. 26. They **fence** with swords. 27. His strength begins to **flag**. 28. Every school should own a **flag** and observe **flag** day.

PAGE 48. *Use each word as a verb, then as a noun:* saw, hail, name, plan, talk, help, smoke, swing, rake, kick, look, part, pat.

PAGE 48. *Use each as a verb, then as an adjective:* better, smooth, light, busy, free, tame, long, board.

PAGE 48. *Use each as a verb, then as a noun, then as an adjective:* fall, feather, pasture, master, work.

PAGE 48. *Use each word as two different parts of speech:* mask, sugar, cut, dirt, shovel, fur, book, pen, cart, safe, trap.

PAGE 50. *Tell whether the verbs make complete predication. If necessary, supply complements:* 1. The messengers rode away. 2. He seemed. 3. I met. 4. All the world is. 5. I go on forever. 6. He tried. 7. Brutus stabbed. 8. He entered. 9. Rip sighed. 10. Wolf wagged. 11. He heard. 12. He stared. 13. He found. 14. He paused. 15. He was. 16. To John it seemed. 17. He could hear. 18. His hand began. 19. Soon his arm ached. 20. He felt. 21. He watched. 22. His ear touched. 23. He was frightened.

PAGE 52. *The indicated words are complements. Tell whether attribute or object:* 1. John looked **tired.** 2. He read the **book.** 3. The day seems **long.** 4. The bread was baked **brown.** 5. Mother baked five **loaves.** 6. The stream ran **red** with blood. 7. He ran his **engine** at full speed. 8. Simplicity is always **right.** 9. The boy painted the **fence.** 10. The fence was **red.** 11. She was his constant **companion.** 12. They believed **they would be sorry.** 13. The buds are the **children** of the flowers. 14. The star showed a great **world** of light. 15. The patient face was **glorified** and **radiant.**

PAGE 52. *Point out the complements, tell whether they are object or attribute, and diagram:* 1. Prince Arthur besieged the tower. 2. I am not an idler. 3. We knew his love for the game. 4. He killed his dog. 5. He looked ill. 6. The indignation was intense. 7. Henry VIII. proved false. 8. King John was insane. 9. Joyful was the song. 10. Be glad. 11. His name was Raggylug. 12. He was lying very still. 13. He saw a robin. 14. The sun was warm. 15. He heard a little sound. 16. He forgot his mother's warning. 17. The snake dropped Raggylug. 18. She led him through the grass. 19. There she made a new nest. 20. Who will be the wolf?

PAGE 54. *The indicated words are object complements, attribute complements, or modifiers. Tell which each is:* 1. He loves **honor.** 2. He loves **nobly.** 3. He gave **liberty** to the slaves. 4. He gave **liberally.** 5. The plowman homeward plods his weary **way.** 6. I see my native **hills.** 7. I see **clearly.** 8. The waves break **gently.** 9. Such partings break the **heart.** 10. It was my **friend.** 11. The apples look **ripe,** but they do not feel **mellow.** 12. We drank the pure **milk.** 13. We heard his last **"farewell."** 14. My friends were **poor** but **honest.** 15. He found **her** by the ocean.

PAGE 55. *Point out the objective complements, and diagram:* 1. Alexander made himself emperor. 2. They elected John Adams second President. 3. The boys dug the hole very deep. 4. Make

ADDITIONAL EXERCISES

yourself useful. 5. They made Charles president of the class. 6. These mills grind flour very fine. 7. The sunset turned the water crimson. 8. His teasing made the dog savage. 9. What power made man master of the world? 10. Cultivation makes plants more productive. 11. He made the slave's cause popular. 12. He always puts his country first. 13. No schooling will ever make him wise. 14. The reflection painted the ceiling a soft green. 15. The big center tore open the line. 16. The railroad rendered possible the wheat fields of the Dakotas. 17. His home made him a man again. 18. The trolley makes the farmer a city dweller.

PAGE 57. *Mention the direct and the indirect objects, and diagram:* 1. The church gave the minister a donation. 2. Provide heavy blankets. 3. Bring me back the old games. 4. Wise men teach their sons wisdom. 5. She did not get her poor dog a bone. 6. The state should give women the right of voting. 7. She wished him a Merry Christmas. 8. Penelope made her husband a feast. 9. Henry sends his friend a kind greeting. 10. Give us our daily bread. 11. I will tell him the story. 12. Sing him a new song. 13. The governor refused him a pardon. 14. They gave him his rights. 15. We offered them freedom. 16. We fed the horses grain. 17. This brought him fame. 18. Do him no harm.

PAGE 57. *Select all complements, tell the kind of each, and point out indirect objects:* 1. The way seemed long and weary. 2. Give me back my heart. 3. The Britons never shall be slaves. 4. Love makes all things beautiful. 5. They called the boy Edward. 6. He had never seen her. 7. We had much cold weather. 8. He reached the summit first. 9. This case requires tact. 10. The world is a curious place. 11. His titles are high, his fame is great. 12. Honor your dear old mother. 13. What a stormy sunset we saw last night! 14. The organ poured its sound into our hearts. 15. Friendship is a gift, but it is also an acquirement. 16. To be a real friend is worthy of high endeavor. 17. They made him a picture of the fox. 18. They made him umpire of the game. 19. The poor brother told him the story. 20. The man offered his nephew the position.

PAGES 61–62. *Analyze or diagram the following and tell how each infinitive is used:* 1. What do you wish me to do with that? 2. I have no jewels to wear. 3. To look poor among rich women is humiliating. 4. Ask her to lend you some jewels. 5. She wished to escape. 6. They feared to display their wretchedness. 7. It will give us time to look around. 8. To hesitate is to be lost. 9. To succeed is every man's desire. 10. We are sure to win this game. 11. Men grieve to see children waste time. 12. He maketh me to lie down in green pastures. 13. We wished to do good. 14. Have you sought to find him elsewhere? 15. I was not sent to you to ask a gift. 16. There I hoped to receive a meal. 17. I kneeled to meet the fatal stroke. 18. It was time to go home. 19. He stopped strangers to tell them about it. 20. The man did not allow him to finish. 21. He wished to be chosen. 22. I heard him say it. 23. He had called to have a talk with me. 24. I have a question to ask. 25. I want you to come with me. 26. The auction is to occur soon. 27. It was my duty to tell him. 28. I wish to go away. 29. He made it run faster. 30. This is the ship to visit. 31. His beard seemed to fill half the room. 32. We are going away to be kings. 33. We want you to show us your books. 34. Is it hard to learn the uses of the infinitive? 35. The man to do that is Mr. Dick.

PAGE 65. *In the following classify the indicated words and tell how each is used:* 1. The man **speaking** is Tom's father. 2. The man's **speaking** interrupted me. 3. The **speaking** automaton interested him. 4. **Seeing** the elephant was great fun. 5. The thief, **seeing** the officer, ran away. 6. The **signing** of the compact was delayed. 7. By **signing** his name Brown became a member. 8. The house **painted** yesterday has already been sold. 9. The farm has an **unpainted** barn. 10. **Working** men have few wants. 11. He was paid for **working** on the train. 12. **Reading** in a moving vehicle may be injurious. 13. The letter **written** yesterday has just been mailed. 14. Our country has a **written** constitution. 15. **Having** one's own wish does not always give satisfaction. 16. **Stealing** property is a crime. 17. They caught him **stealing** a horse. 18. He passed his time in **reading**. 19. By **working** hard he passed the examination. 20. The man was arrested for **forging** a note. 21. **Knowing** I have no right to speak here, I ask your leave. 22. **Painting** is a fine art. 23. The air was **biting**. 24. **Lying** in bed and **listening** to their dreary music had a pleasure in it. 25. Incessant **scribbling** is death to thought. 26. He spent the day in **roaming** over the house. 27. The sergeant's **seeing** these things told him secrets generally hid from young officers. 28. She watched the wonder of the light, and its **increasing**, and **quivering**, and **lengthening**.

PAGES 65–66. *Analyze or diagram the following and explain use of each participle:* 1. We saw the swallows gathering in the sky.

ADDITIONAL EXERCISES

2. By worshiping idols, they sinned. 3. Their worshiping of idols was sinful. 4. The soldiers ran onward, overcoming every obstacle. 5. We found her reading a story. 6. Describing a past event in present time sometimes has a fine effect in language. 7. He deserves being particularly mentioned. 8. By keeping it he has committed treason. 9. Polishing telescope lenses is a delicate process. 10. The soldier, waking in the morning, thinks first of home. 11. Holding office is hard work. 12. Reading in haste gives small knowledge. 13. Your offering me the appointment greatly obliges me. 14. Speaking low, she stepped to his side. 15. Speaking loudly may be offensive. 16. With an ill will, Scrooge, dismounting from the stool, admitted the fact. 17. Knocking down the fire-irons, tumbling over the chairs, bumping up against the piano, smothering himself among the curtains, away he went. 18. The bright stars playing in the sky are the children of the sun. 19. He is a German, unaccustomed to our climate. 20. Lying there, he has neither friends nor gold. 21. I, barefoot and scantily attired, shall tread the burning sands. 22. I'm a prisoner taken at Tebnim. 23. He noticed the officer looking at him.

PAGE 67. *Tell the different kinds of participles, and tell the use of each:* 1. Seeing the thief, they all followed him. 2. Having seen him well started, we returned home. 3. Robbed of his money, the poor man became despondent. 4. His heart stopped beating. 5. Having signed the bill, the president left the office. 6. There he was found, sleeping on the grass. 7. We found him dying. 8. Having been called, I went at once. 9. Being blinded by the flash, he stood motionless. 10. Having been fishing in the lake, I did not know of the accident.

PAGE 69. *Which of the following are phrases and which clauses:* 1. In the summer months. 2. Sensitive to the beautiful. 3. Out of the cold gray fog. 4. Where wine is a rarity. 5. From behind a cloud. 6. After you see him. 7. When the lamp is broken. 8. Breaking the lamp. 9. Like words in a dream. 10. Whatever may come. 11. Of them all. 12. Which come and go. 13. What is told. 14. Which was not all a dream. 15. On the road. 16. In their bloom. 17. To decide for good or evil. 18. Writing in the ledger. 19. When the rocks are gray. 20. Being young.

PAGE 72. *Diagram the following:* 1. It is best at once to sink. 2. That is no excuse for picking my pocket. 3. It is a sin to speak my grief. 4. The child tried to draw his breath. 5. To see the vacant chair brings sorrow. 6. I never said, "Off with your hat."

7. It is hard to settle down. 8. I hope to see my father soon. 9. The men began to climb the slope. 10. Arguing in anger wins no victory.

PAGES 74-75. *Analyze or diagram the following and tell the kind of connective in each:* 1. There are few buildings which have not been painted. 2. This is the spot where they laid him. 3. The scene was enlivened by the dashing of a swollen mountain brook, whose course we followed for miles. 4. He is the only one who cares. 5. The day is coming when wrongs shall be righted. 6. That is the man whom they trusted. 7. There were no men whom one could trust. 8. On the corner is an old shop where toys are kept. 9. That was the day for which they had waited. 10. Lincoln, who was a very poor boy, became president. 11. He who faints is lost. 12. This is all that I can find. 13. Yonder is the house where I was born. 14. There's a land where sorrow never comes. 15. I have found the book which I lost.

PAGES 76-77. *Determine adverbial clauses, tell what each modifies, point out the connectives, and diagram:* 1. After I learned to row, I voyaged often on the lake. 2. No nobler feeling than patriotism dwells in the breast of man. 3. Hero worship will endure while man endures. 4. He had fought wherever the Roman eagles flew. 5. Sing out as the little thrushes sing. 6. If you would be respected, never tell a lie. 7. He came that he might conquer. 8. The clock goes as it pleases. 9. Gather the rosebuds while you may. 10. Wisdom is better than rifles. 11. The wind blows where it wishes. 12. He was so vain that he was proud of his vanity. 13. I am never merry when I hear sweet music. 14. That star was more beautiful than the others. 15. It rose when darkness fell. 16. Let the world run by while you think. 17. I will never neglect a kindness, for I shall live this life but once. 18. The doctor forgets his toils while he bends over a bed of pain. 19. I love flowers because my mother loved them.

PAGES 77-78. *Determine absolute phrases and diagram:* 1. The rain continuing to fall, we remained in camp. 2. I was alone in the house, my brother having stayed at his office. 3. The burglar tiptoed softly across the room, the baby standing silent in the doorway. 4. The struggle for freedom being past, Milton went back to his books. 5. They could not reach me by telephone, the wire being down at some point. 6. The irrigating ditch having been completed, the desert began to blossom. 7. My brother came in, the game having been finished. 8. The machine being broken, I could not use it.

Pages 79-80. *Tell how the noun clauses are used, and diagram:*
1. What he would do next was always a mystery. 2. Pandora was curious to know what was in the box. 3. The thought of where he was going greatly excited him. 4. It was of little consequence where he was going. 5. The people shouted, "Long live the king." 6. How they can do such things is hard to understand. 7. Character is what we are. 8. Men know what we are by what we do. 9. Where the pilgrims landed is a sacred spot. 10. It was known that the Irish were in arms. 11. On which side the truth lay it was not easy to decide. 12. He knew James had defeated the army. 13. He knew what would benefit his army. 14. He knew when the fleet arrived.

Page 81. *Analyze or diagram these simple sentences:* 1. The house was built by Jack. 2. The horse and the cow are useful animals. 3. The boys came home and ate their suppers in silence. 4. In this way we can hope to succeed. 5. They fought and bled. 6. I signed the articles and took the oaths. 7. There is but one course to follow. 8. I came into the room after my coat, having been unable to find it in the hall or on the porch. 9. He and his sister are very pleasant young people. 10. The sun never sets on the British Empire.

Page 83. *Which of the following are simple and which are complex:* 1. Joy, temperance, and repose slam the door on the doctor's nose. 2. Cicero was a famous orator. 3. Alexander wept because there were no more worlds to conquer. 4. He who runs may read. 5. Where he leads let us follow. 6. The man was trapped into making a confession. 7. Spurred to greater effort, they put all their strength where it was most needed. 8. The spots can be removed if you use alcohol. 9. Soda water, if it is pure, is not a harmful drink. 10. He ran when I spoke. 11. I know a place where wild onions grow. 12. Uneasy is the head that wears a crown. 13. Wise men know the place to stop. 14. Darkness which might be felt, fell upon the city. 15. I weep more deeply, because I weep in vain. 16. The man of eminent ability is often deceived by an uneducated sharper. 17. I will go whenever you are ready. 18. That he is a remarkable man cannot be denied. 19. He watched me enter the store and speak to the clerk at the desk. 20. Our sweetest songs are those that tell of saddest thoughts.

Pages 85-86. *Classify the following as simple, complex, or compound:* 1. He again seated himself at his table, and read in that book with silver clasps. 2. Then they bound the prisoner and led him away. 3. Cæsar came, and saw, and conquered. 4. When a lady walks the streets she leaves her frowns at home. 5. "Give the luxuries of life to us and we will dispense with its necessaries." 6. "Good Americans, when they die, go to Paris." 7. "Boston State House is the hub of the solar system." 8. While she was very young, the sister drooped, and became so weak that she could no longer stand in the window at night. 9. When he had five sons, he had five farms. 10. He pointed to the door, and they went out. 11. Drink drives men to crime, but cigarettes make criminals out of mere boys. 12. When it is played by gentlemen who are physically fit, football is the best of all games. 13. A college education cannot make brains, but it can develop whatever intellect a boy may have. 14. Oh, where can I lose myself and whither shall I fly? 15. The author of the story is a lawyer who has written several novels. 16. Early on a dewy morning in the sweet-scented month of June, Marjorie, with her dolls, her quaint little work basket, and her snowy poodle, made her way with tripping step into the blooming orchard.

PAGES 95–96. *Write the following from dictation:* 1. With the close of summer on Wednesday, September 21, autumn began. 2. I saw Governor Stone, but did not meet the president or the secretary. 3. The king of Portugal fled from Lisbon on October 7, 1910. 4. My Aunt Jane praised your uncle's address. 5. Classes are dismissed from Wednesday before Thanksgiving until the following Monday, and soon after comes December and the winter vacation, with Christmas and New Year's.

PAGES 104–110. *Write from dictation:* 1. I invited the Misses Howard and Mr. Hopkins. 2. I asked the three Miss Dicksons. 3. On the vessel were two Englishmen, three Germans, two Brahmans, each with several menservants. 4. They came by twos and threes, all talking about crossing t's and dotting i's, and using many "eh's." 5. The Joneses, the Baxters, the Rosses, and the Dunns were there.

PAGES 123–124. *Write the following from dictation:* 1. The women's vote favored woman's suffrage in determining teachers' pay. 2. Mr. Jones's son works in Holmes Brothers' store. 3. Is boys' clothing sold in a men's furnishing store? 4. It's my son's boat and not yours, theirs, ours, or hers. 5. It's as easy for a school to show its spirit as for girls to show theirs. 6. Dickens's novels are enjoyed by Mr. Hastings's family. 7. He has twelve weeks' work and one week's vacation. 8. Harris's store is next to Olds and Co.'s garage.

ADDITIONAL EXERCISES

PAGES 147-149. *Repeat frequently in class and at home the following:*

I am lying on the couch.	I am laying the book on the desk.
I lay on the couch yesterday.	I laid the book on the desk.
I have lain on the couch.	I have laid the book on the desk.
I shall lie on the couch.	I shall lay the book on the desk.
I am rising from the chair.	I am raising the flag.
I rose from the chair.	I raised the flag.
I have risen from the chair.	I have raised the flag.
I shall rise from the chair.	I shall raise the flag.
I am sitting on the chair.	I am setting the table.
I sat on the chair.	I set the table.
I have sat on the chair.	I have set the table.
I shall sit on the chair.	I shall set the table.
He went home.	He did the work.
He has gone home.	He has done the work.
I saw the boy.	There is (was) a boy.
I have seen the boy.	There are (were) two boys.

PAGES 166-167. *Let the class, individually and in chorus, give a synopsis of each verb in the list on pages 166-167, using the following forms:*

The principal parts of *go* are, Present, *go;* past, *went;* past participle, *gone.*

The sign of the future is *shall* or *will;* the sign of the present perfect tense is *have* or *has;* the sign of the past perfect is *had;* and the sign of the future perfect is *shall have* or *will have.*

The synopsis of the indicative mode of *go* is, Present, *I go* or *I am going;* past, *I went* or *I was going;* future, *I shall go;* present perfect, *I have gone;* past perfect, *I had gone;* future perfect, *I shall have gone.*

The signs of the potential mode are *may, can, must, might, could, would,* or *should.*

The synopsis of *go* in the potential mode is: Present, *I may, can,* or *must go;* past, *I might, could, would,* or *should go;* present perfect, *I may, can,* or *must have gone;* past perfect, *I might, could, would,* or *should have gone.*

The form for the subjunctive and imperative modes and for all of the passive voice may be given by the teacher.

PAGES 169–170. *The following are the common uses of the subjunctive. They should frequently be repeated by the class, both individually and in chorus:*

If I were you.	I wish I were there.	If he were honest.
If he were here.	I wish he were here.	If I were in your place.

PAGES 193–200. *Repeat frequently the following:*

I like that kind of boy. He is the older of the two. She is the oldest of the three.

Tell why:

Say	Do not say
I know my lessons well.	I know my lessons good.
I like that kind of apples.	I like those kind of apples.
I like that kind of horse.	I like that kind of a horse.
I feel bad this morning.	I feel badly this morning.
Please pass that molasses.	Please pass those molasses.
Those data have been secured.	That data has been secured.
These phenomena are infrequent.	That phenomena is infrequent.
He received the title of duke.	He received the title of a duke.
This is more nearly perfect than that.	This is more perfect than that.

DIFFICULT CONSTRUCTIONS OF THE INFINITIVE AND THE PARTICIPLE.

The infinitive and the participle have certain common uses that are somewhat difficult to explain by the usual grammatical principles.

1. The infinitive in its assumed predicate construction (see page 60) frequently becomes the subject of a sentence:

For him to obey promptly is a duty.

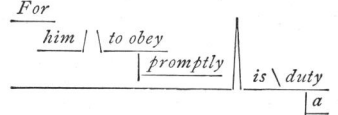

The entire phrase *For him to obey promptly* is the subject of the sentence. The phrase *him to obey* is introduced by *For*, following an idiom of the language. *For*, although necessary to introduce the infinitive, has no meaning, and may be called an expletive. The infinitive *to obey* is an assumed predicate.

Ex. I. *Diagram the following:* 1. For a man to die rich is a disgrace. 2. For him to neglect his studies is foolish. 3. For us to go to the game now seems foolish. 4. For men to waste time in that way always shows thoughtlessness.

DIFFICULT CONSTRUCTIONS

2. The infinitive follows the verbs *please* and *let:*

Please close the door.

$$(you) \mid\mid Please \quad \begin{array}{|l} (to)\ close \mid door \\ \hspace{3em} \mid the \end{array}$$

The infinitive phrase *close the door* is used as a noun, the object of the verb *please*, used in the imperative mode.

Let me go with you.

$$(you)\ Let \mid\mid \begin{array}{l} me \mid \setminus (to)\ go \\ \hspace{3em} \mid with \mid you \end{array}$$

The infinitive in the assumed predicate construction, *me go with you*, is the object of the verb *let*, which is in the imperative mode.

Please let me go.

$$(you) \wedge Please \mid \begin{array}{l} (to)\ let \mid me \mid \setminus (to)\ go \end{array}$$

Ex. II. *Diagram the following:* 1. Please come on time. 2. Let me see your papers. 3. Please let me take that book. 4. Please finish your work promptly. 5. Let me stay alone.

---

1. The participle is used to complete the predicate and to modify the subject:

The child came running.

$$\frac{child \wedge came \setminus running}{\mid The}$$

Running is a participle. It completes the verb *came* and modifies the subject *child*. In that it modifies the subject it is an adjective; in that it modifies the verb it is an adverb. This may be called the **Adjective-Adverb** use of the participle.

Ex. I. *Diagram the following:* 1. He came down the street whistling. 2. The dog bounded along barking loudly. 3. The little stream ran rippling through the meadow. 4. He went away smiling. 5. She came up breathing rapidly.

2. The participle is used as an objective complement:

They kept him waiting. $\quad They \wedge kept / waiting \mid him$

Waiting is a participle used as an objective complement. The words *kept waiting* are somewhat equivalent to *delayed*, — They delayed him.

This use of the participle is infrequent. Care should be taken not to confuse it with the more common assumed-predicate use (page 64).

INDEX.

Figures refer to pages. The letter *f* following a figure means *and the following page*; *ff* means *and the following pages*.

A

a, uses of, 158, 199.
absolute phrase, 77 f.
abstract noun formed from participle, 63.
abstract nouns, 26 f.
active and passive forms, 152 f.
active voice, 151.
acts due to feeling, 265 f, 267 f.
address, of letter, 244.
adjective clause, 70.
   how connected, 72 ff.
adjective phrase, 70.
adjective pronouns, 142.
adjectives, agreement with noun, 200.
   and adverbs, 36 f, 209 f.
   classes of, 193, 194.
   comparison of, 195 ff.
   defined, 34 f.
   errors in comparison and arrangement, 200.
   irregular, list of, 197.
   parsing of, 204.
   punctuation of in a series, 198, 291.
   review of, 201 ff.
   syntax of, 193 ff.
adverbial clauses, uses of, 75 ff.
adverbial objective, 117.
adverbial phrases, 70.
adverbs, and adjectives, 36 f, 209 f.
   classes of, 205 f.
   comparison of, 207.
   conjunctive, 74 f, 76, 205.
   defined, 35 f.
   irregular, 207 f.
   parsing of, 208.
   syntax of, 205 ff.
   that modify a phrase, 207.
   used as coördinate conjunctions, 86 f.
advertisements, 324, 340.
affect, use of, 253 f.
"*aint*," 281.
an, uses of, 199.
analysis, explained, 11.
   of sentences with modifiers, 38.

and, not to be used for *to*, 174.
apostrophe, uses of the, 235.
   and *s*, relation shown by, 114.
apposition, explained, 20.
appositives, case of, 117.
   punctuation of, 20, 284 ff.
argumentation, 332 f.
articles, the, 194.
   correct use of, 199 f.
as, relative pronoun, 139.
as . . . as in equal comparisons, 216.
assert, meaning of in definitions, 11.
assertion made by auxiliary, 171.
attribute, defined, 51.
   seeming to make passive voice, 151 f.
attributive verbs, 49 footnote.
auxiliary verbs, 150.
   assert in potential mode, 171.

B

be, conjugation of, 175 ff.
beside, besides, 302.
bills and receipts, 312 f.
body, of letter, 244.
both . . . and, 215 footnote.
business letter, 245, 252.
but, relative pronoun, 139.
but that, as conjunction, 142.
by-laws, items in, 338 f.

C

can and *may*, use of, 314.
capital letters, use of, 9, 95 ff.
case, explained, 114 f.
   formation of the possessive, 121ff, 235.
   forms in English, 115.
   inflection, explained, 114 f.
   nominative independent, 117.
   old dative, 133 footnote.
   relations, outline of, 116 f.
cases, uses of, 116 f.
character, explained, 240 f.
   way to suggest, 240 f.